THE GREEN
IMPERATIVE

THE GREEN IMPERATIVE

NATURAL DESIGN
FOR THE REAL WORLD

VICTOR PAPANEK

with 162 illustrations, 39 in color

THAMES AND HUDSON

AUTHOR'S NOTE

This book is dedicated to four women:
Deborah, 'Kuniang' of Harbin, and my two daughters,
Nicolette and Jennifer. There were many times when their being there
made all the difference and kept me going.

It is ironic that increasing usage of the metric system has forced me
to include metric measurements. The old measurements, which are
based on human experience of length, height, weight, and so forth, are given
first, followed by the metric equivalents in parentheses. However, miles have
not been converted to kilometres, acres to hectares, tons to tonnes,
because the old terms are still commonly used and understood. The Fahrenheit
scale is given before the Celsius scale, which is also in parentheses.
All references to dollars are to US dollars. A billion as used in this book means
a million million, and not, as in American usage, a thousand million.
Chapter 10 of this book draws on material from Chapters 4 and 7
of my *Design for Human Scale*, published in 1983.

Front cover illustration: *Andy Goldsworthy, Japanese maple leaves,
Ouchiyama-Mura, Japan, 22 November 1987.*
Back cover: *Thorncrown Chapel, Eureka Springs, Arkansas, 1980, designed by Fay Jones,
Photo © Greg Hursley.*

Title page: *Entrance pergola, Guy Hide Chick House, Berkeley, California, 1914,
designed by Bernard Maybeck.*

First published in paperback in the United States of America in 1995 by
Thames and Hudson Inc., 500 Fifth Avenue, New York, New York 10110

Library of Congress Catalog Card Number 95–60281
ISBN 0-500-27846-6

Printed and bound in Singapore

CONTENTS

The Power of Design

With all architects, caring should be a moral imperative.
Fay Jones

Design can only succeed if guided by an ethical view.
John Vassos

ALL DESIGN is goal-directed play. Only our questions change. We no longer ask, 'How does it look?' or 'How does it work?' We are more interested now in the answer to, 'How does it relate?'

There is a sense of wonder, a feeling of completion in design that is lacking in many other fields. Designers have the chance to make something new, or to remake something so that it is better. Design gives the deep satisfaction that comes only from carrying an idea all the way through to completion and actual performance. It can be compared to the emotions aroused by making a kite and then being able to fly it in the sky: a feeling of closure, pleasure and achievement. This enriches us both professionally and as human beings and provides us with a joyous affirmation of what we do.

Where does this element of joy come from? We have been called *homo ludens,* the playful being; certainly among the most profound human traits are curiosity and playfulness, and following from these a delight in learning from trial and error, in experimentation. This is linked to a deep need to bring order out of chaos, or – in the late 20th century – to discover the underlying system of chaos itself. We seem to have a compulsion to bring meaning and pattern to a world that seems random and confused. We are the only 'time-binding' animal,[1] communicating skills, ideas and acquired knowledge across the generations, and so we anticipate many possible futures; the job of designers and architects therefore includes a certain degree of prophecy.

In design – this futures-oriented, trial-and-error process for making meaningful order – we work intellectually as well as from deep levels of intuition and feeling. In all human beings there are fundamental needs for comprehensible order, beauty, fitness, simplicity, anticipatory thinking and playful innovation. Designers attempt to satisfy these longings through their work. In the broadest sense, a designer is a human being attempting to walk the narrow bridge between order and chaos, freedom and nihilism, between past achievements and future possibilities.

The repertoire of a designer's skills and talents include:

1. The ability to research, organize and innovate.

2. The capacity to develop appropriate answers to new or newly emerging problems.

3. The skill to test these answers through experimentation, computer modelling, working prototypes or real-world test runs.

4. The training to communicate such developments through drawings, models, mock-ups and feasibility studies, video or film, as well as through verbal, computer-generated or written reports.

5. The talent to combine form-giving with rigorous technical considerations and with a sense of humane and social factors and aesthetic enchantment.

6. The wisdom to anticipate the environmental, ecological, economic, and political consequences of design intervention.

7. The ability to work with people from many different cultures and different disciplines.

How important is this mix of seven abilities, this synergistic blend of talents and skills? We can play the game of placing this ideal designer in different periods of history, or in different places in the world, with only a slight adjustment of his capacities to accord with place and time. Whether lashing a chipped stone to a stick for the hunt some three million years ago or working as a potter in China during the Sung Dynasty, whether developing the prow of a Viking ship or star charts to navigate the far Pacific, whether building a Baroque church in Austria or designing a diagnostic medical computer in Silicone Valley, our designer fits in superbly well.

If we move from history to geography and anthropology, we can see that innovation, function and delight are treasured in many different milieux, from a simple fishing village in Papua New Guinea to the technologically high-risk environment of a space-station in orbit, from an assembly line in Osaka to the hunting-gathering society of the !Kung bushmen of the Kalahari. Regardless of political systems or religious beliefs, the designer is accepted everywhere as an essential contributor to society.

Both time and place give designers the confidence that the skills and talents that we bring to our work will continue to be valuable in the futures to come. Yet this must make us extremely careful about what we design and why. The changing environment of our fragile planet is a result of the things that we do and the tools that we use. Now that the changes that we have brought about are so major and so threatening it is imperative that designers and architects play their part in helping to find solutions.

The agenda for this book can be put simply. It is vital that we all – professionals and end-users – recognize our ecological responsibilities. Our survival depends on an urgent attention to environmental issues, but even now there still seems to be a lack of motivation, a paralysis of will, to make the necessary radical changes. I want to show that there must be a spiritual underpinning to our ecological consciousness. I feel very strongly that the present world-wide concern for the environment cannot now be dismissed as a fashion, as it was during the early 1970s, nor as pure panic over the sustainability of life on earth. I believe that it is rather a great spiritual rebirth or re-awakening, a desire to re-establish closer links between nature and humankind. Deeply embedded in our collective unconscious is the intuitive awareness of our relationship to the environment. This awareness has gone through wide pendulum swings throughout human history. At times our closeness to nature served as a template for all our actions, our art and our lives. At other periods, fancied differences between humans and other animals, between human life and nature were shrilly proclaimed by religious fundamentalist sects, totalitarian political groups and technocrats.

In his book *The Voice of the Earth,* Theodore Roszak writes: 'If psychosis is the attempt to live a lie, then the epidemic psychosis of our time is the lie of believing that we have no ethical obligation to our planetary home.'[2] I remember a time when food, shelter and clothing were considered to be the absolute necessities of life. This no longer holds true. We have moved backwards and are now far from certain that we can expect fresh air, pure drinking water, food that is safe to eat and an environment that is unpolluted by damaging levels of noise. This raises the question whether designers, architects and engineers can be held personally responsible and legally liable for creating tools, objects, appliances, and buildings that bring about environmental deterioration.

In February 1994 I was speaker at a conference in Vancouver with James Wines, founder of SITE (Sculpture in the Environment). In his remarks he said, 'One has only to look at the bleak and hostile configuration of most cities to see how the ideals of architecture, need for purpose, meaning, and truth have deteriorated. What began as an encompassing socialist and capitalist vision has been turned into a symbol of oppression and a detachment from nature.'[3]

The same has been true for design. In most industrialized countries many people have come to expect a technological fix for every ecological dysfunction. Certainly my friend and colleague Buckminster Fuller felt that future inventions would repair all that was wrong on earth, and pinned a good part of his philosophy on this belief. Experience tells me that in design, architecture or planning, new technological fixes usually come accompanied by dozens of unforeseen side-effects. Some of these side-effects can range from the merely disastrous to the catastrophic, and many of these proposed scenarios wilfully ignore human scale.

There is another view, mostly held by people who misinterpret James Lovelock's Gaia Hypothesis (now the Gaia Theory)[4] – who assume that our planet will adjust to all our devastations by somehow absorbing and filtering pollutants in the air, re-regulating the ozone levels and purifying the toxins. Furthermore they believe that the gradual destruction or complete elimination of tropical rainforests will also be fixed by nature itself, and that the loss of many plant and animal species is of no concern. Lovelock's theory certainly postulates that Gaia, the Earth, has a capacity for self-maintenance and self-repair. It should be stressed, however, that this theory does not assume that there will be a place for our species on a planet that has changed itself as a result of human assaults on its bio-diversity and balance.

Both of these groups are ecologically illiterate. Their mistaken notions are often the result of propaganda by industry or the state. During this century, two major changes have occurred for the first time in the long course of human history. First, we have nearly all – at least in the northern half of the globe – moved indoors. There are still jobs that take people out of doors, but even farmers ploughing their fields tend to sit in a climate-controlled cabin, and most of us spend much of our time in homes, cars, workplaces, cinemas or public buildings whenever we are not shopping in malls, supermarkets or arcades.

The second change, awesome to contemplate, is that we have now truly attained the power to change the natural order of the earth and throw it out of harmony. We manufacture trivial gadgets (electronic tape measures, electric fingernail-dryers, or huge water-guns made from shrilly coloured plastics for children), wasting irreplaceable resources, poisoning the atmosphere during manufacture, and polluting the ground once we have grown tired of them. We cut down forests and create deserts. We poison the lakes and rivers with industrial chemicals or pharmaceuticals, kill the fish, and then drink the water ourselves. We dump waste and toxins in the oceans and overfish them. Not only do we threaten other species with extinction, but also tribes of our own species, who rely on an ancient and intricate relationship with their environment.

We clad buildings with reflecting mirror panels, and then build two such structures so close to each other that the temperature between them can build up to more than 160°F (71°C) during the summer. An incredible amount of energy is wasted in heating and cooling buildings.[5]

What is happening to the once-beautiful landscape is an enormous catastrophe for which the future will curse us. If there is a future. Most contemporary architecture has forgotten the age-old lessons of design which took nature, climate and the elements into consideration. Frank Lloyd Wright once said: 'It is important to work with nature but some architects will say to their client: "Madam, I can't work with nature, how would you like a nice contrast?"'[6] He suggested that much of the Modernist theory was based on a confrontation with nature, and advocated a deeper attention to ecological principles of natural building.

Post-Modernism followed Modernism, and was in its turn replaced by Deconstructivism. This movement started out as a literary fashion that deconstructs meaning and seemingly reconstructs historical reality; its misuse as a justification for collaborating with the Nazi occupation in France during World War II has surrounded it with controversy. It deforms the historic reality by claiming to relate to current conditions in society – fractured cities, families, political institutions. When applied to architecture and design, it continues to dehumanize the tools we use, the rooms we work in and the homes and cities in which we live. It turns us against our own past and against nature. Deconstructivism is an anti-world view according to the ecologist David Orr, who goes on to say: 'It deconstructs or eliminates the ingredients necessary for a world view, such as God, self, purpose, meaning, a real world, and truth as correspondence....This type of postmodern, deconstructive thought results in relativism even nihilism.'[7]

In many parts of the world, our institutions are dysfunctional. Once-bustling cities in North America have changed into wastelands of despair; the number of homeless families, and especially shelterless children, increases steadily. The urban pollution and poverty to be seen in Central and South America is extreme. Societies going through such chaotic transformations desperately need new and radical approaches in design.

Design and architecture are deeply implicated not because designers, architects or engineers are bad people. We work for clients, companies or governments. As Lewis Mumford said: ' Once-local manifestations of criminality and irrationality now threaten our whole planet, smugly disguised as sound business enterprise, technological progress, communist efficiency, or democratic statesmanship.'[8] We are guilty or implicated by not speaking out often enough to our clients whether they are governments, private enterprise or individuals. A designer has always been also a teacher, in a position to inform and influence the client. With the present environmental mess it is even more important that we help to guide the intervention of design with nature and mankind. We must enlarge our own areas of knowledge, and at the same time redirect our ways of working. It is to this task that this book addresses itself.

Wes Jackson, who founded the Land Institute in Salina, Kansas, says that our society is the first to have created 'do-it-yourself extinction'. He proposes something he calls an 'ignorant-based' view of the world to halt environmental deterioration, instead of our present, supposedly knowledge-based system. He argues strongly that things can be changed only by admitting that we can no longer continue under the assumptions that 'we will figure out something', or that 'we know what we're doing'. He makes a powerful case for starting from the premise that we know almost nothing about the future consequences of what we do now.[9] Advertising for cigarettes used to claim that they had been endorsed by doctors as healthy and helpful for respiration – now some forty thousand smoking-related deaths occur each year in the United States alone. Governments, propagandists and 'eco-experts' for industry assure us that 'no clear link has been established between sulphur emissions from factory chimneys and acid rain',[10] and that therefore nothing needs to be done just yet. Scientists believed that CFCs (chlorofluorocarbons) were non-toxic and would not pollute – only after destroying large areas of the ozone layer did we come to realize our profound error.

A world view based on recognizing how little we know might not only protect us from devastating mistakes in the future, but might also require letting go of the arrogance that seems such a strong element in the personality of designers and architects. We could even try to find some sorely needed humility. This may be the cardinal point where design practice meets the spiritual. Buddhism teaches humility and the vanity of material possessions, and, indeed, these are tenets of most philosophies and religions.

Perhaps there should be no special category called 'sustainable design'. It might be simpler to assume that all designers will try to reshape their values and their work, so that all design is based on humility, combines objective aspects of climate and the ecological use of materials with subjective intuitive processes, and relies on cultural and bio-regional factors for its forms.

'Consumers' (or end-users or users as I shall refer to them throughout this book) are also implicated in this ecological crisis. In our greedy rush for more and more material goods in the West (and more recently in the countries of the former Soviet Union and eastern Europe), we have seriously neglected our links with nature and our responsibility to the environment; we are losing love and affection and respect for each other; we are forgetting the joy of the ephemeral and the freedom of owning little in the way of material possessions.

My strongest memory from the two years when I lived on the island of Bali in Indonesia, doing design work for UNESCO, is of the impermanence of things, which may there have been the result of the ever-present threat of volcanic eruption – there are something like eight hundred minor and twelve major earthquakes on Bali each year. A life that is based on change and the ephemeral is subtly spiced. On Bali this is also linked to the rich web of interpersonal relationships, and the fact that everyone participates actively in many different arts. There is wisdom and self-knowledge in their saying: 'We have no art, we just do the best we can.'

Consider the last time that you enjoyed an ephemeral, a fleeting, experience. It may have been a live television show which was fun merely because the unexpected could and did happen, or a concert that was for once not recorded and could never be repeated. The beautiful landscape that you did not photograph probably lingers more strongly in your mind than those you tried to freeze in time. The unique piquancy of the unrepeatable may be the reason why the Balinese routinely spend as much time on constructing an elaborate temple-offering of fruit, blossoms and rice to last only for hours or days as they would on carving a stone statue that might endure for centuries. When everything is temporary, it is life that becomes lasting. This may be why my friend I Gusti Nyoman Lempad of Ubud, who was an acclaimed painter, sculptor, dancer (from the age of eight), composer, musician, teacher, poet, architect, story-teller and cook noted for the subtle flavouring of his dishes, died happy and fulfilled at the age of 118.[11] It seems that by concentrating on goods that don't last nearly as long as we hope and don't age well, we have lost our sense of quality and the temporary. By trying to make art profitable and useful, we have also lost our sense of joy. By elevating the trivial productions of Post-Modernism and Deconstructivism to serious critical discussion, we have abandoned bliss.

This book attempts to develop these thoughts in a more systematic way. It examines the relationship between the disciplines of design and architecture on the one hand, and ecology and concern for the environment on the other. This is the central theme of the chapters 'Here Today, Gone Tomorrow?' and 'Designing for a Safer Future'.

It calls for ethical responsibility and spiritual values in design and architecture to help us find a sustainable and harmonious way of life; this is first explored in the chapter 'Toward the Spiritual in Design'. Our understanding and appreciation of a design or building has been seriously handicapped by concentrating almost entirely on our sense of sight; 'Sensing a Dwelling' shows how we might regain the joy of reading the fabric of a building through all our senses, and why some buildings make us feel good. 'Communities for Human Beings' continues this discussion of building to human scale in relation to town and community planning. 'The Lessons of Vernacular Architecture', the following chapter, is for us all, not just for architects; we can all benefit by looking at and learning from past building traditions.

The following chapters suggest how each of us, as end-users, can contribute to the radical changes in values which are necessary to create a sustainable lifestyle, and points to specific tactics and strategies that users, or 'consumers', might employ. 'Form Follows Fun' explores the narrow division between style and fad, and suggests ways of restoring our enjoyment in fleeting delights. The questions and checklists in the chapter entitled 'Is Convenience the Enemy?' will help end-users to make decisions on what and whether to buy, and 'Sharing not Buying' offers some practical alternatives to the continued acquisition of appliances, tools, gadgets and goods.

'Generations to Come' analyses how design education might help our children and the designers of the so-called Third World to learn from our mistakes. People once judged to be 'primitive' have much to teach us in our turn, and this is discussed in the chapter 'The Best Designers in the World?'

The concluding chapter, 'The New Aesthetic: Making the Future Work', summarizes the general points running through the whole book, and looks at the exciting possibilities if architecture and design were to become environmentally and socially more responsible, and if every one of us were to try to live once more in harmony with nature.

Tanah Lot Temple, Bali
Schumacher College, Dartington, Devon
Fundacion Valparaiso Mojacar, Spain
1991–95

ACKNOWLEDGMENTS

I N MY first book appears the sentence: 'This volume is dedicated to my students, for what they have taught me.' In the intervening twenty-five years I have come to realize that there is still much that I need to understand and learn. It is my good fortune to continue to have students who are still teaching me and providing me with new insights, as well as the varying viewpoints of different cultures and different age groups.

I express my gratitude to Jim Hennessey who was a graduate student of mine at Konstfackskola in Stockholm and at the California Institute of the Arts in Valencia. Later Jim became my Assistant Dean, and he and I co-authored three books. Now Jim is a well-known industrial designer and teacher in his own right, and has recently been appointed to a professorship in industrial design at the University of Delft. My friendship with him and his wife Sara is still as strong as ever after a quarter of a century.

Smit Vajaranant, a former graduate student from the University of Kansas, now works as chief designer for the largest architectural firm in his native Bangkok, where he also takes an active part in preserving the vernacular tradition of Thai dwellings and re-introducing some indigenous motifs into contemporary buildings. His wife Julie is a working industrial designer and teaches at King Mongkut Institute of Technology.

Virginia Diaz de Cisco worked with me on a desert bay on the coast of Mexico as part of her thesis project. She designed an 'intentional community' for some fishermen's families, which included a water-filtration and recycling system, and alternative power sources. She has returned to Venezuela, where she practises and is a professor of architecture.

Imam ('Zainuddin') Buchori studied with me at the Royal Academy of Architecture in Copenhagen. He has gone back to his native Indonesia and spends his time as a working industrial designer and director of an industrial design institute in Bandung.

Takeshi Shigenari says he was my student only through my books. He has specialized in designing and building teaching aids and furniture for multiply handicapped children at a clinic in Kiyushu. He has also published a book about his extraordinary work.

Maria Benktzon was a student on a short-time course in Sweden in 1968. She founded the organization RFSU Rehab in Bromma, where she designs and develops everyday objects for the mentally and physically disabled.

Philip White studied with me both at the Kansas City Art Institute and much later at the University of Kansas. He is among the brightest and most creative of my former students with a deep and abiding interest in the relationship between ecology, the environment and product design for mass production. He has spent several years working in research and design for Philips Corporate Industrial Design Centre at Eindhoven in the Netherlands. He brings great wit and a sense of fun to his work, and I have learned much from him.

I must state that all their work is truly their own, and contemplating their contributions fills me with wonder and joy. Nearly all these former students have visited me, and I have been to their countries repeatedly and learned much from them about the varieties of the creative process and cultural diversity. For this I acknowledge their guidance.

There are other thanks to be given. I must thank the monks and spiritual leaders at the Tanah Lot Temple, off the west coast of Bali, for letting me stay there and work. Satish Kumar, Brian Nicholson, Karen Thomas, Guy Claxton, Stephan, Helen and others at Schumacher College at Dartington, in Devon deserve my gratitude for helping me to find a deeper dimension in design. Satish Kumar's wisdom and friendship have sustained me at difficult times.

Through the generosity of the late Paul Beckett of Copenhagen and his Fundacion Valparaiso, a wonderful workroom was made available to me for almost two months in Mojacar, Spain, last summer where I could write and think. Ian and Barbara Forrest helped enormously to make my stay there delightful and valuable for my work, and my thanks go to them.

The US National Endowment for the Arts gave me a once-in-a-lifetime 'Distinguished Designer Award' and this, together with a completely unexpected 'Outstanding Designer Award' from the IKEA Foundation in Amsterdam, made the work on this book possible.

I must mention Keith Critchlow, Christopher Day and David Pearson, all from the United Kingdom. Their work, writings and wise council have been of profound influence. But neither they nor any of the others mentioned in these acknowledgments should be blamed for any of my mistakes or the conclusions that I have reached, which are strictly my own.

I am very grateful for the strong support of Thomas Neurath, my friend and publisher who, when this book appears, will have been my publisher for a quarter of a century.

Finally, my special thanks go to Janis Brackett, a former postgraduate student. She has helped me with the typing and research on much of this book for the last few months but, more importantly, her skills, profound areas of knowledge and especially her wonderful sense of humour have made working on the manuscript a pleasurable time.

CHAPTER 1

Here Today, Gone Tomorrow?

All thinking worthy of the name must now be ecological.
Lewis Mumford

THERE CAN be little doubt that the environment and the ecological balance of the planet are no longer sustainable. Unless we learn to preserve and conserve Earth's resources, and change our most basic patterns of consumption, manufacture and recycling, we may have no future.

We are all, every one of us, involved with issues of ecology, and we seem to adopt one of two ways in approaching the problems posed by a deteriorating environment. The first is try to do something on an individual or family level. We use less water to flush our toilets, we separate and recycle our garbage, we buy cars that run more economically, we insulate and retro-fit our houses, and generally practise conservation and preservation whenever possible. We join consumer initiatives to campaign against toxic chemicals in agriculture, to keep trees from being cut down or to save the whales. The second way is mentally to shrug our shoulders and decide to 'leave it to the experts'. This amounts to shirking our moral accountability and leaving ethical responsibilities to an ill-defined group of scientists and activists.

I would suggest that we add a third way. We must examine *what each of us can contribute from our own specific role in society*. We must ask the question: 'What can I do as a professor, construction worker, taxi-driver, school teacher, prostitute, lawyer, pianist, housewife, student, manager, politician or farmer? What is the impact of *my* work on the environment?'

There is an ecological and environmental dimension to all human activities. Whatever the subject he or she teaches, a professor can make a personal contribution by cutting down on the immense waste of paper, using computers to store data and reducing the amount of photocopying for classes. The construction worker or taxi-driver must examine how his or her work touches the environment; switching off instead of idling the engine of the cab or the construction machinery, waiting rather than cruising for fares, these seemingly minor interventions can help. Simple acts can empower the individual by providing a feeling of doing *something* to help. Managers, politicians and lawyers are in positions of power; they must sharpen their understanding of the precise balance between ecology and economics – a relationship that is frequently falsely portrayed as confrontational, whereas recent studies show that ecological awareness can have

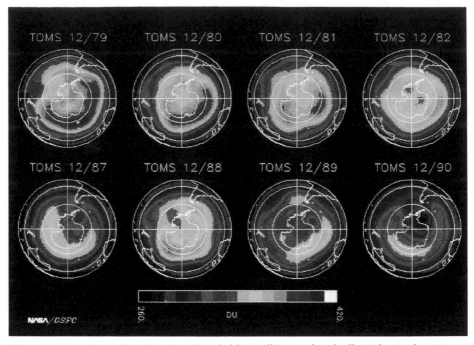

Ozone concentrations above Antartica (recorded by satellite as red and yellow) during the 1980s.

positive economic consequences. The question of ecological intervention will be explored throughout the whole of this book.

OUR DAMAGED PLANET

Between 1981 and the end of 1994 major climatic changes have occurred all over the world. The summers from 1990 to 1994 were among the hottest ever record-ed in northern Europe, with the autumn of 1994 in Sweden the warmest for two hundred and fifty years. During this same thirteen-year period, winters in North America and Europe were generally much warmer, yet interrupted by brief cold snaps with the temperature descending as low as -37°F (-37°C). Australia was plagued by huge firestorms caused by prolonged droughts. Summers in northern Argentina and north-eastern Brazil were also much hotter than usual, and the winters there since 1987 warmer than ever previously recorded. In May 1994, we learned that the warming of the Earth and the holes in the ozone layer were increasing at nearly twice the speed predicted in 1987.

During the summer of 1993, enormous floods in the Midwest of the United States wreaked havoc through nine states, and for nearly three months the Mississippi river was six times wider than normal. The Sahel, the sub-Saharan part of Africa, has seen a dry, desert-like climate moving southwards starting in the late 1970s, and these continuing droughts have devastated Niger, Chad,

Senegal and the Ivory Coast. The incidence of major typhoons in south-east Asia doubled between 1990 and 1994. Bangladesh suffered the two worst floods in its history in 1982 and 1983; during the second an incredible 81% of the land surface was under six feet (2m) of water for several days.

The most devastating hurricane to strike Florida occurred in 1992, and major hurricanes continue to batter the east coast of the USA. El Niño, the recurrent warming of the westward ocean currents heading towards South America, led to heavy rains that resulted in killer landslides in Colombia, Ecuador and Venezuela.

The completely unpredictable temperature and weather patterns of the last few years suggest that we are living through a time of massive environmental change. In June 1993, when this chapter was written in southern Spain, which normally has a desert-like climate, the ambient temperature was distinctly chilly and a heavy rain was falling. At the same time a colleague arriving from Helsinki reported that for the previous few weeks there had been a heatwave there that would have been considered tropical in August.

THE HISTORICAL VIEW

Yet humanity has withstood ecological, environmental and energy crises before. I have been working with a historian, helping to turn her scholarly interests towards ecological and environmental studies, and learning a great deal in the process about the effects of climatic changes in the past.

The first great energy crises came long before the OPEC oil embargo of 1973. Twelve thousand years ago agriculture (the transformation of wild annual grasses into domesticated cereals) began in the southern Levant under the simultaneous pressure of drought, high temperatures, over-population and over-exploitation of natural resources. This forced foray into plant genetics brought about massive changes in nutrition, trade and settlement patterns.

The 'Little Ice Age' in western Europe lasted roughly from 1550 to 1700 and helped to shape ways of living, farming, and, as a consequence, artistic expression.[1] More time spent indoors during the longer winters led to a flowering of the crafts that made life more comfortable, such as quilt-making, blanket and carpet-weaving, and pottery. Mirrors and crystals were used in experiments to enhance candlelight, and interest grew in choral singing and in decoration for home and church. Conditions during the 'Little Ice Age' must have been very like those in the isolated, dark and snow-bound farms in Finland during the 18th and 19th centuries. This home-centred mode of living nourished all kinds of artistic expression, especially in music and literature which sprang from story-telling and narrative poetry. One of the most obvious results of the colder climate in England was the disappearance of much of the common land (due to the increase in sheep farming) leading to great changes in land ownership, travel and class structure.

The depletion of forests occurred not once, but many times and in a great many different places. An energy crisis was developing in England by the 16th century, forcing people to burn coal or peat – foul-smelling, inconvenient and dirty – to keep off the chill during the winter months. Yet in a landscape drastically deforested and turned into sheep pastures in the northern Midlands and Scotland, a roaring log fire was no longer practical.[2] Coal-mining not only changed the structure of settlements through the building of mining towns and row upon row of working-class cottages, but also ushered in the 'dark Satanic mills' and the beginning of pollution through the use of fossil fuels. The precipitation of soot and coal-dust could soon be measured by the changes in the appearance of the peppered moth (whose wings turned from silvery-white speckled with dark spots for camouflage against birch bark, to a uniform dark brown, matching the birch trees now blackened by soot).

In China the overcutting of forests caused a fuel shortage that lasted from 1400 to 1800, a vivid dress rehearsal for the oil embargoes of the 20th century. The Chinese were forced to burn straw and – by learning to build with bamboo – developed a bamboo-based structural technology equalled only by that of Latin America before the conquest.[3] Historian-ecologists now have much data on China and are preparing to study the possible relationship between rainfall and drought cycles in the development of treeless terrain and the subsequent expansion of the Central Asian steppe peoples.[4] The inhabitants of India, Pakistan, Sri Lanka and Bangladesh, lands where forests have been destroyed, burn dried cowdung, lacking other fuels.

It is salutary to remember that almost all the deserts in the world – with the exception of the central Australian outback – are human-made. Recent studies suggest the influence of climate and eco-catastrophes on the shifting fortunes of the Mayan civilization of Central America.

The historical view also makes clear the alarming increase in the speed of change in the last few decades. I now live in Kansas and learned that in the western part of the state, one June day in 1860, it was as dark as night – the light of the sun had been blotted out by a flight of between three and five thousand million passenger pigeons, breaking trees when they came down to roost.[5] Now, a little over a hundred years later, there is only one passenger pigeon left – it is stuffed and stands in my university's museum of natural history.

The sooty coloration of the peppered moth c.1850–1970 indicates the period of worst pollution.

THE ACCELERATION OF DISASTER

Our present concern with the biosphere is the result of a whole series of recent catastrophes. One of the first indications of the potential hazards to human existence posed by industry started in Japan in 1932 and lasted through the 1950s. Mercury was pumped as waste into the Bay of Minamata, poisoning thousands of local fishermen and their families in the Chizo Prefecture of Japan. It was not until 1953 that there was scientific proof that this had been causing great genetic damage and had led to the birth of many severely handicapped children.

This was followed by large-scale dioxin poisoning in Sardinia and other parts of Italy, which started in 1949. Since then we have had, among hundreds of smaller nuclear accidents, the thermonuclear-reactor near-meltdown at Three Mile Island in Pennsylvania in 1982; the Chernobyl disaster in the Ukraine in 1986; we have had the poisoning of thousands by a US chemical corporation in Bhopal in India in 1984; in 1986 a Swiss pharmaceutical factory accidentally released large amounts of toxic chemicals into the Rhine, poisoning the river from its sources in Switzerland throughout its course in Germany, France, Belgium and the Netherlands, eliminating fish-life for more than five years.

We have had *an average of one major oceanic oil spill every second day for the last eighteen years*. The *Exxon Valdez* oil-tanker spill in 1990 affected wildlife and the Alaskan coastline and fishing grounds, and will continue to do so into the next century, putting into jeopardy the cultural life and very existence of the native peoples of Alaska who subsist from hunting and fishing. In August 1994 the US courts found the Exxon Corporation guilty of criminal negligence and it was ordered to pay five thousand million dollars to the native peoples and fishermen of Alaska, in addition to almost two thousand million dollars already awarded as direct damages.

The explosion of the Siberian oil pipeline of June 5, 1989, in Russia, also derailed two trains killing hundreds of people. *On an average of three times a day, towns or villages have to be evacuated somewhere in the world because of the spillage of toxic chemicals from train wrecks or truck crashes.*[6]

People often seem to be far ahead of their governments in concern for ecology. The second greatest man-made ecological tragedy in the 20th century was the burning of over five hundred oil wells in Kuwait at the end of the Gulf War. By far the most terrible ecological disaster in our time was the systematic destruction and defoliation of the south Asian forests in Vietnam, Laos and Cambodia from 1968 to 1971 through the use of Agent Orange and other chemical and biological 'goodies'.

There are other disasters, no less devastating for their more insidious development. The slow death of northern European and North American forests and lakes is largely caused by effluvia from factory smoke stacks which turns rain acid;

Sealions on oil-covered rocks in Alaska after the Exxon Valdez oil spills in 1990.

the gases given off by factories in the American Midwest cause acid-rain damage in Canada; factories in the Ruhr district of Germany and the Czech republic are affecting Sweden and Denmark.

There is the terrible threat of the increase in 'greenhouse' gases. Some of the heat from the sun is radiated back from the surface of the earth and much is trapped by several naturally occurring gases in the atmosphere, such as carbon dioxide, nitrous oxide and methane, which act like the glass in a greenhouse. Clouds also work as magnifiers: cirrus clouds let in sunlight, yet trap rising heat. This effect is necessary for the existence of life as we know it, for without it our planet would be considerably colder. On the other hand, human activity, compounded by the explosive rise in the population, has increased the production of greenhouse gases so alarmingly that scientists predict a wholescale global warming, which may already be apparent in the recent climatic changes.

Through sample drillings in rock, Arctic ice and soil it has been established that the carbon-dioxide content in the air *never rose above 280 parts per million during the last twelve million years. By 1958 it had risen to 315 parts; to 340 parts by 1988, and to 350 in 1993.*[7] This is the result of the burning of fossil fuels (coal, oil and gas) and the diminishing of tropical rainforests which absorb large amounts of carbon dioxide as well as producing oxygen.

Nitrous oxide is also produced by fossil-fuel burning, and more comes from the increase in the use of fertilizers in agriculture. Enormous amounts of methane are generated by cattle (now bred in increasing numbers by a fast-growing human

Burning oil wells in Kuwait in 1991 emitted 200 million tons of carbon dioxide.

population, particularly for the meat and dairy products of a Western-style diet), by waterlogged soils such as rice paddies, oil and gas production, and by landfill.

CFCs (chlorofluorocarbons), not invented until 1930, are responsible for the holes in the ozone layer, increasing the risk of skin-cancer, leukaemia and birth abnormalities all over the world as we lose protection from the sun's ultraviolet rays, and – more ominously – contributing to the radical warming of the Earth's climate. CFCs are being phased out because of their threat to the ozone layer, but are being replaced as refrigerants, solvents, blowing agents for foam plastics, by related gases, the HCFCs and HFCs, which, though less powerful ozone-depletors, are long-lasting greenhouse gases.

Our best computer-modelling tells us that we may expect a rise of temperature of 1° to 1.5°F (0.6° to 0.8°C) by the year 2000, and a consequent rise in sea levels of about three feet (one metre). This doesn't sound too threatening until one stops to calculate that on a sloping beach, such a rise could bring the ocean as much as 295 feet (90m), above its current tideline.

The razing of tropical rainforests has to be halted now. Sadly some of these natural green lungs of Earth have already been eliminated within the last few years. The destruction of the huge rainforest areas in Sarawak, which started at the beginning of 1991, had eliminated *all* rainforests in northern Borneo by mid-September of that same year. The Amazonian and other rainforests are still with us; besides their great importance to the Earth's atmosphere, they contain millions of species, many still unknown to us, some of which are in danger of being eliminated forever. The rosy periwinkle, native to the shrinking rainforest of Madagascar, yields two compounds that are successful in treating two cancers – lymphocytic leukaemia and Hodgkin's disease.

Even in the United States there are examples of previously unknown beneficial plants, such as the Pacific yew whose bark and needles have proved to be helpful in the treatment of ovarian and cervical cancers and some breast cancers. Hoping to cure or at least control AIDs, pharmaceutical companies continue to study plants, lichen, spores, moss and other botanical specimens as well as various rare soils. Among the many experimental drugs released for laboratory study in 1993, one contained constituents from a tree mushroom in the Brazilian rainforest.

Even such seemingly trivial changes in the environment as the enormous increase of tsetse flies and malaria-bearing mosquitoes, can be directly traced to human activity. There are approximately three thousand million car and truck tyres in dumps in the United States alone. Tyres collect stagnant water and provide a perfect breeding-place for these insects.

These accelerating man-made catastrophes make it vital for the survival of the world as we know it that industrial designers, graphic designers and architects, contributing from their particular areas of knowledge and influence, and joining with other disciplines, should involve themselves in environmental issues.

HEALING ON A HUMAN SCALE

There is a secondary problem. It is the problem of human scale, the threat of bigness. My primary conviction as a human being, a designer and an ecologist is: *Nothing Big Works – Ever!* One only has to look at General Motors, General Dynamics, General Electric, or General Westmoreland and all his armies for that matter, to see the truth of this proposition. It is equally true of those large countries made impotent by their own ungovernable size, such as the former Soviet Union, the United States, China, India and – to a lesser degree – Brazil, Indonesia and Nigeria. This curse of bigness holds true of large corporations, huge school systems, mushrooming bureaucracies and other megastructures. *Nothing Big Works – Ever* is a simple natural fact, elegantly stated by the biologist D'Arcy Thompson: 'The elephant and hippopotamus have grown clumsy as well as big, the elk is of necessity less graceful than the gazelle.'[8]

Hope for the future springs from witnessing small reversals of the damage we have caused. Animal species have, through the good works of individuals, been brought back from near-extinction. The Lincoln sheep from Lincolnshire provides a virtually cholesterol-free milk and an extremely fine wool. The Devon cow is, to my knowledge, the only species providing very low cholesterol meat. Collectors of Navajo carpets are aware that the best Navajo rugs were made before 1870 or after 1960. The reason is that before 1870 saddle blankets and rugs were made from the wool of Churro sheep – a breed of sheep that simultaneously yields four different kinds of wool, some of it extremely fine and silky, other parts tough and long-wearing. Nearly a century later Churro sheep were bred back from the edge of extinction, and their wool is again used for weaving by Native Americans.

These dangerous times for Earth call not just for passion, imagination, intelligence and hard work, but – more profoundly – a sense of optimism that is willing to act without a full understanding, but with a faith in the effect of small individual actions on the global picture. The actions of the city council of Irvine in California, reported in the *New Yorker*, vividly illustrates this point. Laws were passed in 1989 restricting the sale and use of chlorofluorocarbons inside the city limits. This would affect local businesses and raise local prices, but any improvements to the atmosphere would be so tiny as to be almost unnoticeable; any benefits would be global not local, for future generations and not now.

> It's idealistic, even quixotic, for little Irvine to take responsibility for the sky. And yet on an emotional level the action seems exactly right. As global problems become overwhelming, the idea of locality assumes a new political importance.... It may be that authority – the power to take responsibility – can at this point be recovered only on a local level, and that this is why local politics has acquired new significance.... Irvine's step does not come anywhere near solving the problem of ozone depletion, but the Irvine City Council did not claim that it would: so large is the sky and so small is Irvine that the relationship of the city to the problem is automatically acknowledged as that of tiny beings to something utterly beyond their control. In this acknowledgment, true scale is recovered, and, with it, effectiveness. The problems of the environment are beyond the power of Irvine to solve, but because the city took responsibility where it could, it is no longer helpless. It examined its own contribution to the destruction of the ozone, asked, 'If not us, who?' and heard the answer, 'No one.' [9]

The problems may be world-wide, yet they will yield only to decentralized, human-scale and local intervention. This is partly due to the fact that we are still unable to assess the impact of what we do as designers and as consumers – only if our intrusions are modest in scale are the chances of major miscalculations reassuringly remote.

Most architects and designers – especially younger industrial designers – feel that high technology is bound to disturb the ecological balance even more profoundly. They express this concern through a nostalgic longing for the past, in an attempt to return to a seemingly simpler, more primitive way of life. Yet one cannot turn back the clock, however good the reason may seem. Others – equally concerned with the environment – are convinced that the problems of high technology require a 'techno-fix', that is, the use of even more technology to solve the technology-based problems that we face on the planet.

Tropical rainforests help to maintain the atmosphere of the planet.

The rosy periwinkle, a rainforest plant, is valuable for the treatment of certain cancers.

Both viewpoints are wrong. Useful answers to many of these problems will frequently come from areas we normally associate with high technology, such as electronics, computers, and microchips. The importance of computer modelling in exploring the growth of ozone depletion cannot be overstated. Remote sensing from space satellites has given us a profound understanding of how far pollution, desertification and droughts have already changed the land, the oceans and the climate of the Earth. But equally informative clues to the true nature of the difficulties we face will come from the life-sciences, as well as anthropology, cultural geography and geology. Still deeper insights will be derived from biological, botanical and biomorphic sources, as well as the study of history, ethnography and the so-called 'old technology'. We are all in it together and we need all the information we can get.

IS TIME ON OUR SIDE?

Most people agree that these ecological catastrophes pose enormous dangers, but we tend to shrug them off with the assumption that changes in nature occur slowly through many periods lasting millions of years – the Cambrian, the Triassic, the Cretaceous, and so forth. For nearly two hundred years, writers dealing with nature have tried to understand the almost incomprehensible length of what the anthropologist Loren Eisley, called 'the immense journey'.[10] The age of the trilobites began six hundred million years ago. The dinosaurs flourished for about one hundred and fifty million years. Since we have trouble imagining even a million years, we feel that nothing happens speedily, any change takes unfathomable, 'geological' time.

Yet this concept of time is misleading. The time-span of the world we know, in which human beings first formed into some sort of civilization, can be quite easily comprehended. Peoples began to assemble in prototypical social groupings in the north of Mesopotamia approximately twelve thousand years ago. If we assume twenty-five years to be the length of a generation, that means that civilization began only 480 generations ago. As I write this, I can think back some five generations, and through my teachers a common bond is formed, reaching from Frank Lloyd Wright back to Louis Sullivan, to George G. Elmslie and the sculptor-theorist Horatio Greenough in 1789.

I have family photographs of five generations, from the late 1840s to the present, which means I can actively think myself back one ninety-sixth of the way to the start of human settlements. Furthermore, my family's records can be traced to the year 1280, so I have a concept of my own family going back one thirty-third of the way to the beginnings of civilization. Plays, books, historical accounts, and the works of archaeologists give me some sense of daily life at least as long ago as the Pharaohs in Egypt, which is nearly half way. About three hundred and twenty generations ago, Jericho was a walled city with three thousand inhabitants. Of course, three hundred and twenty is a large number, but not quite as incomprehensible as six hundred million. Yet even within these last twelve thousand years from Mesopotamia to the present, our sense of time is not particularly uniform. The world we understand goes back only to the Renaissance. The world as we *really* know it dates back to the Industrial Revolution, and the world we feel comfortable with probably began – depending on our age and feeling for history – sometime between 1945 and 1973.[11]

Thus our view of an unlimited future is a chimera. During a lifetime, a decade, a year, or even a day, profound and impersonal dramatic changes take place. We have come to understand the concept that continents can drift over the course of aeons, and that continents could perish in one thermonuclear second. But we feel that 'normal time' is isolated from such great changes. Yet most of the ecological and possibly irreversible damage has occurred only during the last thirty years. Time is running out.

CHAPTER 2

Designing for a Safer Future

*The epidemic psychosis of our time is the lie of believing we have
no ethical obligation to our planetary home.*
Theodore Roszak

ECOLOGY AND the environmental equilibrium are the basic underpinnings of all
human life on earth; there can be neither life nor human culture without it.
Design is concerned with the development of products, tools, machines,
artefacts and other devices, and this activity has a profound and direct influence on
ecology. The design response must be positive and *unifying*. Design must be the
bridge between human needs, culture and ecology.

This can be clearly demonstrated. The creation and manufacture of *any*
product – both during its period of active use and its existence afterwards – fall into
at least six separate cycles, each of which has the potential for ecological harm.

When we speak of pollution as related to products, we usually think of end
results: the exhaust fumes from automobiles, the smoke from factory chimneys,
chemical fertilizers or truck tyres in a dump poisoning the ground-water. But
pollution falls into several phases.

PRODUCTION AND POLLUTION

1. The choice of materials
The materials chosen by designer and manufacturer are crucial. Mining metal for
cars creates atmospheric pollution, and uses oil and petrol, thus wasting natural
resources that cannot be replaced. The designer's decision to use foam plastics to
make cheap, throw-away food containers damages the ozone layer. This is *not* a
prescription for doing nothing at all, but an attempt to make designers aware that
every choice and dilemma in their work can have far-reaching and long-term
ecological consequences.

2. The manufacturing processes
The questions facing the designer are: Is there anything in the manufacturing
process itself that might endanger the workplace or the workers, such as toxic
fumes or radio-active materials? Are there air-pollutants from factory smokestacks, such as the gases that cause acid rain. Are liquid wastes from the factory
leaking into the ground and destroying agricultural land or – worse still – entering the water supply?

Scarcity of materials for many Third World countries has made recycling a necessity and a way of life for generations. When life is hard, nothing is wasted. Bottles and card are collected in China for recycling (above) and old tyres are made into water carriers in Nigeria (opposite).

3. Packaging the product

Further ecological choices face the designer when developing the package in which the product is transported, marketed and distributed. Foam plastics, which pose acute dangers to the ecological balance, are used by designers as a protection for fragile products. It is now known that propellants (such as CFCs) for lacquer sprays and other products are directly implicated in the depletion of the ozone layer. Considerations of materials and methods are therefore crucial in the packaging phase of ecologically aware design.

4. The finished product

There are too many different versions of the same item available in many cases. Since the manufacture of most industrial or consumer products uses up irreplaceable raw materials, the profusion of objects in the market-place constitutes a profound ecological threat. To give a typical example: in western Europe, Canada, Japan and the USA there are now more than 250 different video cameras available to consumers; the differences between them are minimal – in some cases they are identical but for the name-plate. The choice of consumer products in the West is highly artificial.

Other products threaten the ecological balance even more directly. Snow-mobiles, which are largely sold as winter-sports and recreation equipment, are so noisy that when they go into roadless terrain they destroy breeding grounds and habitats. Yet, at the same time, they have assumed an important role in hunting and herding cycles and are now important tools for survival among the Inuit of Canada and Alaska. 'Off-road' vehicles and 'mountain bikes' affect the precious layer of topsoil and humus that can grow crops. 'Dune buggies' harm the sand-dune layers at the critical edge between ocean and land.

5. Transporting the product
The transporting of materials and products further contributes to pollution by the burning of fossil fuels, and by the necessity for a whole complex of roads, rails, airports and depots. There is transportation from the mill to the factory, the factory to the distribution centre, from there to the shops and, eventually, to the end-user.

6. Waste
Many products can have negative consequences *after the useful product life is over*. One only has to see the huge automobile graveyards in many countries to under-stand that these vast amounts of rusting metals, decaying paints and shellacs, deteriorating plastic upholstery, leaking oils and petrol are leaching directly into the ground, poisoning the soil, the water-supply and the wildlife, besides visually destroying the landscape. It has been estimated that the average family in the tech-nologically developed countries throws away some 16 to 20 tons of garbage and waste a year. This is not only an environmental hazard, but is also an enormous waste of materials that could be recycled responsibly. This is one area in which the so-called Third World countries are leading the way – because of material scarcities, recycling is an accepted way of life there and has been for generations.

PRODUCT ASSESSMENT
The relationship between design and ecology is a very close one,[1] and makes for some unexpected complexities. The designed product goes, as shown, through at least *six* potentially ecologically dangerous phases. Product Life Cycle Assessment is the evaluation incorporating all of them, from the original acquisition of raw materials, through the manufacturing process and assembly, the purchase of the complete product (which also includes shipping, packaging, advertising and the printing of instruction manuals), the use, the collection of the product after use, and finally the re-use or recycling and final disposal. It can best be understood through the hexagonal diagram, the six-sided 'Function Matrix' (p.34). At the moment Life Cycle Assessment is very new, and can be profoundly complicated, demanding a great deal of study, testing and experimentation.

*The vast Smokey Mountain rubbish tip in Manila in the
Philippines provides home and livelihood for the very poor.*

Environmental issues in Life Cycle Assessment
- The exhaustion of scarce or finite resources
- The production of greenhouse gases
- The production of chlorofluorocarbons leading to ozone depletion
- The production of acid rain
- Habitat destruction and species extinction
- Materials or processes that harm plants, animals and humans
- Air, soil and water pollution
- Noise pollution with its deleterious effect on the human psyche
- Visual pollution

PACKAGING AND SHROUDING

Most goods need to be packaged. The package protects the contents in transit and
in store from spoilage, vermin, moisture and damage. It can serve as a powerful
marketing tool through design, colour and texture. Furthermore, as explored in
Chapter 7, it will frequently signify not only the contents, but also lend identity to
the product-line. In terms of goods that are nearly identical – washing-up powders,
breakfast cereals or cigarettes – it can be said that *the package is the product.*

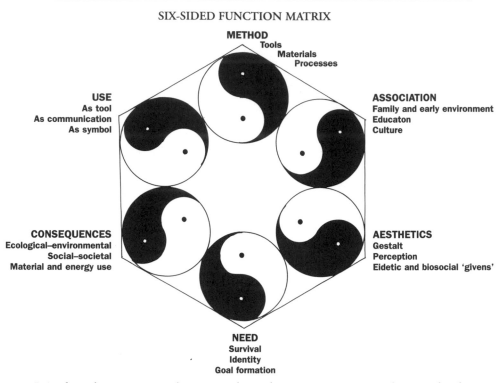

SIX-SIDED FUNCTION MATRIX

METHOD
Tools
Materials
Processes

USE
As tool
As communication
As symbol

ASSOCIATION
Family and early environment
Educaton
Culture

CONSEQUENCES
Ecological–environmental
Social–societal
Material and energy use

AESTHETICS
Gestalt
Perception
Eidetic and biosocial 'givens'

NEED
Survival
Identity
Goal formation

It is clear that we routinely over-package things. In some cases this is to lend a visual charisma to luxury goods such as perfumes that sell at enormously inflated prices. But the less luxurious package can be equally destructive of the environment. Fast-food suppliers have for decades used small coffins made of a plastic known as styrofoam in North America in which to serve their cheeseburgers and Big Macs. Some years ago, McDonald outlets in the American Midwest proudly proclaimed on an automatically changing neon sign: '*Seventy billion* sold so far' (italics supplied). More recently the McDonald corporation has been convinced of the ecological soundness of switching to paper containers.

Foam plastic is a very useful packing material, yet profoundly damaging to the environment. After it has been discarded, it is doubtful whether it is possible to re-use it, and it continues to be an environmental and toxic hazard in spite of the optimistic assurances of the manufacturers relayed to the public by their public relations people. The advantages of foam plastic are that it makes an extremely lightweight protection for precision parts, is easily formed around delicate optical instruments or electronic assemblies, and is quite inexpensive. But there are alternative and organic ways of packaging.

It is a valuable concept that there is really nothing new in the world that needs to be packed and shipped. The immediate objection will be that this is sheer nonsense. After all, there were no computers, CD players or camcorders in the distant past. Yet Van Leuwenhoek had to ship his microscopes from the Netherlands to Padua in the 16th century, Galileo needed to send telescopes to the Danish astronomer Tycho Brahe on the island of Hven off southern Sweden, and forward 'philosophical instruments' and optics to various other parts of Europe. More recently, during the Civil War in the United States, delicate surgical instruments had to be shipped from northern factories to the front. The materials used to pack such early precision instruments were Spanish moss, other dried mosses, sand, sawdust, crushed and dried leaves or dried grasses, thin cotton bags filled with down or feathers, wood chips, and much else. The one thing that these materials have in common is that they can be recycled; they are all organic and will return to the natural environment.

My earliest introduction to this way of packing was my first job as a young boy in New York. I worked in the basement of the Museum of Modern Art packing small sculptures or ceramics to send to members of the museum who were renting art objects for a few months at a time. I remember that, in addition to shipping-boxes (which were made of wood or cardboard), we had two gigantic popcorn machines, and made popcorn – unsalted and without cheese, I may add – in which to pack the sculpture pieces; polystyrene 'worms' did not then exist. It was an intelligent and decent way of packing which in 1992, to my delight, began to be revived by some mail-order firms as an ecologically responsible way of dealing with fragile objects.

In 1989 I was hired by a Japanese corporation, specializing in computers, cameras, and other high-tech products, and spent three years conducting research and feasibility studies in the use of organic packaging materials. Research eventually concentrated on plants that, when maturing, surround their seeds with an enormous protective cradle of fluffy material. The specific seed we researched expands its bulk to more than forty times the original volume.

The package was for a professional precision 35mm camera and its lenses. Normally, expensive small cameras are cradled in a shaped foam-plastic cushion that has been covered with an equally plastic fake-velveteen fabric. This in turn is topped by another velvet-like foam-plastic lid on top, and both are bedded in a sarcophagus-like box, made of high-impact polystyrene. The box is held, or suspended, by two foam-plastic spacers within an outer (again plastic) case. Lenses are normally placed in plastic tubes that are upholstered with foam on the inside, and covered with a leather-like vinyl, called 'leatherette' (the very word makes one's flesh crawl), or a plastic called 'naughahide' on the exterior. A hideous example of over-packaging and transparent make-believe.

Eventually we created a small quilt, about 15 inches (37cm) square. The 'shell' of the quilt is made of rice-paper, filled with fluffy plant fibres and then sewn into quilt squares with a hemp-derived thread. The quilt is wrapped around the

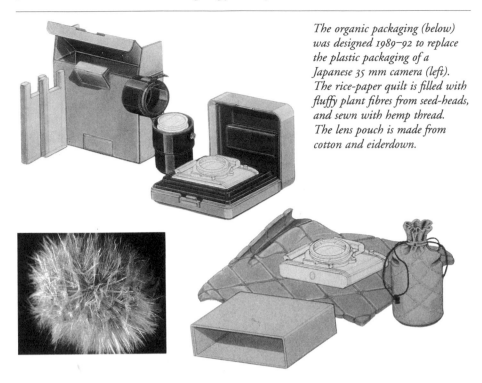

*The organic packaging (below)
was designed 1989–92 to replace
the plastic packaging of a
Japanese 35 mm camera (left).
The rice-paper quilt is filled with
fluffy plant fibres from seed-heads,
and sewn with hemp thread.
The lens pouch is made from
cotton and eiderdown.*

camera body and inserted into a cardboard sleeve. Quilted pouches, made of 'green' cotton and filled with eiderdown, protect the lenses. In Japan this method of softly cradling precision parts is already in experimental use, and will probably soon be used for export models. The great advantages of this package are obvious. Reliance on oil-based plastics and the hazards of their manufacture are entirely eliminated. The new package is wholly organic, and will return to the soil. To exaggerate somewhat, theoretically it may be possible in a year or two for someone to buy a camera or CD player and literally dump the wrapping in the back garden where the recyclable, organic components of the package – augmented by trace amounts of nitrate boosters – will actually help the garden grow.

At the moment, packaging generally involves the use of plastics (discussed in detail later in this chapter), metal, wood, cardboard and paper. The use of paper has two major effects on the ecology. One of these is the cutting-down of trees and forests, the other the pollution that occurs in the paper production itself. Nine-tenths of paper products come from forests in northern temperate zones – Canada, the United States, and northern Europe. It is now widely known how to manage such forests commercially so that they can continue to function as renewable resources, but the timber industry generally refuses to engage in selective harvesting from multi-species mature forests, and continues to plant monocultural forests and to employ the clear-cutting of established woodlands.

Chlorines used in paper production as a bleach for wood fibres also pose an ecological hazard. Chlorine creates dioxins that are mutagenic, that is to say, they create genetic changes by bonding to the DNA structure of living cells. Furthermore the runoff of water tainted with dioxin and chlorine has endangered aquatic life (such as salmon in the Pacific north west of North America), as well as poisoning ground-water.

There are packaging items that are inherently impossible to recycle. Manufacturers can easily avoid using high-gloss papers, highly coated or plastic-coated papers, glues that are not water-soluble and plastic windows on envelopes. Instead designers could specify non-bleached papers or those whitened with new, bleach-free methods. More than three-quarters of all paper types can be recycled, but usually a percentage of new fibres are added. Recycling waste paper can be 50% more energy efficient than the use of virgin pulp. It is good practice to use paper with the highest percentage of recycled material. The Simpson Paper Company of San Francisco has emerged as one of the leaders in this field.

Lead, mercury, arsenic, chromium, cadmium, beryllium and vanadium are all carcinogenic and neurotoxic. They are frequently used in the composition of printing inks on packages, and pose a severe threat when they leach into the water supply from landfills. De-inking is difficult and costly. Vegetable-based inks, made from soya for instance, can be used effectively, and here again the Simpson Paper Company has led the way.

There are other materials that are dangerously poisonous to human beings and the environment. Some countries have already restricted polyvinyl chloride (PVC)

Recycling plants do not have to be a blot on the landscape. This trash recycling plant near Lund in Sweden is unobtrusive and uncluttered.

Three hazard symbols for harmful, flammable and toxic materials respectively, and (on the right) the Blue Angel symbol for safe materials, introduced in West Germany in 1977.

since, unless it is burnt in special handling ovens, it releases dioxins and hydrochloric acids into the air. It has also been established that the making of PVC is directly linked to kidney cancers in workers. There are many other substances, such as cadmium-based pigments, certain flame-retardants and chlorinated solvents, that are still unrestricted in the United States and the United Kingdom, yet pose major health threats. A series of labels and symbols have been developed and accepted internationally, and more specific national or regional markers also exist.

> **Terms for hazardous materials, products or processes**
> - **Carcinogenic:** can cause cancer either in manufacture or in use
> - **Mutagenic:** can cause genetic mutations in human beings or other organisms
> - **Neurotoxic:** can attack the nervous system of human beings or other animals
> - **Biocidal:** destructive to the environment and ecology

In January 1993 a comprehensive set of laws was introduced in Germany to deal with the reduction of packaging waste. These include requirements that producers and suppliers take back all sales and transport packaging. Manufacturers are also obliged to remove wrapping when selling to the end-users, and to inform them where and how to return the rest of the package. Furthermore, the law states specifically that manufacturers must take back, sort and recycle the following:

> Electrical or electronic appliances in the sense of this ordinance are household goods, entertainment electronics appliances and appliances and installations for office, information and communications technology, banking machines, electrical tools, measuring, steering and lighting technology, toys, clocks which contain electrical or electronic component parts…component categories such as casing, screens, keyboards or plates.[2]

Furthermore, these laws decree that packages are merely for the protection of the contents and are not be used for advertising messages or point-of-sale graphics.

Packages come in various guises. With complex mechanisms and electronic parts forming a machine or device, the package in industrial design frequently turns into a 'shroud', that is, an external cover or shell that keeps dust from the working parts, protects them, and cuts down the visual confusion of a complicated working arrangement that can no longer be understood by the end-user.

THE PROBLEM WITH PLASTICS

Virtually all plastics in common use today are based on fossil fuels. Their manufacture therefore contributes to the greenhouse effect, as well as utilizing irreplaceable resources. Although many plastics can be recycled in one form or another, there must be an upper limit to the number of dark grey, rough-textured counter-tops that can be usefully employed. Plastics that contain similar molecular structures can be co-recycled, but it is better procedure to keep plastic materials separate.

There is a continuing need for plastics in medicine, optics, animal husbandry, research into and storage of food and chemicals, where nothing else will do the task as effectively. Plastic is, at the moment, the best material we have for replacement heart-valves, heart pacemakers and artificial joints, filtration and liquid storage devices. But as vast quantities of indestructible plastic waste are washed up on the shoreline and lie unmouldering in our rubbish dumps, we must analyse the whole question of how we use it and how we throw it away.

The 'environmentally friendly' recycling initiative started by the plastics industry should be welcomed with great caution. American householders are encouraged to separate plastics from the rest of their houshold trash, but it seems that thousands of tons of both household and industrial plastic waste, instead of being recycled in the United States, are being shipped to less industrialized countries, particularly in Asia, where the waste is reprocessed under much less stringent rules for health and environmental safety, or is merely dumped in landfills there. Although waste imports are banned by law in the Philippines, over 7500 tons of plastic waste were shipped there from the USA in 1991. Indonesia was receiving thousands of tons until November 1992, when the Indonesian government banned imports of plastic waste; since then, however, illegal container shipments of plastics from the Netherlands, Japan, Korea and the USA have been accumulating in Indonesian ports. By far the largest importer of US plastic waste is Hong Kong, from where much of it goes to China.[5]

One of the main difficulties then lies with the fact that plastics just won't go away. It has been estimated that a discarded plastic bottle will be around for between two to four hundred years. Approximately 25% of all trash in the United States consists of plastics – some ten million tons every year. Landfills can no longer absorb such enormous quantities.

California, Minnesota, Wisconsin and scores of cities and towns are considering banning non-degradable plastics, and are advocating paper for packaging. This approach sounds reasonable at first, until it is realized that this would require a hundred and seventy million acres of extra forest land for paper production, an area the size of the United Kingdom. This alone would add fifty-five thousand million pounds (twenty-five thousand million kg) of trash a year world wide, and would also raise annual energy consumption by more than 225% each year. Researchers are therefore currently attempting to develop plastic materials that can be biologically degraded, either into many inert, minute fragments, or, ideally, into carbon dioxide and water.

Not only designers but also recyclers and users of products need to know what kind of plastic or elastomer (an elastic rubber-like material) they are dealing with. Thermoplastics and elastomers are easy to recycle. Thermoplastics melt at a specific high temperature and therefore can be compared to glass. Thermosetting polymers – a loaf of bread could serve as a metaphor – do not liquefy and are consequently extremely difficult to recycle. Thermosetting materials can be ground up and used as a 'filler' in newer thermosetting materials, but less than a third of the newly constituted material can be recycled filler. Thermosetting plastics, such as melamine, phenolic, epoxies, urea, unsaturated polyester (UPE), or thermosetting polyester (PE) are extremely difficult to re-use.

The use of such terms as 'biodegradable' and 'biodegradation' lacks precision and is too simplistic. Even within the plastics industry and scientific circles, these terms need clarification. The table opposite gives a short explanation of the meaning of various terms in relation to the different categories of plastics and the alternatives presented to the product designer.

At present the designer has a choice of at least seven strategies that employ plastic materials in an ecologically benign way – a repertoire that is sure to expand greatly over the next few years. Yet there are many other possible materials available, and the designer should bring about innovative new ways of utilizing what we already have. In May 1990 an industrial design student at the Gerrit Rietveld Akademie in Amsterdam, on a short-term Eco-design course with me, demonstrated that layers of paper no heavier than ordinary typing paper could be laminated into an all-paper armchair with organic glue so that the entire structure could be recycled or – better yet – abandoned to return to the earth.

The necessity for choosing materials with extreme care is emphasized by the problem of landfills – dumping sites where unsorted rubbish is buried in the ground. Frequently such landfills are then used as building sites. Recent research excavations of older landfills have shown that, if closely packed, even organic waste and waste considered biodegradable can last from twenty to forty years without significant changes.

CATEGORIES OF PLASTICS

Permanent

For products for which there will be no secondary use.
Applications in medicine and related fields for products in direct contact with organic parts, e.g. parts of an implanted hip-joint, shell of heart pacemaker, artificial veins, blood-storage bags. Material characteristics and lasting quality performance of primary importance, e.g. **nylon 66.** Quantity used negligible.

Re-usable

Product can be used over and over again unchanged, e.g. plastic bucket. Complex tools or appliances can be repaired, upgraded in whole or in part, for resale. Enormous numbers of items involved. Wood, tin, enamel, glass, ceramics ecologically and aesthetically preferable.

Recyclable

Thermoplastics and **elastomers** melt at a specific high temperature like glass and are easy to recycle. **Thermosetting polymers** do not liquefy and are very difficult to recycle; research is continuing into better methods.

Co-recyclable

Compatible materials can be recycled together to form a useful new material.

Biodisintegratable

Attempts have been made to embed a biodegradable trait into synthetic polymers so that they turn into mulch. These compounds perform badly in landfills through lack of moisture, slightly better when composted. Radical improvements have produced plastics, now commercially available, that degrade 100% less than 2 months after being discarded. Research continues into further control of the start of degradation.

Biodegradable

100% biodegradable rather than biodisintegratable. **PHA (polyhydroxyalkanoate),** a member of the polyester family discovered in 1925, is 'manufactured' directly by micro-organisms. Since then scores of bacteria that produce this organic polymer have been found, including **PHBs (polyhydroxybutyrates),** one of the first to be commercially available. PHA plastics can be moulded, melted and shaped like petroleum-based plastics, and have the same flexibility and strength. The same production methods can be used, e.g. melt-casting, injection-moulding, blow-moulding, spinning and extrusion. Manufactured under the name Biopol in Europe by ICI and PHBV in the United States. Too expensive for routine use for soft-drink bottles or grocery bags, but the cost should drop with full-scale production.

Bioregenerative

Union Carbide researchers have produced a type of **polycaprolactone film** that completely biodegrades within 3 months, leaving no residues. Research into paper products laminated with layers of corn-based cellulose materials prove they can resist water for 6 to 8 hours and could serve as containers for drinks and fast-food items.

Bioenhancing

Carry additives to stimulate plant growth, or, as with the artificial burrs designed in the 1970s to prevent erosion in arid climates, carry plant seeds and seedlings embedded in growth stimulants.

MILLIONS OF TYRES

My own particular concern is scrap tyres. In the United States alone there are presently more than three thousand million tyres in landfills, illegal dumps and stockpiles, increasing by another thousand million every four years. The largest pile of tyres in the world is in Westley, California, where thirty-four million scrap tyres cover nearly 200 acres, sometimes forming seven-storey high mountains. Apart from providing ideal breeding conditions for disease-carrying insects, tyres are also profound pollutants of the atmosphere when they burn, producing spectacular clouds of stinking oily smoke; these fires can last for years. In landfills tyres can capture explosive methane gas and 'float' upwards – sometimes shooting to the surface with enormous force. In 1984 seven million tyres began burning in Winchester, Virginia. The fire lasted for more than nine months and nearly seven hundred thousand gallons (two and a half million litres) of oil oozed out.

Less than 20% of tyres are re-used in the United States; most are exported. All tyres, from a child's tricycle to the monsters on earth-moving machinery, are made of near-identical ingredients. There are several types of natural and synthetic rubber, fabric, steel and carbon black, and each must be recycled separately, further complicated by the fact that tyre rubber is vulcanized, that is, the sulphur and carbon in the rubber are bonded inseparably – the rubber is 'thermosetting' rather than 'thermoplastic' and, like a loaf of bread, it cannot be remoulded.

Tyres can be made into a new product called rubber-modified asphalt; a mile of road uses sixteen thousand chopped-up tyres. American laws now require that at least 5% of asphalt laid in any American state must contain recycled rubber; this will rise to 20% by 1997. A tyre road lasts twice as long as a normal asphalt one according to the National Solid Wastes Management Association.

Pyrolysis is a costly process that can vaporize tyres at 1000°F (538°C). A new process has been developed that can do this at 450°F (232°F), yielding light oil and also methane gas which is used to power the machinery.[4] Experiments are proceeding with dissolving tyre scraps in oil at 700°F (371°C)[5] which produces a light oil that can be refined into diesel gas, heating fuel and other chemicals and also smaller amounts of heavy fuel oil. It has been estimated that *presently there are over twelve thousand million gallons (forty-five thousand million litres) of oil locked up in tyre dumps around the world.* Our resources lie deeply embedded in recyclable scrap – the mines and reservoirs of the future are the rubbish tips of today.

GREEN DESIGN

Design for Disassembly (DFD) is a profoundly important new development in design, take-apart technology which facilitates recycling. There is also Design Diversification, the imaginative discovery of new applications for superfluous components. There is also the use of manufacturing waste and production fall-offs which has not yet been sufficiently investigated; it is a brand-new approach to benign recycling. All these developments will be examined later in the book.

The exploitation of solar power seems to be going in two different directions. American scientists are attempting to improve the efficiency of solar cells, whereas Japanese engineers are reducing their cost through mass-production methods. Yukinori Kuwano, general manager of research and development at Sanyo, began to make solar cells of amorphous silicone after the energy crisis of 1973. Sanyo has since become the world's leading manufacturer of amorphous-silicone cells which are now used – essentially as free give-aways – in calculators, wristwatches, cameras and other small consumer goods. Yukinori Kuwano is quoted as saying that within seven and a half years the *entire* energy needs of the world could be supplied by 323 square miles of solar panels covering 4% of the world's deserts. Super-conducting cables would carry the power to areas with less sunlight.[6]

Commercially viable small-scale solar devices should be more readily accepted following ideas for suburban and garden pathway lighting with self-sufficient solar lamp standards, as well as my own concept for amorphous silicone roof tiles.

In 1981 I was commissioned by the United Nations to develop a non-electric refrigerator to be used in developing countries for storing medicines and bulk food. The design is based on a classic experiment by Michael Faraday in England over one and a half centuries ago. Faraday coupled two glass retorts together, one containing silver nitrate crystals, the other ammonia. When a bunsen burner heated the glass vessel, the resulting mixture made the other retort extremely cold.

Early in the 20th century, the Crosley Radio Corporation in America produced a refrigerator based on Faraday's experiment which was widely marketed under the name of the 'Crosley Icy-Ball'. This fridge worked well for years, since the chemical mixture was contained in a closed system and did not need to be renewed. It was much more convenient than the old-fashioned ice-chests. With the introduction of electric or gas-driven refrigerators, however, the Crosley Icy-Ball lost the advantage of greater convenience, and quickly faded into disuse.

My design research team re-defined the unit, which is now powered by a parabolic solar mirror, with lithium bromide substituted for the earlier chemical charge. The unit is produced in a number of Third World countries, primarily for the storage of medical supplies. It has proved itself effective in more than ten tropical countries. My team considered it for re-design in technologically highly developed, or overdeveloped countries, but this has been overtaken by the introduction of CFC-free refrigerants, such as Suva MP-39, and the production of environmentally safe coolers by Siemens A.G. in Germany among others.

There are hundreds of ways in which industrial designers can participate in helping the environment and forestalling further ecological damage. I shall

This solar cooking stove was developed through UNESCO
for India and Pakistan where millions are now in daily use.

confine myself to a few solutions explored by my colleagues, my graduate students and myself. Only a selection from scores of important topics will be covered in the hope that these kaleidoscopic fragments will form a meaningful pattern. These design interventions may seem trivial – they *are* trivial as they are the first small attempts to reverse the ongoing trend of 'bigger is better', and to challenge the received wisdom of design 'progress'.

A portable solar cell, about the size of two sheets of typing paper, has been developed and is now on the market to provide power for charging batteries on boats, automobiles and some small tools. A simple solar cooking stove has been developed through UNESCO for India and Pakistan, and some 40–80 million units are now in daily use. This stove will cook meals over a five-hour period using only sunlight, and the unit can be self-built on a village level of technology. (It must be pointed out that this lends itself only to the preparation of traditional Indian foods and is not suitable for quick cooking methods.)

Studies in preventing future oil spills have resulted in the design of modular oil-storage containers. These hollow, tetrakaidekahedral-shaped units[7] measure some 36 feet (12m) in diameter and can be assembled into transportation floats that will bring oil to the surface from submarine drilling, transport it across the ocean surface and to onshore refineries. The containers are virtually impervious to puncture – should something go wrong however, the spill would be restricted in size and therefore limited in its destructive effect.

In 1981 I was able to start a user-initiative for ecological controls in Papua New Guinea, which had only recently achieved independence and was still emerging from a virtual Stone Age culture. Nonetheless it proved feasible to organize clean-up squads, and to mount parades and rallies that focused attention on recycling, litter control, the use of biomass conversion, geothermal power, and so forth. The press in Papua New Guinea took up our initiative and continues to push for sane

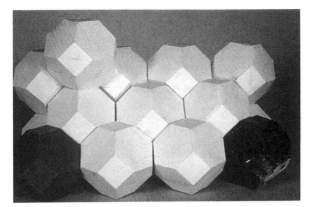

Design study for tetrakaidekahedral modular units for the safer transportation of oil.

environmental controls. Through a simple organization and the development of a consumer movement, Papua New Guinea was fifteen years ahead of many technologically developed societies in ecological awareness.

It is in the soft-energy technologies that the excitement of Green Design can be found. The Egyptians, the Greeks, the Romans and others used passive solar power. In downtown Los Angeles one can still see solar mirror panels – or rather the remains of them – that date back to 1905 and that provided light and some power to offices, a fact that young students today find startling. Now solar furnaces at Mount Louis in the USA and Odeillo in France and vast solar mirror concentrations in Colorado and California are providing power.

The first geothermal power station was built at Ladarello in 1904; both volcanic as well as hot-water geothermals have been used in Iceland for more than three centuries, and in New Zealand for generations, to warm buildings and provide power. Tidal power has been harnessed in France at St Malo, Garonne, the Loire, and has been studied intensively since 1989 in the Bay of Fundy in Canada.

Wind farms (consisting of large clusters of wind-turbines) have been in use in North America and Israel since 1978. Methane digestion has been in use in Gothenburg and other Swedish towns since the 1960s. When working in Chad (in North Equatorial Africa) in 1972, we researched the exploitation of the great differential in desert regions between night-time and daytime temperatures; such systems, using pipes filled with water, alcohol and other liquids, are now used as power generators in Libya, Egypt, Morocco, Iran and Saudi Arabia.

Biomass conversion, that is, the conversion of dead plant-material, has been used in Brazil since 1973 to make an alternative fuel for cars from banana leaves and cane sugars. Maize is used as a propellant in the USA, and Austria has pioneered the use of 'raps' (a combination of rapeweed and turnip) as an automobile fuel, and this is (in 1994) available in filling stations in Vienna.

Before the re-unification of Germany, serious research was being carried on in East Germany on 'co-generation', which is the use of industrial waste to generate electricity as well as the re-use of heat generated in the manufacturing process. Forest waste is being turned into liquid fuel in eastern Colombia and Venezuela; and in the Alps near Mt Blanc French scientists are studying the possible use of glacier movement for power generation. In Indonesia and Malaysia research goes on to study tropical downpours of rain as an energy source.

Some years ago the first trans-Australian solar-powered automobile race was held; since then, in subsequent trials, vehicles have improved enormously. The *Gossamer Albatross,* a solar and muscle-powered aircraft, has crossed the English Channel, and Commander Cousteau's research vessel *Alcyone* has covered most of the oceans and rivers of the world, relying entirely on its vertical wind-turbines.

Even though few of these experimental devices will find immediate applications, these and other benign techniques provide exciting challenges for industrial designers to explore new technologies that will do less harm to the environment.

Whenever high technology achieves greater speed at greater financial and energy cost, it would be useful if a slow but cheap alternative way could be developed. The time may have come for serious consideration of the re-introduction of abandoned railtrack, canal boats and transoceanic sailing ships as an alternative to speedy but costly air shipment. Sailing ships were phased out largely because a large crew was needed to swarm up the rigging and re-set the sails. Because of modern computer-controlled rigging and servo-mechanisms, 'tall ships' now cruising the Caribbean frequently have a crew of only twelve handling the sails, working in three shifts. In previous books I have suggested the re-introduction of Zeppelin-like aircraft for leisurely transcontinental travel, as well as for the direct silo-to-population transfer of emergency food and aid to various parts of the world.[8]

PROFIT AND POLITICS

Industrialists, primarily in Germany, Japan and Sweden, have recognized the current environmental and ecological hazards for what they really are: vast new challenges for humankind that must be solved, and *vast possibilities for future earnings, since few governments or industrial powers yet take these threats seriously.*

The beneficial connection between economics and ecology has been systematically misrepresented by industrial and governmental apologists. When the Pacific Electric Company distributes thousands of low-wattage and therefore energy-saving fluorescent light bulbs (that retail at $16.95 each), at no cost to its domestic customers, and insulates private houses for free, this may be done out of altruistic concern for a benign environment, but it also saves 185 million dollars otherwise needed to build a new power-generating station.[9]

Jacques Cousteau's research vessel 'Alcyone', powered by vertical wind-turbines.

The slogan 'Re-use, recycle and dispose responsibly' is a familiar one. 'Use less', however, should should be our over-riding maxim. Manufacturers and their designers are frightened by the idea of using less. It implies that less will be bought and that profits will shrink. Yet if we disengage ourselves from this linear way of thinking, we see that quite the reverse may happen. In a world in which less is used and less is bought, products that are designed to last longer and are more carefully crafted and assembled will obviously need to cost more.

Most designers today don't seem to feel comfortable with a term like 'social responsibility' in reference to the built or designed environment. The Post-Modern condition can be characterized as a vacuum of conscience in which such socially responsible notions as fair housing, a clean environment, health care or access to services are considered somewhat of an embarrassment. Product culture has been allowed to run wild, and has substituted trendy objects for community values, many of them provided by industry and their captive industrial designers, designers and architects.

The richer countries of the world should feel guilty for a statistic that has often been cited since 1970: 6% of the world's population consumes more than 35% of its resources. A riveting fact is that individual sentiments of guilt or shame have done little to alter collective or governmental or professional accountability. Each new insight into the environmental crisis has led to a normalization of a Green Apocalypse – global warming, acid rain, soil and water depletion and the toxification of the land – all these have become accepted penalties for our high-entropy way of life. The consequences which seemed far off and uncertain, are now with us, and yet are treated with the same inattention as the weather.

The great threats which have contributed to this crisis – mechanized agriculture, dirty industry, and rapid urbanization – are well-known. Roughly 70% of the energy used in the United States (which produces more than 25% of the planet's greenhouse trace gases) is attributable to urbanization: this includes transportation, heating, lighting and power, and the generation of that power itself.

Yet it is stupidly optimistic to imagine what *might* happen if we don't know *how* it will happen. This is why concern for the ecology involves ethics and social responsibility. Using less, preserving for the future, conservation and softer energy sources are only drops in the bucket unless these activities are linked to a greater social process that can influence industrial design, industry and policy.

The question of ecology as a socially-based priority asks that design and planning consider sustainability and social justice as reciprocal conditions – that saving the planet and saving the community become one – inseparable.

DESIGN IN THE 21ST CENTURY

As we move towards the 21st century, there will be an increasing need for *some – a few* – designers who are specialists in ecological design. However, in my opinion, *all* design education must be based on ecological methods and ideas. This will include studies in the scientific method, as well as in biology, anthropology, cultural geography and related fields. Social and human ecology and philosophy and ethics will form an integral part of this training.

The future of design is bound up with the key role of *synthesis* between the various disciplines that make up the socio-economic-political matrix within which design operates. I list some examples of how an ecological world-view could change design:

1. There will be a greater emphasis on quality, permanence and craftsmanship in designed products, as people and designers come to understand that obsolescence or bad workmanship waste natural resources that can't be replaced, and contribute to shortages on a global scale. The style of the future will be based on products that age gracefully, and will be more timeless than the quickly changing fads, trends and fashions of the late 20th century.

2. Designers and manufacturers will need to question the ultimate consequences of a new product being introduced. Questions of profit balances and production quotas are not enough.

3. New product ranges will appear, especially in areas such as catalytic converters, afterburners, scrubbers for factories, air, water and soil-quality monitors.

4. It will be understood that no design stands on its own: all design has social, ecological and environmental consequences that need to be evaluated and discussed in a common forum.

5. There must be a greater concern for and a deeper understanding of nature, and this will be a preserving and healing force for the global environment.[10]

CHAPTER 3

Toward the Spiritual in Design

It may be true that one has to choose between ethics and aesthetics,
but whichever one chooses, one will always find the other
at the end of the road.
Jean-Luc Godard

AT FIRST sight, there is no such thing as a piece of industrial design that is invested with spiritual values. There can be no transcendental refrigerator, no righteous chair, no moral tea kettle. We cannot find a spiritual advertisement, a soul-stirring logo or trademark. In the fields of fashion and textile design it is impossible to locate an immaculate cotton print or a saintly dress.

The question of whether a design is spiritual or not seems easier to answer in relation to architecture. Architecture can – at times – touch the spiritual. The why and how of this will be explored in the following chapter, 'Sensing a Dwelling'.

THE FUNCTION OF BEAUTY

Can the spiritual exist in design? The men and women working and studying in Germany in the 1920s at the Bauhaus (possibly the most influential school of design in history), would have answered affirmatively and without hesitation. Their conviction was: 'If it functions well, it will be beautiful – and therefore have spiritual value.'

Looking at this proposition from the vantage point of the mid-1990s, things are less clear. The cool elegance of the Bauhaus style has gained some cachet. We are also somewhat seduced by the fact that age has bestowed the seeming blessings of permanence on these buildings, pieces of furniture, tools, crafts and graphic designs. We respond affirmatively to the daring and revolutionary re-structuring of the human environment reflected in the work. At the same time we have also gained greater detachment from the shock of what was formerly new. We are more able to diagnose the 'cool elegance' as cold sterility. We may applaud the attempt to build a 'Cathedral of Socialism'[1] and the effort to 'join artists, workers, industry and the crafts', but we are well aware that the experiments at Weimar and Dessau found their admirers amongst a comparatively small group of artists, the intelligentsia and the *haute bourgeoisie*, rather than the workers and farmers that the designers and architects had envisaged as their target audience. In short, the Bauhaus style was élitist and seen as alienating by many.

This Bauhaus lamp of 1923-24 shows the cool elegance typical of the style.

To the statement, 'If it functions well, it will be beautiful', we now add the questions: 'If it functions well, doing what ? It will be beautiful in what sense ? Function and Beauty in what context?'

We have also seen many of the pioneering works of the Bauhaus domesticated, trivialized and cheapened. The cantilevered tubular steel chairs with cane seats and backs were a truly new concept of tool and material. Marcel Breuer used the bending moment of steel to build in a 'feathering' action that added comfort without visual or mechanical clutter. However we have seen the descendants of these chairs – in kitchens and 'dinettes', and in some of the seediest cafés around the globe – shoddy and cheap, the caning replaced by flamingo-coloured plastic.

Is a bullet-shaped shade on a flexible arm, both enamelled shiny white on metal, really the most appropriate task-light? Or would it be more fitting in a laboratory making false teeth? Can we find no better way to serve a fine sherry or port than from a clear glass bottle resting on a cork ring – obviously adapted from a flask in some chemical laboratory? Ironically, I am presently designing a birthing-chair for a women's group, a design that is based on a reclining lounger developed at the Bauhaus. Let me emphasize quickly that I am adapting the Bauhaus original for ergonomic reasons only. Aesthetically the original is far from satisfying since a birthing-chair needs to communicate associations of safety and comfort – the sterile-seeming cleanliness of the original did not carry these reassuring patterns.

Latter-day apologists for a strictly utilitarian idea of beauty will frequently point to, say, a 747 aeroplane, an F-16 fighter aircraft, or a high-performance sailplane such as the Mini-nimbus. Their form is – allegedly – based on pure aerodynamic considerations, 'purely functional' (in the narrowest sense). Things aren't that simple. The 747 is an awkward compromise between seating capacity, ticket sales and class separation; engineering logistics, aerodynamic factors and fuel capacity are among many other modifiers, and also the trade-off between leg comfort, safety and square-foot cost of each seat written off over ten years. The fighter-bomber strikes a balance between high speed, close turning ratios and fuel capacity; it must also carry bombs, cannons, machine guns and heavy armaments. The design of the Mini-nimbus demands an advantageous descent ratio, and

The spare functionalism of Shaker furniture, like this stove of 1840, sprang directly from the sect's belief in austerity and the reduction of worldly goods.

extreme lightness in weight, coupled with strength; the reason that it seems so 'right' for its purpose, and therefore beautiful, is the complete absence of unnecessary ornamentation or decoration. *Unnecessary* ornamentation. This is equally true of the 747 and the F-16.

At the same time, we know that decoration is deeply satisfying to human beings and has been throughout history. When I lived among the Inuit I was struck by the time devoted to carving ornament on tools. Some of the objects of 35,000 years ago unearthed from Willendorf and the Neander valley in Austria show detailed chipping and colouring. We take pleasure in adding adornment to plain areas – yet this is functional decoration: it fulfils the aesthetic part of the six-fold function complex (see p.34) by relieving the monotony of the large, plain areas. It is only when we are dealing with survival conditions in design that we are forced to abandon the extraneous 'beautifying', and a dynamic form may be revealed that we experience as satisfying.

We can sift through the history of designed objects. In so doing we must beware of the distortions when we gaze at anything through a rear-view mirror. We will find much that enchants us with its restrained elegance and simplicity: the ceremonial tea whisk, cut from a single joint of bamboo to serve in a traditional *cha-no-yu* tea bowl in Japan; the water bucket made of birch staves for a Finnish sauna; a Viking boat; furniture made by the Shakers in America during the 18th and 19th centuries; a Chinese rice bowl of the T'ang dynasty.

A whisk for a Japanese tea ceremony, cut from a single joint of bamboo.

We can try to probe the mechanism at work here. To begin with, we are guilty of the sin of 'Presentism'.[2] Living in overdeveloped countries with underdeveloped taste, we excel in ornamentation, visual braggadocio and excess. Our natural sense of order and simplicity makes us overly impressed by the austere, yet we flaunt the flashy and ostentatious. In order to extract the essence from these objects, we must examine them against the cultural and social matrix from which they developed. When we do so, we find that all of them are related to spiritual values in some sense.

The tea whisk is pure ceremonial gear. Powdered green tea is not normally consumed as refreshment; it is reserved for the traditional tea ceremony. Nor is tea-water whipped in Japan, except as part of this rite. The bucket used in the sauna – like the sauna itself – goes far back in Finnish history to pre-Christian traditions. It is a purification ceremony that is still surrounded by some mystical values, occupying a similar place in their view of the universe to Navajo sweat-lodges, Bedouin sand-cleansing and the Inuit smoke-igloo. Over the centuries the few sauna utensils became simplified to the point of anonymity.

For the Vikings, deep spiritual values were interwoven with wood technology, the resistance and strength needed to cut cleanly through ocean waves, and considerations of safety for the voyagers. Out of this web emerged the Viking boat as a metaphysical tool for exploration and a transformative journey. The sparse simplicity of Shaker furniture directly reflects the sect's religious values and rules,[3] which, in promoting austerity and order, attempted to reduce wants and false needs and to permit a journey unencumbered by worldly possessions. The traditional Chinese rice bowl speaks eloquently to the unique symbolic – almost holy – place of rice in traditional southern Chinese culture.

The fighter-bomber gives us a hint. When I organized an exhibition of great Finnish design, a number of designers and architects were deeply shocked by my choice of a 22mm rifle as one of the exhibits, explaining to me that anything that was dedicated to death could not have beauty – let alone spiritual value.[4]

We seem here to have reached a key point in our examination of what separates all industrial design from architecture. Through the manipulation and orchestration of interior spaces, it is possible to release transcendental feelings, hints of the sacred in people. This can't be done as directly in any tool, object or artefact. We may admire the pure lines of a birch-bark canoe, or a glider, but this aesthetic response – caused by simple elegance – may only infrequently release in us intimations of the sublime.

THE DESIGNER'S INTENT

I firmly believe that it is the intent of the designer as well as the intended use of the designed object that can yield spiritual value. The European word 'form-giving' may express best what industrial designers do – always being careful to include the workings of the device in the form-giving and making sure that a degree of inventiveness is part of the design process. As we practise our art and skill, what we do moulds who we are and what we are becoming.

- When we become the hired guns of greed-driven corporations, we are driven to **conform**.
- If we generate status kitsch for a jaded élite, and allow ourselves to become media celebrities, we **perform**.
- When we twist products to reflect the navel-gazing of market research, we **deform**.
- If our products divorce appearance and the other functions – a telephone that looks like a duck and quacks instead of ringing, a clock-radio that looks like a female leg – we **misinform**.
- When our designs are succinct statements of purpose, easy to understand, use, maintain and repair, long-lasting, recyclable and benign to the environment, we **inform**.
- If we design with harmony and balance in mind, working for the good of the weaker members of our society, we **reform**.
- Being willing to face the consequences of our design interventions, and accepting our social and moral responsibilities, we **give form**.

All this can be done only if we learn to recognize the ethical dilemmas of our profession. This means thinking dispassionately about what we do. This is desperately difficult for designers. Our professional education is deeply divisive, almost schizoid. On the one hand we learn many aspects of high technology. We study mass-production methods, industrial techniques from explosive moulding to micro-chip regulators, CAD-CAM (computer-assisted design and computer-aided manufacture) to random extrusion bundling. We investigate materials-technology and explore many aspects of plastics and electronics engineering.

On the other hand we are encouraged to think of ourselves as artists. This part of our education frequently leads towards totally self-indulgent aesthetics. In our age, it is the nature of aesthetic processes that users are never consulted. This may give great freedom to a painter or sculptor to express his or her convictions,

Bookcase, 1981, designed by Ettore Sotsass for Memphis; a reaction against late Modernism.

dreams, demons or hopes. In a wider public art, such as the design of everyday things, this can only encourage the peacock's strut, eccentric perversity, the fraudulent posturing of the charlatan.

Designers asked for more than a hundred years: 'How can I make it more beautiful?' After the Bauhaus and the lessons of Scandinavian form-giving, this changed to: 'How can I make it work better?' The logical question, 'Can it work and look better?' isn't put often enough. Just look around at our buildings, cities, automobiles, furniture or tools. It is tempting to think that form-givers – faced by this false choice between appearance and utility – answered: 'Neither!' The 'statement' or 'gesture' have replaced the object, and designers emerging from this bifurcated education tend to ask themselves: 'How can I make it different?' Theoretically this might lead to an endless and lackadaisical repetition of stylistic mannerisms, varied by frequent sorties into the past.

Into this zany mixture caused by a misconceived education and a social structure devoted to no higher aspiration than, 'Take the money and run!', we now introduce the question of the spiritual in design. As if by magic, we can begin to see clearly. I repeat, it is the intent of the designer as well as the intended use of the designed object that can yield spiritual value. The questions that must be asked are:

Will the design significantly aid the sustainability of the environment?
Can it make life easier for some group that has been marginalized by society?
Can it ease pain?
Will it help those who are poor, disenfranchised or suffering?
Will it save energy or – better still – help to gain renewable energies?
Can it save irreplaceable resources?

A positive answer to these or similar questions does not make the design visibly spiritual. But the performance of such services to our fellow humans and the planet will help us inwardly. It will nourish our soul and help it to grow. That's where spiritual values enter design.

The organic shape of a prototype camera by Collani, 1974.

New directions in design and architecture always arise out of real social and cultural changes. The monotonous sterility that still existed in household products, especially furniture and furnishings in the early 1970s, eventually led to a counter-revolutionary movement in the upper levels of the market. Both Memphis (led by the witty style of Ettore Sotsass) and Alchimia were stylistic protest movements – primarily in the field of furniture – that tried to expose the visual poverty of the late Modern movement through promoting non-functional pieces that were carefully designed to violate all the strictures of the Modernist gospel. The effect of these movements on furniture design are comparable to that of Dadaism, the 'anti-art' movement, on the arts immediately after World War I. Memphis and Alchimia gave us chairs that could not be sat on, bookcases that could not hold books and other non-functioning devices. The results were 'camp' or 'funky', but found little appeal outside a few museum exhibitions and the more avant-garde salons of Milan. Memphis and other Italian counter-functional movements, however, have forced industrial designers to lighten up in the design of tools and objects.

Following yet another new direction, the influence of the designer Luigi Collani has been strong in the fashion for biomorphic, organic and fluid shapes. His published materials are a major influence combining ergonomic considerations with shapes that seem almost to have grown around the electronic and mechanical parts.

The sometimes subversive influence of design-styling on a simple tool is shown by seven fish hooks that I collected in Papua New Guinea. The simple hook made

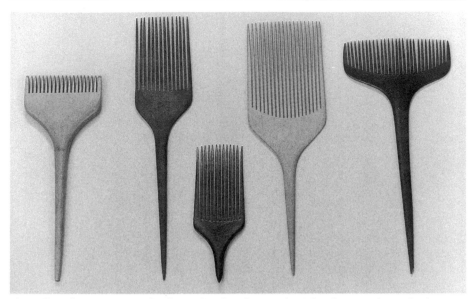

A set of wooden Japanese combs, designed so that the attendant's hands are made to take the best and visually most elegant position to fashion the traditional geisha hairstyle.

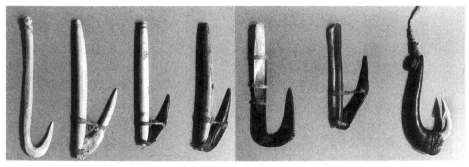

Design development (left to right) in fish hooks, Papua New Guinea.

of bone worked fairly well for centuries, but later it was realized that a barb independent of the shank, yet attached with twine to give it a slight 'feathering' action, could be larger and catch fish more effectively. Then someone made a barb of tortoiseshell whose light-reflecting properties would be attractive to fish; at the same time he decided to straighten out the shank, with the result that the hook hangs at a useless angle. The fourth hook shows that the designer has learnt his lesson; the shank is curved and the tortoiseshell barb is larger.

Possibly the robust egos of designers make them feel that bigger is always better, and biggest is always best. The designer of the next stage decided that if a medium-size tortoiseshell hook worked in attracting fish, then an enormous one would work even better. He also replaced the shank with a highly-reflective abalone shell. From my own observation, fish would come for miles to look at this shining object, but it never occurred to them to put it in their mouths. The sixth hook marks the decadent stage of design development. The shank is made from the most rare and precious material in Papua New Guinea, part of the plastic canopy of a fighter aircraft shot down over the island in the 1940s. It was soon found that the plastic shank dissoved in saltwater, making it useless as a fish hook, so the designer decided to sell it as an amulet, forgetting that human sweat is also salty. The seventh hook shows that by rethinking the problem statement, it is possible to go beyond degeneracy and develop a better design. It is made of heavy teak, containing enough natural oils to be impervious to saltwater. The shank has been artfully curved with the line somewhat offset so that it will hang at the most opportune angle. The barb has two retro-hooks and is carved from bone. It is secured to the shank with tarred hemp twine permitting the 'feathering action' that works it more deeply into the fish.

There is a point at which beauty and high utility through good design interconnect. If both conditions exist simultaneously in an object, and are furthermore clear expressions of the social intent of the people who designed it, it is possible to speak of the spiritual in design. We have seen that the old Modernist saying, 'If it works well, it will be beautiful,' is false. We are surrounded each day by hundreds of objects that nullify this approach. At the same time we know that the reverse, 'If it is beautiful, it will work well,' is ridiculously wide of the mark.

The OXO corkscrew and the jar-opener (illustrated on p.58) are superb examples of high aesthetic function married to utility; both were designed and are made with the needs of arthritic and elderly people in mind. The sensuous curves of the corkscrew don't just look inviting, they also sensibly and sensitively guide the hands through correct use. This tool looks remarkably handsome when closed, open or in the various mid-range positions. The designers have exhibited unusual understanding of plastics as a permanent and good-looking material rather than a substitute for something else. The jar-opener is as much of a conceptual breakthrough, a great solution to the difficult problem of removing a tight lid, though it does not have quite the same sensuous flair as the corkscrew. In using these two tools it becomes clear that nothing could possibly be added or taken away – they seem perfect statements just as they are.

Betsy Wells Farber is the design director of OXO International. She is an architect who suffers from arthritis herself, and the jar-opener is her concept. The design development was by Stephan Allendorf, who also with Peter Stathis designed the corkscrew for the industrial design firm 'Smart Design' of New York. Both appliances are part of a series of kitchen, garden and measuring tools marketed under the name of 'Good Grips' which have won several design awards.

We are still looking for a new reality-based aesthetic direction. Concern for the environment and for the disadvantaged of our society are the most profound and

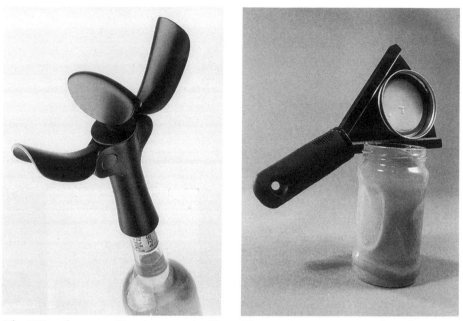

The OXO corkscrew combines beauty and utility.   *The OXO jar-opener is a satisfying design.*

powerful forces with which to shape design. They may indeed develop the new styles that are so desperately needed. Whole technologies, based on alternative power sources, have to be invented and designed. Lifestyle changes will be required to make many of the most radical changes acceptable.

DESIGN FOR DISASSEMBLY

Around 1990 a new direction in industrial design was introduced called 'Design for Disassembly' (DFD), or take-apart technology. It takes the environment into account by designing the whole object in such a way that it can easily be disassembled and recycled once its useful life is over. It is increasingly acknowledged that a mix of glass, metals, plastic, paint, shellacs and fillers on a motorcycle or car body makes separating and sorting after use almost impossible and certainly prohibitively expensive; further developments should ensure that individual parts will be made of single rather than compound materials. Screws, glue and other mastic agents, as well as many welding and soldering methods, also defeat take-apart technology, whereas two-way fasteners, pop-in pop-out rivets, for instance, become necessities. Some of the aesthetic possibilities that DFD opens up for design are examined in Chapter 12, but it seems appropriate at this point to stress the effect that this new technology may have on the whole spirit of design.

Assemble for disassembly? Construct to destruct? It sounds odd, yet with serious concern for environment and ecology, designing things to come apart efficiently is as important as to design them well initially. This approach may be obscurely troubling to older designers. Their schooling and early work prepared them to design for obsolescence, fashion-orientated consumer products that would be discarded for the 'brand-new latest'. This had its roots in the strictly functional need to replace the moulds used for car bodies when they wore out after a few years.

During the late 1940s, consumer demand for new cars in the United States increased annual production runs to a point where these moulds wore out within a year – industry began using mould-inserts to extend the use of the 'sloppy' moulds, leading to minor and superficial changes in the appearance of the car (tailfins, altered front grilles, and so on); this in turn conditioned customers to look forward to annual model changes and long for the latest, futurist incarnation of the same old car.

EXPLOITING EVERY SCRAP

Concern for the ecology points to yet another possible new direction in design, that is, the exploitation of off-cuts from manufacturing, which are normally wasted. This can best be illustrated through small-scale and modest examples.

When I saw handsome leather goods of light-coloured oxhide, handsewn by saddlers in Poland, I became interested in how leftover scraps were used. I was told that they were thrown away as 'too small even for a wallet'. Talking to the small manufacturers in Poland resulted in my inventing a 'bookweight' for people who like to read whilst eating, which has been widely sold through mail-order houses. The oxhide darkens with use to a golden honey colour, quite distinct from the inferior copies, now mass-produced in the Orient, stained the colour of cheap milk chocolate, and finished with a shiny polish.

But there are still smaller scraps left over from the original oxhide. They could be used for form-fitting handles for cutlery to meet the specific needs of people with hands crippled by arthritis or other disabling afflictions; this could provide work and therefore independence and self-esteem for people with learning difficulties. The eating utensils could come in many configurations,[5] including one for so-called 'normals', so as not to isolate the physically disabled from their families or friends. Innovative design can solve this ecological challenge – wasting less – and at the same time tackle three different problems of human performance and psychology.

PEOPLE PARTICIPATION

The job of the designer is to provide choices for people. These choices should be real and meaningful, allowing people to participate more fully in their own life decisions, and enabling them to communicate with designers and architects in

This leather bookweight is made from manufacturing off-cuts.

Design for cutlery handles to be cut from the smallest leather scraps.

finding solutions to their own problems, even – whether they want to or not – to become their own designers.

The old are just one of many groups either not sufficiently served by industry and its designers, or not served at all. Just designing for the needs of the ageing could keep most designers and architects busy for the next fifty years. This segment of the population is increasing more quickly than any other; most old people still have enough money to get by – in many cases even fairly large disposable funds – and are the best people to consult on ways of easing the difficulties of old age.

In a project, undertaken by one of my students, it was possible to recycle mattresses and plastic (the sort that dry-cleaners use to protect clothes) to make a highly portable bathing or sitting cushion that would ease the daily life of women in the last months of pregnancy. Small-scale, decentralized production, or working at home on a do-it-yourself level can combine with re-use to form a new process and a benign ecological intervention.

Babies and small children have specific needs for recreation, educational environments, exercise and general health. There are also a number of health hazards and disabling diseases where design intervention can help. These are but a few of the areas to which designers can and should address their talents. From such activities some very real spiritual values will accrue to the designer and the producers.

The requirements for decent design are far too complex for a designer to solve alone, (or even by several designers working as a team). It is essential to work with people from other fields. For many years, my own practice has been to set up a multidisciplinary team as soon as I have moved into a new locality or established my studio in a new country. The basic members of such a team will usually include an anthropologist, a psychologist or a member of one of the other social sciences, an environmental scientist with a strong bent towards biology and ecology, a doctor, an electronics and mechanical engineer, a lawyer and a graphic designer, as well as myself for product innovation and design. At other times specialists from different fields (architects, chemical engineers, child-care specialists, nurses, cultural geographers, historians, film-makers) may be needed temporarily to help with some special research. Obviously, I consider it absolutely essential that representatives of the users also participate in the team's work and discussions.

All this must sound formidable – in actual practice the team that works together intensively will number only four or five most of the time. With a group totalling around twenty-four who all share the dream of providing fewer but better goods for people in need this mode of operation enables us to approach our work with greater insight. The necessity of explaining what we are doing to members from many different disciplines means that we can look at possibilities through new eyes. An additional benefit has emerged. We are quicker to spot gaps – things that would answer to a specific need, yet don't exist at all. Our 'throat-cancer robot' may help to explain.

Oesophageal cancer requires the surgical removal of the larynx, and the patient then has to learn to use an external, artificial voice-box in order to talk. In the United States, this device is about the size of a packet of king-size cigarettes with a metal casing; sticking out of the top is a bent tube, which is inserted in the corner of the mouth; with months of patience and practice, the metallic-sounding speech (amplified by the external voice-box and lacking any underlying

A toy robot with electronic voice synthesizer to enable children to 'talk like a robot'.

The redesigned artificial voice-box which is based on the robot toy.

melodic structure) can be understood. This device costs nearly a month's wages for many people. The total cost of the components at retail prices is less than 1% of this!

This is where cross-disciplinary team-work comes into its own. Mr Paul Werner of Nebraska – a patient himself – discovered a Japanese toy on sale in the United States that works almost exactly like the clinical prosthetic selling for fifty times as much! The toy is a robot, six inches (15cm) tall, and made of bright red and blue plastic. It also has a tube, which is inserted in the mouth so that a child can – with a bit of practice – sound exactly like a robot. Werner showed it to speech pathologists at the University of Nebraska's Medical Centre, and the medical man on our team brought it to our attention. We decided to redesign the medical version, using the toy as a starting-point. It was a great temptation to distribute the toy itself, but the number of respectable people of a certain age who are willing to hold a brightly coloured robot to their throat is reassuringly small. The final device is black, and a simple neutral shape that fits well to the hand. It can be produced for the same price as the robot. As a further design improvement, we are presently exploring simple microchip technology to see if we can convert the rasping speech into a pleasant contralto or baritone.

Since the 1970s the wave of demythologizing various professions has grown around the world. In the field of self-administered diagnostic testing, the United States has made some interesting contributions. This is partly because of the steadily rising charges of the testing laboratories, partly the waiting-time for the results, especially when the test has to be sent away. There are also many more

The movable playground structure was designed so that the children, parents and teachers, working in co-operation, could easily assemble it.

tests and types of tests performed which increases the chances of wrong findings, accidentally switched samples and misdiagnosis. Consequently our belief in the whole testing-laboratory procedure has been shaken. Self-testing kits are available for blood pressure, pregnancy, diabetes, AIDS, and many other medical applications. We still prefer to pack our own parachute .

A design can serve several different groups and make direct participation by each separate constituency both possible and necessary. A post-graduate student from Britain investigated design applications in the social field, using the geometric solid tetrakaidecahedron. There were several objectives. The physical design goal was to build a exercise environment combining jungle and gym that would also be fun, a shelter from the rain, and would look different from routine schoolyard equipment. The social agenda was to develop a scheme that encouraged the schoolchildren, parents and teachers to co-operate in building the equipment. The creative teaching strategy was to give the children hands-on experience with photography (in the form of 35mm colour slides) and the making of audio tapes. They would also investigate the relationship between image and sound, edit their individual productions and share the results. Other factors influencing the brief were that the structure had to be vandal-proof, inexpensive and safe, movable, easy to put together and take down.

The result was an organic-looking cluster of four to eight tetrakaidecahedral nodes. The geometry of polyhedra is directly related to the growth and form of crystals, and their shapes are consequently satisfying at deep levels of the collective unconscious.[6] The children and teachers working together would put together the flat squares and hexagons that formed the 'skin' of the environment. Parents and teachers together would then erect the actual play-structure from these parts. A bulky box contained a standard Kodak Carousel projector for 35mm colour slides, and a smaller unit held an audio-tape cassette player. The lens on the projector was modified into several facets so that it could project images into two or four different spaces simultaneously.

The schoolchildren's mission was to provide the 'software' for the entire system, that is, the slides and tapes. They received simple automatic 35mm 'do-everything' cameras and some plain tape-recorders. Instructions were minimal to encourage the children's immediate and intuitive response. They supplied the schools with almost endless streams of slides and tapes, documenting their friends at play, their homes, adventure walks, their pets, and much else.

It all came together better than expected. The sound-slide presentations by the children were moving and entertaining; they were also beginning to master cameras and recorders and to develop a selective eye. The play-shelter was so popular with the children that when the time came to photograph it we asked just a few to pose, otherwise the structure would have been completely hidden by more than a score of children swarming all over it.

DESIGNER AS ENTREPRENEUR

Many of the tools and devices illustrated in this and other chapters exist as prototypes only. High risk and low return discourage many firms from producing them. My proposed solution to this societal neglect of valuable ideas is a combination of small, highly decentralized factories (to give autonomy to owners and workers, as well as to conserve the energy wasted in long-range transport of goods). There is a need for both design enterpreneurship and governmental incentives that would protect such new enterprises.

I left university in 1957. In the field of product design alone almost everything has changed. There is one circumstance, however, that is even more relevant today. I remember my professor telling us repeatedly that no large company could ever afford to compete in the market through design excellence. With an established large assembly line or production method, only low prices and massive numbers can move the merchandise. And, once the law of such large numbers operates, economies of scale make it difficult to change models – designs are frozen. Small firms on the other hand, Professor Arnold told us, can change rapidly, profit from new directions, innovations and changing lifestyles. This picture has not changed. Some rather large corporations in Japan, America and Germany have started to create independent divisions within their organization.

Because these divisions are small and have real autonomy to compete freely against others within the parent company, they can be quite successful.

General Motors discovered to its chagrin that dissolving the Pontiac division into the general workforce was disastrous. All over the world cars are looking more alike. The few deliberate exceptions, such as the Porsche 911 or the Morgan Plus-4 from England, sell as soon as built. Since only about 400 Morgans are made each year, there are waiting periods of up to six years in the USA. Attempts have been made over the years to develop cars along different lines (the Kaiser 'Henry J.' and the Tucker in the US, the DeLorean in Ireland, and an adaptation of Raymond Loewy's Studebaker 'Avanti' in Canada.) All have failed. This is in part due to a determination among large automobile manufacturers to keep anything new off the market at all costs, but to a larger extent because of the vast marketing plans of these ventures.

Young people in the United States spend four thousand million dollars each year to 'customize' their cars, that is to make them look different. The Volkswagen 'bug' with a fake Bentley grille, the fibreglass body shaped and painted to look like a human penis, another Volkswagen 'bug' covered by its proud owner with replicas of William Morris wallpaper are only slightly more extreme than most. The 'high-riders' and 'low-riders', custom-painted vans, the Cadillacs from Texas (why always Cadillacs, why always Texas?) are all statements of a sort, and deserve serious study by designers. I don't accept the routine explanation by sociologists and other classifiers and pundits of vernacular taste that these are the mere outpourings of popular culture. I think people are trying to tell car manufacturers and their captive designers that they are fed up with the dreary sameness of cars.

We need small factories and workshops. Most people think of factories as gigantic buildings forming the equivalent of half a city, with belching smokestacks and vast parking lots. There are places like that, but not that many. The size of the average factory in the American Midwest is about the size of a two-storey family home, and it employs around twenty to thirty-five people. Assuming only basic skills among its workers, and reasonable tools and machines, it could manufacture almost anything. Risks can be taken safely; if something doesn't sell, the place is flexible enough to change. The large-scale competition has no chance against it in design or innovation, nor in custom-making goods for special needs. It can make a decent profit for its owners and pay proper wages to the workers. There is just one thing such a place cannot do: grow huge and make millions!

If one of the products suddenly succeeds far beyond expectations and capacity, the factory should market the idea under a 'closed franchise contract' to another small producer elsewhere. The buyer of the idea undertakes to make only a small, agreed number of the product each year and – should demand again outstrip capacity – sell to another producer elsewhere under the same conditions. In this

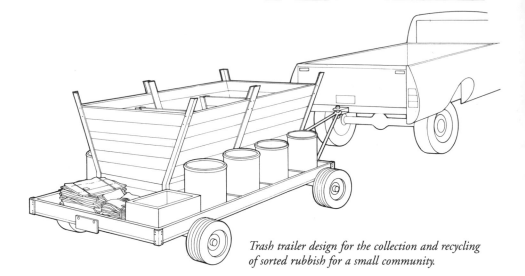

Trash trailer design for the collection and recycling of sorted rubbish for a small community.

way, all stays flexible and human in scale, and the means of production remain decentralized. This would cut down on energy uselessly spent in transporting things up and down the country (or all over the world), and make possible greater variety suited to local conditions. A recent example from my own design praxis illustrates the point.

In 1991, a young man, deeply concerned with environmental issues, and living in a community with no recycling service, decided to use his pickup truck to collect trash (presorted in each household into ten categories and left at the curb) for a small monthly fee. The service flourished, things were recycled properly, householders felt some pride in 'doing their bit' for the environment.[7] Peter asked me for design advice when lifting heavy bags into his truck resulted in back trouble. After several days with him in the truck, doing the rounds, I designed a simple trailer with low sides (nearly at curb height), and a large central hopper into which he could toss lightweight bags. I designed it so that Peter and his friend could build most of it themselves and have the rest cheaply made by any garage or car-repair shop. It attached directly to the small pickup, which could now be used exclusively for highly toxic materials.

When they asked me if they could buy the design – that is, the idea of the design – and start making trailers for other small-scale recycling groups, I decided to put my theories to the test. I arbitrarily suggested that they should restrict themselves to only two hundred trailers annually, all to be sold within less than two hundred miles. They could obtain the rights from me to sell the idea to any other person further away – but with the same restrictions on numbers and area. They agreed. By 1993 the trash trailer was made in more than thirty small communities, with certain adaptations to desert roads, mountainous terrain, and so on.

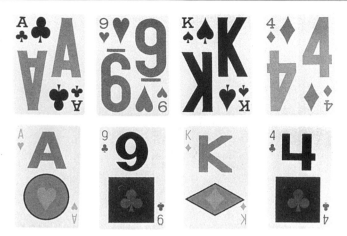

*Playing cards commercially available for those with low vision
(top) where the A and 4 are very similar, and the deck designed
by Melissa Duffner.*

There are two other case histories that deal with the role of the designer as his
or her own entrepreneur. During the last thirty years of working intensively with
disabled and handicapped people, my colleagues and I have learned several
important lessons. It is important that designs for special needs don't become
exclusive, but instead are – whenever possible – broadly inclusive. A designed
object that isolates or marginalizes an individual (or a group of people) is generally unacceptable. There is, for example, a fairly large constituency united by
difficulties in walking fast and getting up and down steps or curbs – people in
wheelchairs, pushing prams or shopping-baskets, the sight-impaired or those who
walk with the aid of sticks or crutches. The recognition and analysis of such
groups is of great importance in order to keep specialized design from remaining
special, and instead to be as comprehensive as possible.

A graphic design student, Melissa Duffner, decided to design for 'low-vision'
people (that is, people whose vision is 20:600 or less). Her researches at a Kansas
City clinic showed that many enjoyed playing card games, but because of their
restricted eyesight it was difficult for them to distinguish the various suits and
numbers on the cards. Melissa experimented with various simple shapes to
determine which they found easiest to recognize. Eventually she decided on a
square, a circle, an equilateral triangle and a diamond on its side. For people with
impaired vision, there is confusion between 4 and A (for Ace), 6 and Q (for
Queen), and the numbers 9 and 6. After making the design changes, however, she
found that normally sighted, visiting friends or family members found triangles,
circles and squares confusing substitutes for clubs, hearts and spades. Melissa
decided to include the original symbols of each suit within the new symbols but
to screen these images down to minimal contrast. The cards were now instantly

Wrist pill box with different receptacles for each medication, and which also includes a digital watch with an alarm.

recognizable by those with normal eyesight, whereas the images of the original suits were too faint to confuse those with low vision. A design judgment worthy of Solomon!

Melissa then contacted a playing-card manufacturer with details of her low-vision deck. She was told that low-vision cards didn't sell 'because of a complete lack of public interest'. We sent for a sample pack. It was not hard to see why they didn't sell. Both numbers and symbols were in the traditional red or black, but two of the suits were printed in sky-blue and leaf-green. This novel colouring naturally disconcerted normally sighted players, whereas low-vision card aficionados couldn't recognize the colours at all. Through a staggering design error, the card-manufacturers had managed to confuse both constituencies that might have a simultaneous interest in card games! Furthermore, the deck contained two extra cards that – in the smallest possible type-size – attempted to explain the colour-coding in harrowing detail to people who are virtually incapable of reading. Melissa, I am told, now prints decks at home after work, and sells them through mail-order to clinics and individuals in many parts of the world.[8]

Elderly people are often on several medications that have to be take in various combinations at different times of the day. Under my direction, one of my students developed a 'wristlet' that contained five colour-coded small receptacles. Each held the pills (measured out by pharmacist or nurse) to be taken at a particular time, and was clearly marked with an appropriate symbol. A small digital watch with an alarm was part of the wristlet, which was small enough to wear yet could also hang from the refrigerator door handle as a reminder to take some medicine with the next meal. The wristlet may soon be produced commercially, and is an interesting example of a design where the function and the package become one.

EVALUATING NEW TECHNOLOGIES

There is the question of whether new technologies are applied in a meaningful manner. A few years ago some Japanese cars came equipped with micro-chirping; a disembodied tone would announce, 'The door is ajar!' if one switched on the engine before shutting the door. Electronic strip-scanners at supermarket check-outs now use microchips and synthesized voices to read prices aloud to customers who – according to recent research – find it extremely irritating. In both cases I feel that the technology is misused, with predictably annoying results. This is 'additive' design ('what else can we stick on, George?'), and is applied for the simple reason that adding a three-cent microchip will justify charging an extra twelve dollars at the point of sale, and will be explained as 'added convenience'.

Since the 1970s, the People's Republic of China has produced and exported a simple two-wheel walking tractor (known as the 'barefoot tractor') which is extremely popular in many developing countries. The instructions are hard to communicate to rural populations that are still largely illiterate, separated from other tribal societies by different languages or patois, and unfamiliar with the country's 'official' language (frequently a legacy from colonial times). There was a similar problem with the tin-can radio that I designed in Indonesia in the 1960s, as well as Batta Koya ('Talking Teacher'), the cassette player designed for Tanzania and Nigeria in 1980; both had to be explained to some pre-literate users.[9]

It would be easy to 'gang' several microchips together that could give step-by-step instructions for use in any number of dialects or tribal languages, This could be built on to the tractor handle to guide the new user through a hands-on training experience. Alternatively, the chips could be arranged in a tubular con-figuration that could slip over the existing tractor handle-bar. It still surprises me that both audio-tape cassettes and microchips are not more extensively used for instructions,especially when most pre-literate societies come from an oral, story-telling tradition and still tend to learn better aurally than visually.

DESIGN ETHICS

The examples above may help to make the connection between the spiritual in design and the intent of the designer. But there still remains the question of design ethics.

Before we can honestly address this question, we must first eliminate the red herring of 'professional ethics' or 'professional codes of conduct'. These are generally rules that some trade group or professional organization has drawn up to further its own fortunes and eliminate competition between members. They also usually protect the group, or its members, from public scrutiny and criticism. To evaluate whether the ethical rules of a group are really more than a self-protection racket is fairly easy. All we have to do is ask some simple questions:

1. Is the code of ethics simply self-serving?

2. Does the 'code of conduct' really protect the public?

3. Is this code truly regulative, that is, do the members comply with it, and can the public make its own judgments about the compliance of the members?

4. Are these rules clear and specific about the possible pitfalls inherent in the particular profession or work performed by its members?

5. Can non-members observe and judge compliance with the rules by members, and is it enforceable?

6. Is this code of ethics, as well as the group or association, so constructed as to anticipate future changes, and therefore willing to teach, learn and inform its membership as well as the public?

7. Can the professional leadership of such professional organizations be made aware that, due to the modern media, we are living in an increasingly transparent society, in which secret deals, whitewashing and stone walling will no longer work?

With these 'cover your own backside, boys!' ethics out of the way, we can think about the interaction between design and moral values.

Properly speaking, ethics are the philosophical basis for making choices about morals and values. Moral decisions are made through recognizing that a dilemma exists and consciously weighing the alternatives. Values provide direction when decisions about alternative courses of action must be made. Values do not have to be based on truth. They frequently stem from beliefs or convictions that certain things are true – even if false. Many values in the United States, for instance, are based on the statement: 'All men are created equal.'

Most decisions in daily life have ethical implications or moral overtones. Issues in a post-industrial society are even more complex and baffling. This is especially true in product design since designers – like it or not – need to have one foot firmly planted in the future. The time-lapse between being assigned the brief to design, say, a refrigerator and its first appearance at a store can be as long as three years. This is not just an arbitrary example. A German firm began to design a new model, but was forced to rethink the entire appliance by the first discoveries of the effect of freon gases (CFCs and HFCs) on the ozone layer. The result was the first refrigerator that poses no threat to the atmosphere, but research, design and engineering time increased to nearly six years from brief to product. During this time, entirely new and unanticipated fiscal and aesthetic constraints had come into play.

To think dispassionately about what we design and why, as well as what the eventual consequences of our design intervention may be, is the basis of ethical thinking. It gets easier with practice.[10]

The most direct link between values, creativity, beauty, art and the transcendental is probably demonstrated by Abraham Maslow's seminal writings on the 'hierarchy of values'. The higher motives that Maslow recognizes have to do with self-transcendence and the eventual loss of self that can be experienced at the moment of high artistic creation, the process of invention or during the ecstasy of religious experience. He writes movingly about these 'metamotivational' needs that we are all capable of approaching and satisfying.[11]

When I first lived in Toronto in the 1950s, a client asked me to design a free-standing structure to house a florist's showroom. He said, 'I know you have studied with Frank Lloyd Wright; well, I want to have a showroom that looks as if Mr Wright had designed it!' The last thing I wanted to do was a Wright pastiche, yet I felt that I could not turn down my first and only job offer. I have regretted my lapse of ethical judgment ever since, especially as it later turned out that there were several scores of my client's showrooms clear across Canada. This early, negative experience first turned my attention to the ethical dimensions in design.

Nearly everyone seems to feel that a designer, faced by a job that is ethically unsound or offensive, has only two choices: reluctant acceptance after much soul-searching, or outright dismissal. When discussing this in a seminar, my postgraduate students urge me to react differently. 'Why,' they ask, 'don't you say, "I feel that this commission is morally wrong, here let me explain why." ' It is a sad fact that I have never yet had a client willing pay me one hundred and fifty dollars an hour whilst I attacked his proposal and lectured him about pop-psychology, ethics and personal value choices. Just unlucky, I guess. The fourth way of handling the situation is to tell him that I won't do the job (without going into details), then adding: 'But George will be glad to do it, and is an extremely competent designer. Let me give you his address.' This solves absolutely nothing. The job is still done (by someone else, it's true), your own office has lost income and helped the competition.

TRANSFORMING THE ASSIGNMENT

Over the years I have managed to develop a way out of the dilemma, and the case-history which follows may explain an actual working procedure, a system of dealing with ethically repugnant design assignments.

A large chocolate manufacturer asked me to design a new wrapper for their standard chocolate bar, which was sold predominantly from automatic vending-machines. The manufacturer wanted a more distinctive design for the wrapper, to rival that of his main competitor. I faced a real dilemma in social and ethical responsibility in design. On the one hand I was being hired by a company then more than a hundred years old and the main employer in the small city named after it. It was losing money to its competitor, and this endangered the fiscal and social well-being of thousands of employees and their families. The town and the entire economy of the region seemed to depend on the successful survival of my client's plant.

On the other hand, my principles made me uncomfortable in the role of souteneur for a chocolate-maker. Sweets, chocolates in particular, can cause dental caries. I also knew enough about the medical problems caused by improper eating habits to be worried by the fact that many of my students breakfasted on chocolate bars from the nearest vending-machine. Executives munch chocolates as a quick mid-morning or late-afternoon pick-me-up; they are too valuable to lose to candy snacks! I felt that it was wrong to help to promote a junk-food that had little to recommend it. It was up to me to invent a positive option.

I realized that, since the scruples were mine, I would need to take some risks. I explained to the CEO (Chief Executive Officer) of the company that I would accept the brief and design a new wrapper and packaging. Without disclosing my reservations about the work, I suggested that I had dimly conceived a way to increase sales and at the same time provide some positive publicity. I volunteered to do some speculative research – at no cost to them and on my own time – in parallel to the packaging assignment. If the board liked my research proposal and decided to go ahead with it, then they would pay me my expenses, and my professional fees. If they didn't accept it, it would cost them nothing. It was an offer he couldn't refuse.

I was quite clear about the risks I was taking. The original design assignment was a routine job, rather time-consuming, but essentially simple and would be well paid. The other work, however, would take me weeks (possibly months) of research, funded out of my own pocket. It would require travel, discussions of my requirements with several experts outside the field of design who would charge me their standard fees, the preparation of a lengthy feasibility study and situation report, and a great deal of artwork, charts and colour slides for a final presentation. There seemed no other way to satisfy my client and my social conscience simultaneously, so I began.

I knew that vending-machine snacks should ideally be high in proteins and vitamins, but free from artificial flavourings, colours and preservatives. We decided to try three different products, two savoury and one sweet: a combination of desiccated chicken and cheese forming a small sausage-shaped roll; a vegetarian version with soya instead of chicken; carob, almonds and raisins for the sweet snack. Then we consulted doctors, dieticians, specialists in food preparation and preservation. Without preservatives, food in vending-machines has to be replaced nearly twice as often, and, since serving the automats is a major cost of such 'convenience snacks', we could expect the retail price to rise by nearly a third. We were advised against the carob-and-almond confection – there were similar items already competing for a market share. We finally succeeded in producing two versions of the savouries that tasted decent without any artificial 'taste-modifiers'. By making a series of careful trade-offs among some of the ingredients, the nutritionists also managed slightly to extend the shelf-life, reducing costs.

Meanwhile the official design task of a new image and wrapper was complete. At the same time my assistant began turning our medical and dental statistics into brightly coloured graphs and pie-charts. At this juncture I consulted an acquaintance of mine who earned a surprisingly high income from concocting names for new products. I explained the situation – including the fact that I was contributing my own time and money to this experiment in design ethics. To my delight he offered to make a 'name-search' and develop a product designation at no cost. From his three or four proposals, one stood out: Pro-Teen. It sounded its contents, protein, and looked right for a country in which teenagers have been a cultural ideal for decades. Furthermore we were aware that half the eventual buyers would be in their late teens or early twenties and knowledgeable about nutrition and health.

A visual identity was developed, and packaging and other graphic material designed. We presented the original project for which we had been retained, the new wrapper. It was well received and instantly accepted. We then went on to present our new proposal, describing the process from the original research to the final packages for Pro-Teen, giving sample snacks to the directors. I argued that the company would gain enormous goodwill from the public (and much free publicity in the media) for having had the courage to switch to a new product that was demonstrably healthier.

Design intervention can help to encourage the choice of nutritious snacks, such as the Daintree Sports Slice, instead of chocolate and junk foods.

To our surprise, the board decided to accept our proposal and feasibility studies for further investigation. Knowing how difficult companies find it to entertain radically new ideas, we were extremely happy. Not long afterwards the two Pro-Teen products were test-marketed in six university towns. Acceptance levels were high, and, unexpectedly, highest for the vegetarian version. Present results justify serious distribution plans.

For legal and professional reasons I cannot give any further details of the Pro-Teen bar. Barry Crone, who runs the Design Synergy in Melbourne, Sydney and Singapore, a friend and colleague, has recently worked on a similar design intervention, which has resulted in the Daintree Energy Sports Slice. Design Synergy adds the following nutritional information: branch-chain amino acids have a different molecular structure from all other amino acids, providing a high rate of nitrogen to the body for fast muscle growth, and are quickly transferred from the blood into muscle to meet reserves.

There is both a cautionary note and a lesson in this case-study. When faced with an unappetizing design brief, I practise this two-track approach. Perform the requested work, but do a voluntary study of an alternative solution as well. Find a way to appeal to the client's 'enlightened self-interest' by demonstrating that public goodwill, favourable press notices and profit can accrue by following the alternative. The caution lies in the fact that this approach has been successful in only about four out of ten cases. Actually, I think these odds are quite good. Pro-Teen might have cost me nearly twelve thousand dollars for consultants and nutritional experiments, as well as about two hundred hours of research, discussion and design time. Looking at it from an ethical viewpoint, however, the issue is simple. Through my work and the risks I have taken, I have done my best to alter a difficult problem of values. Even if a client only accepts the work on his brief as given, at least I have the satisfaction that I tried, and made some personal sacrifices to attain a better solution.

Even in the trivial exercise of finding a substitute for a chocolate bar, and the aggressive vulgarity needed to 'sell' a design approach to an executive board, the satisfaction of succeeding is immense, and, whatever the outcome, there is still a profound growth of experience and self-esteem. I have an irrational belief in the virtues of intelligence and optimism. This tells me that although a blunting of moral sensibility is connected with the marketing of designs or goods, it is only when one treats people squalidly that they will behave squalidly. By never losing sight of one's higher aspirations, spiritual growth increases and is nourished.

CHAPTER 4

Sensing a Dwelling

Think with the whole body.
Deshimaru

We are born indoors, live, love, bring up our families, worship,
work, grow old, sicken and die indoors. Architecture mirrors every
aspect of our lives – social, economical, spiritual.
Eugene Raskin

THE OTHER day a friend visited me at my office. While waiting to see me, he picked up a magazine and looked at some pictures and floor plans of a recently completed building in Portland, and then said, 'What a beautiful building!' I replied, 'How can you possibly know?'

Before one can begin to think about the place of the built environment in our time – an age that is increasingly concerned with ecological and environmental issues – it is evident that we must learn to look at buildings, homes and settlements in a different way. Architecture has to be experienced by all the senses rather than just *seen*. The visual image may provide us with pictorial information, yet beauty is never skin-deep.

Architects, architectural students and the general public experience buildings that are considered 'important' largely through television images, slides projected on to a screen or photographs in a book. It is André Malraux's 'museum without walls' for space and place, with all the distortions inherent in reducing the three-dimensional to two, and shrinking a building to the size of a page in a periodical. In fact there is now a whole area of architecture that can be described as 'non-dimensional' that exists only in the form of projects and drawings in coffee-table books, architecture that is purely conceptual or fantasy-driven, was never intended to be built and never will be. Even the 'virtual reality' provided by computer programmes is unrelated to the total sensory experience of idling away a few hours in a building that leaves us with a strong aftertaste of trickery and illusion, 'smoke and mirrors'.

A three-dimensional structure is – or should be – designed specifically for its site, and should be closely and contextually related to the topography, the local plant material, landscape and climate. The seasons of the year, and the quality of light at different times of the day, all play an important part in the appearance of a house, both the interior and the exterior. This visual presence is strengthened through the plasticity and changing spaces and volumes in a dwelling, and this cannot be reflected accurately in a colour slide or a black-and-white photograph. If one compares the vivid adventure of walking through and around any building and its setting with the attempt to experience it through drawings, slides, photographs or films, the difference is profound.

Our response to architecture is very like our response to the human face. We often say about a man or woman that he or she is 'not photogenic'. What this really means is that the face possesses animation and signals shifting moods and feelings through great mobility of expression; it seems to be forever changing. Most visually compelling faces – Albert Schweitzer, Georgia O'Keeffe, Wanda Landowska, Rabindranath Tagore, to name a few – have this in common: their profile presents an unexpected contrast to their full face. A portrait – especially a photographic one – can select only one view and just one of many expressions or moods. In the same way, it is impossible to photograph a building and freeze that one thin slice of time. We may succeed in obtaining a superb picture, yet we won't achieve an intelligent understanding of dwelling, site or context.

Scientists tell us that we experience the world primarily through our eyes. Researchers on the payroll of advertising agencies and 'media consultants' assure us that television, films and illustrated magazines make our experiences increasingly visual, and we are further promised 'high-resolution video', computer screens, multi-media productions, holography and 'three-dimensional wall-to-wall TV'. The fact that these prophets are all employed by the owners of these visual media, should, however, give rise to a healthy scepticism.

We are endowed with five senses and more: we have sensory nerves which make us aware of the body position and movement in relation to a space (kinaesthesia); we have thermal receptors which register warmth and cold; we have visible and involuntary micro-muscular responses that psychologists have recorded when we watch sport or look at paintings, (haptic muscular sensitivity); a 'third eye' (intuition) and much else. It is in the interaction of all our senses that we can begin to really see – to experience.

MOOD AND ENVIRONMENT

Why are we only now becoming increasingly aware of the impoverishment of our sensory abilities? It is only since World War II that the majority of people in the Western world have moved indoors for the first time – 'protected' from bright sunshine and sealed off hermetically from the waterfalls, forests, rivers and mountains that carry large amounts of small-air ions (clusters of molecules with negative electrical charge). Today most of us live in highly artificial environments that dull all our natural senses with artificial substitutes, or deny part of our sensory and sensual apparatus by neutralizing organic stimulus. In countries with a highly developed technology, most people spend nearly all their time inside build-ings with fixed windows, breathing climate-conditioned recycled air and under artificial lighting. In Canada and the United States, once-a-week shopping patterns allied to speculative land use, have resulted in enormous, enclosed shop-ping malls. Here, in a controlled environment with piped-in synthetic fragrances designed to stimulate the shopping urge, and music to induce a state of passive yet acquisitive enjoyment, we are turned into 'competent consumers'. These malls are developing a secondary use as year-round jogging and walking spaces, gossip-ing places for the elderly, and hang-outs favoured by teenagers. Dr Richard Wurtman, a professor of brain and cognitive sciences at the Massachusetts Institute of Technology, says, 'We are all unwitting subjects of a long-term experiment on the effects of artificial lighting on our health.'[1] We must take conscious responsibility for creating man-made environments that won't do even further damage to the performance of our senses and brain-body systems.

We experience beauty in the spaces in which we live or work in a multi-sensory way, and parts of that experience lie entirely hidden from us in the subconscious or preconscious layers of our mind. Biometeorologists and micro-biologists have found that air containing a certain amount of small-air ions, will lower the quantity of serotonin, a hormone associated with anxiety, in the mid-brain. Experiments in pschycology and psychiatry at Yale University have demonstrated that some smells have the same effect as meditation on lowering blood pressure, and that some of the light entering our eyes in bright sunlight bypasses the cortex entirely and acts directly upon the hypothalamus, the spinal cord and the pineal gland, where it suppresses the production of a hormone called melatonin that affects moods, fertility and and many other body functions. It has been known for decades that a certain red-orange colour will kick into high gear several psycho-physiological systems that deal with aggression and sexuality; recent studies in colour therapy and photobiology seem to show that 'passive pink' (the bubble-gum colour), has an almost immediate effect on aggressive behaviour. When people displaying berserk behaviour are put into a small passive-pink room, they tend to calm down within minutes and go to sleep.[2]

In the 1950s Dr Abraham Maslow, one of the founders of humanistic psycho-logy, conducted some of the first experiments on the effects of environment. He built three rooms: one beautiful, one 'average' and one ugly. The ugly room had a naked light bulb hanging from the ceiling, an old mattress on the floor, battleship-grey walls, torn window shades, brooms, mops and a good deal of trash and dust. The beautiful room had large windows, a superb Navajo rug on the floor, off-white walls, indirect lighting, a bookcase, soft armchairs and a wooden desk, paintings, plants and a small sculpture. The 'average' room had 'the appear-ance of a clean, neat "worked-in" office with grey metal furniture'.

Volunteers were given photographs of people and asked whether these faces displayed 'energy' and 'well-being'. The volunteers were supervised by three examiners who were themselves unaware of the real objective of the experiment, that is, people's reactions to work-spaces. The results reveal that in the beautiful room the volunteers found the faces energetic and happy; in the ugly room, they thought they looked tired and ill. The behaviour of the examiners also varied: in the ugly room, they rushed brusquely through interviews, exhibited 'gross behavioural changes' and complained of monotony, fatigue, headache, hostility and irritability. They knew that they preferred not to work in the ugly room, but they were quite unaware that their own behaviour was closely related to the appearance of the rooms. Furthermore, the reactions of both volunteers and examiners to the average room were more closely related to their reactions to the ugly room than to the beautiful one.[3]

THE DIMENSION OF LIGHT

Light – our first visual experience at birth – can be direct, indirect or dispersed. It also has a colour quality that is influenced by geographic location (longitude and latitude form a locus that the sun strikes at a specific angle), the season of the year, the time of day, and the weather. Sunlight will cast strong shadows, creating great contrasts in tone and temperature, and may create glare, shining directly into a room through a window. Indirect light is reflected, ricocheting from surfaces both outside and inside the room. The reflecting surface may mute the quality and affect the colour of the light. But not always successfully.

The Pasadena Museum of Art, designed by Thornton Ladd and completed in the 1970s, was characterized accurately in *Time* magazine as a regrettable hybrid of cruise-ship lounge and California bathroom. The grounds outside the museum form a sort of optical moat: crushed white marble chips and crystal in the unshaded sunlight produce a harsh glare. After passing this visual booby-trap, some museum visitors need several minutes to adjust their eyesight so that they are able to recognize the colours of paintings inside the museum.

Dispersed or diffused light is produced when it passes through a screen or filter. Blinds, translucent curtains, frosted glass or glass bricks, bamboo shades – all these create light that is soft and virtually shadowless. Sliding *shoji* screens (room-dividers of white rice-paper or plastic on a slim wooden frame) will model the light entering traditional Japanese houses; the sundeck in Mojacar on Spain's southern coast where this chapter was written, is partially covered with horizontal bamboo slats that allow for a marvellous dappled light, as well as providing a cool space.

Frank Lloyd Wright used white linen-canvas as material for the tent-like structures at his original Ocotillo Desert Camp in Paradise Valley, Arizona. He prized

The quality of the light is soft, diffused and virtually shadowless as it enters through the traditional 'shoji' screens in Japan. This screen forms a delicate division between interior and garden.

the quality of the soft, diffused light so highly that in building Taliesin West he used these same canvas-covered stretchers for the roofs and upper part of the walls. These textile roofs not only screened out the harsh Arizona sunlight, but, because they were permeable, also allowed for ventilation. When the sun was low on the horizon, the roofs could be folded back, allowing for the cooling evening breezes. The architectural critic Lewis Mumford wrote at the time: 'Coming upon Taliesin West in the desert of Arizona is like encountering an armada of sailing ships, with their white sails unfurled.'[4] Wright's original design for the Guggenheim Museum in New York was planned to modulate light in a similar way through the use of a large, clear central dome surrounded by nine smaller subsidiary domes. Natural light would have flooded the entire snail-shaped interior central court as well as the gallery extensions, even on overcast days. A series of white canvas sails were to act as movable light modulators, to keep the light on bright days from being too 'shrill'. (This scheme was abandoned with the re-design of the dome into a smaller, faceted one.) Frei Otto's tensile structures at the Munich Olympiad and at the airport in Riyadh are further examples of designs which filter sunlight through fabric.

The use of overhangs and louvres takes advantage of both direct and diffused sunlight at different times of the year. Carefully calculated extensions of the eaves

*Interior light effects from the circular windows
of Grand Central Station in New York.*

facing south will ensure that the room is flooded by sunlight during cold winter days when the sun lies low on the horizon, whereas the overhangs will shield the space from the harshness of the summer sun, turning direct sunshine into reflected light and keeping the room cool. Bernard Maybeck, an architect practising in the San Francisco area after the turn of the century, carried this approach further in an ecologically apt manner. At the University of California at Berkeley, he created a south wall that consisted entirely of small glass panes. Suspended from the roof overhang and about three feet (a metre) from the wall itself, are masses of deciduous plants or hanging gardens. These filter out the heat of the sunlight and give a pleasing green cast to the room; more importantly, the air-space between the window-wall and the plants acts as insulation from heat. In the autumn the plants lose their foliage, and the weaker winter sun warms the room.

We walk through three-dimensional spaces with light changing through windows, clerestories and other penetration of walls or roof. Not only do we see this light, but we also feel ever-changing thermal messages of warmth, coldness, comfort or irritation which trigger endocrine messages and involve galvanic skin responses. The light will assume its own dimensional quality, as in the focused rays of the late afternoon sun pouring through the circular windows of Grand Central Station in New York, through the Hagia Sophia in Istanbul or through the textile roof over an Arabic souk. Light through a rose-window in church floods the space with brilliant colours. Le Corbusier's Church of the Pilgrimage at Ronchamps moulds the interior space through the seemingly random penetrations of the enormously thick walls – Corbu himself called the interplay of shafts of bright daylight, darkness and shadows 'visual acoustics'.

Behavioural scientists have found that a room with daylight flooding in from windows set at right angles to each other will increase serotonin levels and – in many cases – provide its inhabitants or users with a more positive attitude. The British architect Christopher Day has used this method of enlivening rooms in the dwellings and Waldorf schools he has designed and built in the Welsh countryside.

Light streaming into the interior of Hagia Sophia in Istanbul creates its own dimensional quality.

We tend to feel depressed and apathetic when winter days are short and dark and become more energetic as our nervous tone improves with the longer and brighter days. In Europe, North America and the temperate zones of the southern half of the world, winter sunlight is only about one-tenth of the intensity of that in summer, quite apart from its duration. These seasonal cycles of light intensity and duration affect our endocrine glands. Melatonin, which is produced during prolonged dark periods or in dim light, causes sleepiness, melancholia and – if overproduced – depression.

Studies of climate and human responses in the Nordic countries, England and the United States, have found that the lack of daylight in the middle of winter can cause severe clinical depression, suicides occur most frequently during the late winter months, manic depressives feel worse and alcohol-related problems increase. This dysfunction has been named 'SAD syndrome' (for 'seasonally affective disorder'). It is associated with fatigue, increased craving for carbohydrates in the diet, weight gain and lethargy.

In the United States 'light therapy' treatments have been used successfully since 1984 for severe cases; for about two hours a day, sufferers sit in front of full-spectrum, bright-light boxes that are five to ten times brighter than normal room lighting. When I lived in Finland I found that some people there had adapted to the extremes of light in that far northern country. I lodged with a young couple who could function on only three or four hours of sleep during June and July, whereas in January they would go to sleep as early as 7.30 in the evening and sleep soundly for twelve hours or more before returning to work or university classes.

Again, light may come from flickering candles – entrancing, tranquil and romantic – and a log-fire in the hearth will supply us with psychic as well as physical warmth. We may be imprinted by millions of years of gathering around camp fires to cook, eat and socialize – an open fireplace still yields up strong feelings of companionship. Now that we can control both the colour and the intensity of electric light, we need to re-educate our eyes to the subtleties of candles and oil lamps. Designers will plan subtle and sophisticated lighting effects to influence moods and keep us intrigued with the spaces we inhabit or explore. But task-lighting or indirect mood-lighting is only the beginning. Light needs space: it is the room that dictates the flow of the light – it is the light that modulates the volume of the room.

FOOTFALLS

We feel the changes in the surface under our feet. We enjoy spaces with bare hardwood floors dotted with small rugs; delightful as this contrast between wood and textiles may be visually, it is even more beguiling to our ears as the sound of our feet or shoes becomes an ever-changing acoustic accompaniment to crossing a room. Finished wooden flooring gives a different springiness to our steps; it reverberates quite differently from brick or concrete, and from carpeting, cobblestones, slate, quarry tile or bamboo matting. A temple in Kyoto has floorboards tuned to sing like nightingales as one crosses the floor wearing only socks or *tabi*. In indigenous homes in West Java and Thailand, I have observed that walking on bamboo steps gives off sounds similar to those heard made by the *anklung* (a bamboo instrument), and this is not by accident but by design; the bamboo for the steps has been tuned carefully before being installed. I have been told by my graduate assistant from mainland China that there are similar 'musical steps' in vernacular dwellings of some of the minority groups in that country.

We treasure the feel and sound of fallen leaves or pine-needles underfoot, the literally footloose pleasure of running on fine sand, the crunch of snow. From the way snow feels to their fur-clad feet the Inuit can tell how recently more snow has fallen and the ambient temperature when it fell. Most experienced skiers can determine what wax to use by the feel of the snow.

Stepping-stone paths in Japanese gardens are laid in various numerical patterns to direct the feet and the eyes.

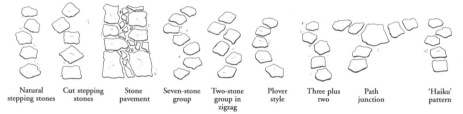

| Natural stepping stones | Cut stepping stones | Stone pavement | Seven-stone group | Two-stone group in zigzag | Plover style | Three plus two | Path junction | 'Haiku' pattern |

The buildings of the ancient Ise Shrine near Nagoya are ceremonially rebuilt every twenty years. The carpenters go to the sacred forests to cut new cedar and cypress logs, and the building is crowned by soft thatching. The feel and sound and especially the smell of these virgin materials are profound experiences.

Like Ariadne's thread, stepping-stones in traditional Japanese gardens can direct our feet to changing vistas and fragrances. In Japanese landscape gardens a series of cylindrical stone plinths will send us on a meandering voyage across a reflecting pool, forcing our aesthetic experience to be more astringent through our muscular control. The Japanese have scores of asymmetrical path patterns, from the seemingly chaotic *chidori-kake*, or 'plover style', to the zigzag pattern of the 'wild geese', or *gan-kake*. The groups of stones making up the paths are carefully designed and constructed in one of several numeric series, such as 5-7-5 or 3-5-7, thus reiterating the structure of *haiku* and *manga* poetic forms, so that rhythm and a sort of subconscious counting-game are added to the textural adventure of walking through a dwelling, temple or garden – an odd combination of an easy-going stroll and an architectural minuet.[5]

The architect Gunter Nitschke has this to add: 'We can find a presentation of space as a time and mood-structured process in the layout of traditional Japanese stroll gardens and, on a smaller scale, in the placement of *tobi-ishi*, [skipping stones] used to make garden paths. By a sophisticated placing of the stones, our foot movements can be slowed down, speeded up, halted or turned in various directions. And with our legs, our eyes are manipulated, and our visual input from spatial phenomena is structured over time.'[6]

FEELING THE FABRIC

Obviously our sense of touch is not constricted to what we feel through our feet. Tactile receptors are located all over our body surface, a fact to which all lovers will testify. We can even feel things that aren't there: pain, heat and all other sensations from so-called phantom limbs that have been amputated. All tactile sensations, whether real or from 'ghost'-parts of the body seem to relate back to a small, orderly, although distorted, version of oneself – an eidetic homunculus – outlined somewhere on the dura mater of our brains.[7]

But sensing a building through touch? We can brush our hand across lichen-encrusted rocks forming a cottage wall in the Hebrides, or the tall stones dreaming silently at Stonehenge, and derive profound sensory (and sensual) satisfaction. We run our fingers along a smoothly planed teak column, or the oak-planks forming an inside wall. And with this tactile pleasure goes once more the sense of smell – the odour of wood, rock or lichen. The stone walls of a Gothic cathedral – especially on a hot summer's day – exude a rich mineral smell that stays with us and provides us with healing coolness. Conversely, a thick adobe wall – well warmed by the sun – will then radiate out its warmth at night as the desert temperature dips toward freezing. The cool feel of the copper siding contrasts with the sun-warmed stones at the student-union building at Dipoli, just outside Helsinki. As we walk through a wine cellar, or the catacombs in Vienna or Rome, we can literally taste the structure.

THE SENSE OF SMELL

The sense of smell may be the most evocative of all our senses. It transports us magically to long-forgotten scenes of childhood: grandmother's parlour, joss sticks burning at a shrine, the censer breathing incense during Easter services at the cathedral. In a Finnish smoke-sauna, the smell is a subtle cocktail of sheer heat, wet birch leaves and wood smoke. It recalls log cabins and farmhouses heated with peat on Ireland's west coast. It tantalizes us with hints of the smoky tang of malt whisky or the oddly similar flavour of bowls of Lapsang-Souchong tea. There is a strong physiological and psychological connection between taste and smell; people who lose their sense of smell frequently also lose their ability to taste nuances and to call up those memories linked to a particular fragrance.

Of all our senses, smell gives us our most direct link with the environment. With every inward breath we gather microscopic particles of the outside world and bring them into physical contact with odour-receptive nerves in our nose. Smells are wired directly into our emotions and memories. Signals speed from our nose to the olfactory bulbs at our brain's base, and from there these stimuli continue on to the limbic system – that ancient part of the brain that deals with moods, sexual urges, and powerful emotions such as fear – moving on to the hippocampus, which controls memory functions. As Vladimir Nabokov wrote, nothing revives the past so completely as a smell that was once associated with it. Finally the signals spread to the neocortex, which is believed to give rise to conscious thinking.

In a warm climate and always assuming that we can escape air-conditioning we can begin to experience our surroundings through smell. The olfactory cues given off by a sun-drenched quarry-tile floor at midday are very different from those of the chillier late afternoon. I am not referring to temperature, but rather to a sort of odour-balloon that surrounds us and provides us with some spatial definitions. The scent drifting toward us from the kitchen leads us towards it and even provides cues telling us where to fruit is stored and where the stir-fry is cooking on the stove.

When I first arrived in New York as a student, to save on expenses, and – more importantly – to enlarge my own cultural horizons, I lived as a boarder with a Chinese family just off Mott Street, deep in New York's Chinatown. After a few days, the grandmother, who managed the whole family, told me to change my diet or move out. After she had convinced me that to her all 'pink' people stank, I followed her dietary suggestions and lived happily in Chinatown for almost two more years. I carried a sort of pungent, scent-drawn street map of shops, restaurants and apartments in my head and could – to use two hackneyed phrases – find my way blindfolded by following my nose.

The aroma of *fusuma* and *shoji* (paper screens), *tatami* (mats of seaweed and reeds), *ishi* and *kiri* wood (aromatic woods used for interiors), will define the space in a traditional Japanese room, just as the fragrance given off by the rain-washed pebbles and moss under the roof overhang will indicate to us the perfumed boundaries of the house and the edges of the garden. Research has shown that scents can affect us powerfully: the odour of spiced apples can lower our blood pressure, whereas the smell of freshly cut wood sets our pulses racing. At the end of the day we sink gratefully into a hot bath and – having added a few drops of an essential oil that pleases us – are brought back through scent, space and temperature to equanimity. Smell seems to have a major role in this evening feast of the senses, since it re-creates precisely the one sense we miss most in our daily, synthetic lives.

RESPONSES TO SPACE

Think back to the last time you were in a great European cathedral. As you looked up to the arched vaulting under the roof, your whole body was engaged. Your neck muscles expanded and contracted again, putting a small temporary strain on your neck, re-focusing eye muscles and slightly compressing the lower back, bringing ligaments into play, working your whole body kinaesthetically. This kinaesthetic experience was intended by the architect. When the low entrance to a Japanese tea house forces us to bow as we enter, this unavoidable obeisance forces us once more to a spiritual and muscular effort, designed into the structure.

This is not the only way our musculature is engaged in 'reading' a building. When we walk up a spiral staircase, the balancing mechanisms of the inner ear become involved, feeding information back to brain and body in rich and subtle ways. And there is direct haptic involvement as we involuntarily lean slightly inward to the centre of the stairs, and shorten or lengthen our step. We feel the movement from level to level. The height of the ceiling varies, becoming low and sheltering around the fireplace, rising up exultantly in the living space, and providing a feeling of security and privacy where we sleep and make love.

When we sit in meditation, we again lower our sight-line, we become more centred, we experience a closeness to the horizontal, the nourishing earth. It is in this act that we change the space around us and – to paraphrase rather loosely Winston Churchill's remark about the architecture of the Houses of Parliament – the space in turn then changes us.

Architects and designers have always been aware that our kinaesthetic and muscular responses to space and place can be used to manipulate perception and emotions. Foreign dignitaries visiting Hitler and Mussolini had to walk though seemingly endless halls, only to find that there was still a long walk to approach the desk, all designed to make the visitor feel insignificant and to disarm him psychologically. Yet emotional responses to muscular participation in a structure depend on many other cues. The path along Maya Lin's Vietnam memorial in Washington DC, covers roughly the same length as the walk to an interview with *Der Führer* or *Il Duce*, yet the feelings aroused are sorrow, awe and humility. Maya Lin's Memorial is possibly the most spiritually moving structure designed and built in the 20th century.

The ramp spiralling downwards in Frank Lloyd Wright's design for the Guggenheim Museum was originally carefully calculated to eliminate 'museum

The long dark wall of the memorial in Washington, designed by Maya Lin and finished in 1982, is a moving and dignified commemoration of the Americans who died in Vietnam.

feet', the tired leg muscles that we experience after walking for hours on the unforgiving floor surface of galleries.

When the sculptor Alexander Calder lived in Paris as a young man, he nailed wire coat-hangers to his floors with the hooks sticking straight up. This was to sharpen and alert people to the tactile possibilities of the surface underfoot, the sixth side of the room, he explained to his friends.

SOUNDS AND RHYTHMS

Our sense of hearing also helps us to understand spaces. We experience echoes and other more subtle acoustic effects. An architect or designer will enter an empty church or music-hall and clap hands to judge the acoustic properties of the space, and opera houses and concert halls were carefully designed to yield the best possible aural conditions for the audience. Architects have always enjoyed playing with sound in space, as attested to by the number of 'Whispering Galleries' in European Baroque churches and the small whispering or spy-vestibule at the refurbished railroad station (now a shopping mall), in St Louis, Missouri. Certain architects, such as Louis Sullivan, Alvar Aalto, the Saarinens, Frank Lloyd Wright, possess an intuitive sense for shaping opera houses and concert halls to provide superb acoustics. The way we define acoustic quality, however, has undergone profound changes, and, consequently, our expectations for reverberation, pitch and resonance have altered. The introduction of high-fidelity sound equipment in the home during the 1950s, and, above all, the advent of compact-disc players in the early 1980s, have exposed people to a drier, echoless sound, which has influenced architects and designers. These days many performance halls are designed to hold as large a crowd of concert-goers as possible and the architect then relies on electronic amplification and ceiling baffles to enable the music to be heard. One can only regret this development: it robs us of a 'living sound', a vivid experience. Conversely, since 1993 the recording industry has begun to play with artificially added 'concert-hall' resonance and echo-effects in the recording of classical music.

A generation ago, the comedian Mort Sahl used to say when describing his high-fidelity set-up that 'the human ear is the weakest link in the system'. It is amazing how much we can learn about the relationship between hearing and architectural space through exploring music and its reproduction. I teach at a large university in the American Midwest. On the walk to my office, I pass students plugged into their personal stereos. The trouble is that I too have to hear the music they are listening to! It simply doesn't occur to them to turn down the volume to a level that won't permanently damage their ears.[8] Many have already irreversibly affected their sense of hearing by attending 'heavy-metal' concerts, where the sound can reach a level of 120 decibels – the equivalent of standing within a few feet of a jet-fighter taking off from an aircraft carrier. At the start of every autumn semester the Registrar's office tells me how many of my first-year students suffer from partial or full hearing-loss, and therefore need to sit where they can see the interpreter who translates my lecture into ASL (sign language); the percentage has jumped from 2% to almost 16% in only twelve years.

When visiting a cinema in this university town, I always insert earplugs so that I can listen to the action at a 'normal' level (and protect my hearing). The projectionists turn the volume to maximum to make the sound-track intelligible to the majority of their youthful patrons. When a new restaurant and micro-brewery opened its doors, I found the local brew outstanding and the food extremely fine, yet the place was so noisy that it was difficult to have a conversation. In 1970, I had developed a virtually cost-free sound-proofing system for the Gallery of Contemporary Art in Toronto, and now offered it to the owner at no cost – just to ensure that my friends and I, when dining and drinking here, would not have to bellow to make ourselves heard. To my surprise he said, 'My friend, about one quarter of the students come here because of the hullabaloo, and the vast majority can no longer tell that it's noisy at all!'

An architectural solution for providing auditoriums that can be used by increasing numbers of the hearing-impaired is the 'Reflex Seating System'. Frank Lloyd Wright was the first to experiment with this way of seating around 1936, and the system was finally permanently installed at the Kalita D. Humphries

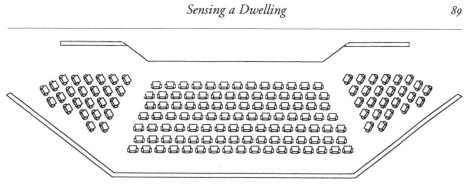

Stretched half-hexagon seating after the design by Frank Lloyd Wright.

Theatre in Dallas, Texas. It is based, in plan view, on a 'stretched' half-hexagon (as shown), and has excellent acoustic and visual properties.

Thick curtains and carpets will add a feeling of warm intimacy to an interior, and the mixture of absorbent and hard surfaces will enrich and soften the sound of music. The wonderfully peaceful tone of a fountain playing in an interior courtyard provides us not just with visually satisfying stimulus, but also gives us tranquil 'white noise' that becomes a defence against the intrusion of harsh sounds. Trees and bushes, grasses and reeds planted in the garden will rustle and whisper continually even in a slight breeze – defining the building much as a whispering silk dress will define the wearer through sound. Wind chimes under the eaves or aeolian harps will extend the defensive sound zone around a house and add their ethereal notes and haunting melodics.

In the quiet of traditional Japanese gardens, one is startled about every fifteen minutes, by a loud clack, like the sound made by hitting two wooden blocks together. The *sozu* consists of a bamboo tube, closed at one end and balanced on legs so that it can tip. It is constantly filled by a stream of water trickling from a bamboo water-pipe. When the tube is full, it tips forward, empties and falls back to its original position, loudly striking a rock. Originally these *sozu* or *shishi-o-doshi* were used to frighten away birds, deer and even wild boar that invaded farmland and gardens. Zen Buddhists, however, will explain that they were first introduced by the Zen mentor Rikkyu some six hundred years ago 'to give a sudden "clack" a few times during each hour so that one can hear the silence more clearly'.[9]

When we listen to rain falling on cedar shingles, the corrugated-tin roof of an Australian farmhouse, soft thatch, slate roofing, Mexican tile work or the tent we pitch in the

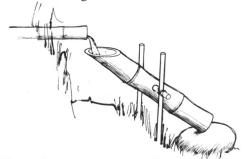

The 'sozu' in a Japanese garden fills with water and then empties itself, striking the rock as it falls back.

high Sierras, we can hear the roof and consequently sense something about the interior space-bubble. While living in Bali I observed the people in my village each morning as they took their songbirds out of the houses and hung the cages outside under the eaves. This was partly to make the birds feel less confined, yet it also helped to fill the air with beautiful songs. Pigeons were tethered on long silk lines with tiny bells or whistles fastened to their feet. This aeolian ululation from the skies, mixed with the trills of the songbirds, established a small and ghostly parasol of music over every home.

One of our most primitive senses is rhythm, which resonates from our heart beat and makes us respond to the drumbeats of a tribal celebration or jazz group. The *Art of the Fugue* by Johann Sebastian Bach may be the nearest construct to the spatial imagery of architecture in the West, just as the complex ornamentation of *suling* flutes and the *kantilan* (gongs) in the music of a Balinese Gamelan orchestra recalls the carefully controlled gestures of High Baroque buildings.

Architecture has been called 'frozen music' since it brings this same sense of rhythm into play by the repetition and spacing of windows, floorboards, wall spaces. Frank Lloyd Wright would manipulate these signifiers of rhythm, as well as room heights, to 'tune' the design of his houses to his clients' eye-height and provide a wholly new sense of psychic comfort from such visual modulations, best experienced in his Meyer May house.[10]

Ceiling heights and windows, floors and walls create a pleasing visual rhythm in the interior of Frank Lloyd Wright's 'Fallingwater', the Kauffmann house in Pennsylvania, 1935-39.

ORGANIC GEOMETRY

The shape of a room, besides creating various kinds of resonance, also provides a space for the movement of energy in a particular pattern. Since energy – including spiritual energy – flows in spirals and circles, rectangular spaces tend to accumulate stagnant pools of energy trapped in their corners. On the other hand, Native American tipis, Inuit igloos, pagodas and other indigenous dwellings, temples and shrines, tend to create a spiralling vortex of rising and diminishing energy streams. Every structure has a unique resonance arising from its proportions, and thus serves as a template for dynamic energy depending on its particular shape. This is equally true of the round domes of Buckminster Fuller's followers, the circular dome-shaped structures intuitively built by the so-called 'hippies' in places like Drop City at Trinidad, Colorado, or the Lama Foundation at San Christobal, New Mexico, of the late sixties and early seventies. Since nature seems to abhor straight lines in habitable spaces, this will also support Christopher Day's search for alternative spaces in his houses, as well in the Rudolf Steiner and Waldorf schools that he has designed and built.

If one views the meditation room of a Zen monastery, or enters a Zuni or Hopi *kiva*, one is impressed by the harmonious flow of space that leads inwards to centering oneself. In contrast the sacred spaces designed and built by the American architect Fay Jones – Thorncrown Chapel and Thorncrown Worship Centre in

Drop City, Colorado, was built 1966–68 and abandoned in 1972. The dome-shaped structures are made from old car tops.

© Norman McGrath

Interior of the Baha'i Temple,
Delhi (above), designed by
Fariburz Sahba, 1987. The
temple is based on a lotus, in
India the symbol of purity.

Interior (right) and exterior
(opposite) of Thorncrown
Chapel, Eureka Springs,
Arkansas, 1980, designed by
Fay Jones, an example of the
spiritual values in his work.

Arkansas, the Mildred Cooper Memorial Chapel in Arkansas and Pine Eagle in Mississippi – are outwardly oriented like John Lloyd Wright's Wayfarers' Chapel at Portuguese Bend in California. Their magic lies in a strong rhythm of light and darkness, warmth and coolness, cues of texture, nature and the human-made. The strong contrast is in a harmonious balance, a perfect *yin-yang* experience. On a near-mystic level, various sensory and subconscious triggers released by such structures flood our minds with a sense of joy and well-being.

Most, if not all, ancient buildings located at sacred sites derived their spatial geometry from organic sources that lie deeply buried (and frequently unrecognized) in our psyche, and those systems of proportions that govern growth patterns throughout nature, the proportionate organization of our bodies, the energy structure of the cosmos, as well as the harmonic intervals of the musical scale. In the West we are familiar with the 'golden proportions' of Leonardo da Vinci's drawing of a male figure defining both a circle and a square by being inscribed within these two shapes, illustrating the 'golden section' or the 'golden mean'. According to some research, the echoes in Gothic cathedrals resonate at the same frequency as the Earth itself – at seven and a half hertz – which happens also to be the frequency of the brain whilst in its most receptive and relaxed Alpha state. We find ourselves attuned to the Earth both psychophysically and spiritually. One is led to speculate that these ancient architects and builders knew how to use the golden mean in their form-giving to make temples, shrines and other enclosed environments resonate with a specific frequency, and recent research measurements have proved this.

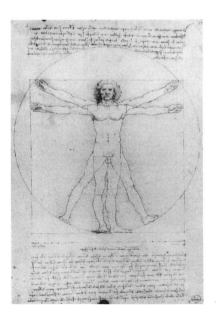

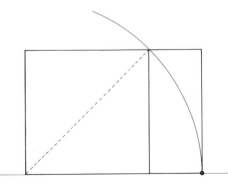

'Golden proportions' in Leonardo's famous drawing of a male figure defining both a circle and a square (left).

The 'golden rectangle' is determined by taking the diagonal of a square as the radius of a circle, which in turn marks the longest side of the rectangle with its circumference.

The sound of the waterfall comes from beneath Frank Lloyd Wright's 'Fallingwater', 1935-39.

Resonant spaces can also establish greater community among a group of people. Chanting or group singing, provided it is in a place that is acoustically 'alive', profoundly affects the participants and endows them with a sense of unity and common purpose. If such a group makes sounds like 'Om' together, yet in an arbitrary and individual 'free-form' way, without a leader or a scripted programme, the group sound will in the end reach a single pitch, duration or chord. Pendulums placed together in a room, swinging at random, will synchronize within half an hour. The very words we use to describe community or communitarian endeavours are used in music – accord, attunement, harmony.

Recently I was enchanted to hear choral pieces sung in Russian Orthodox churches in Moscow and St Petersburg, and the authentic resonance between the massed voices and the cupola and rounded interior niches of the church produced a deep feeling of joy and awe. The Christmas carol service at Stephansdom in Vienna, or Gregorian plainsong at Grace cathedral in Kansas City, yield a similar entrancing blending of space, stone and voices and provide a profound underpinning to the idea of viewing architecture as 'frozen music'.

Although entirely different in terms of massing and spatial treatment, most of Frank Lloyd Wright's dwellings and public structures have a strong link through this interplay of resonance and proportion, and so do many of the buildings of

The powerful interior spiral of the Solomon R. Guggenheim
Museum, New York, 1956-59, designed by Frank Lloyd Wright.

Water provides a sense of space, light and calm at the East Texas Medical Center, Athens, 1987.

Christopher Day uses organic shapes and fluid interior spaces in his designs, as for this kindergarten at Nant-y-Cwm, Dyfed, in Wales, 1990.

Alvar Aalto. In design and architecture we are dealing with profound forces that need to be better understood. Frank Lloyd Wright's design for the Guggenheim Museum forms an unusually powerful interior spiral. Many visitors have reported a strong desire to jump into the inner court, the centre of the spiral. Far from contemplating suicide they felt that they would slowly and gently float down to the floor, 'like a piece of down, like a feather'. This desire was deeply instinctive, since intellectually they were fully aware of the consequences of such a literal 'leap into the absurd'. Part of the same architect's most dramatic and famous house, 'Fallingwater' at Bear Run in Pennsylvania, is cantilevered out above a waterfall; some visitors report feeling somewhat disorientated by the sound of falling water coming from under the dwelling.

The most telling proportions in architecture seem to be those that are truly organic, linked to the Fibonacci series – 1, 1, 2, 3, 5, 8, 13, 21, 34, 55, 89, 144, 233, 377, 610, and so on, each new number generated by the sum of the two previous ones. Fibonacci was the nickname of the monk Leonardo of Pisa who in 1280 discovered that this series determined the number of leaves grown and extended by any plant for optimum chlorophyll production. It also governs the spiral seed display on pineapples, sunflowers, pine cones; the spirals generated by snail shells and the chambered nautilus; the horn configuration of deer and antelopes; and the mating patterns and number of generational descendants of bees, rabbits and other small mammals and insects. During the 19th century the French mathematician Edouard Lucas fleshed out the Fibonacci series by demonstrating

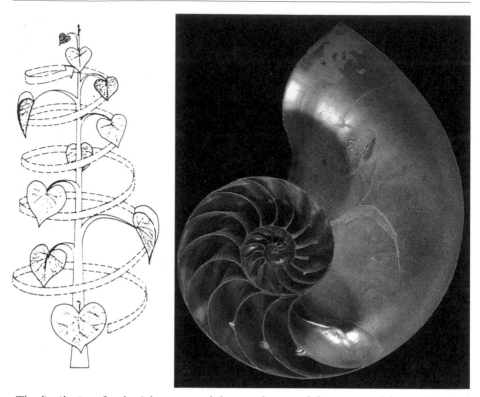

The distribution of a plant's leaves around the central stem and the structure of the nautilus spiral follow mathematical ratios common to countless forms in nature, including the human body.

through fractions (⅝ = 1.6 and Leonardo da Vinci's 'golden fraction' of ¹³⁄₈ = 1.625) a close relationship with the ratio of the golden section, but also with another 'magic' number, Pi. Other determinants of these proportions are deeply embedded in our biogenetic heritage which yields ratios between various parts of our bodies (in adults the relationship of head size to total body height, forearm to upper arm, length of leg to hand, and so forth).

THE COLLECTIVE UNCONSCIOUS

There is also the collective unconscious, as postulated by Carl Jung, which makes us feel comfortable with some places and spaces but distraught with other proportions. Jung himself designed and built a tower at his home at Bollingen.[11] For reasons still unknown, rooms that are pentagonal in plan cause great restlessness and psychic discomfort in most people. Many young designers and students in the 1960s and 1970s invested hard work and money in building a living dome based on Buckminster Fuller's original prototypes, and they argued passionately that a circular dwelling was somehow more 'organic' and conferred greater psychophysical comfort on its inhabitants. To strengthen their case they would cite igloos, kraals, tipis, Stone Age settlements, Mongolian yurts, and South American round-houses. Their opponents, leaving aside questions of practicality, existing furniture, linear arrangements, and so forth, argued for houses that were square or rectangular in plan. Yet no one has ever bothered to research which configuration provides greater comfort and which – to use current jargon – is more 'dweller-friendly'.[12] An enormous amount of research still awaits enquiry into many of these aspects of well-being and human comfort – research that ought to be approached with intellectual rigour, yet with a strong intuitive bias.

By entering spaces that were designed with a conscious recognition of some of these principles, one can experience what a human-scale, divinely proportioned building feels like, and speculate about a world in which such dwellings would be the norm rather than the exception. The villages in Egypt designed by Hassan Fathy and employing Nubian vault-makers, Christopher Day's buildings, most of Keith Critchlow's work, are marvellous examples of architecture that awakens our innermost mythic responses. The temples and houses of worship by Pietro Belluschi in Oregon and Washington, Herb Greene's early houses in Nebraska, and especially the dwellings and chapels by Fay Jones in Arkansas, Texas and Mississippi – all these reflect more than the adroit orchestration of space.

Yet these qualities could be achieved in the houses and flats in which we live, and were achieved on the whole until the last quarter of the 18th century. In the West, the houses of the rich and powerful were influenced by Renaissance and Graeco-Roman mannerisms, Baroque and Rococo spacing, and found their resolution in the work of Palladio. All this influenced the design of mercantile establishments, factories and apartment blocks. The dwellings of poorer folk frequently adapted the style of the residences of the wealthy, but were still equally informed by a vernacular tradition which gave them a sense of aptness and organic fit.

It is only since the height of the Industrial Revolution, during the last century and a half, that – as if through some vast act of inattention – architects and their clients became oblivious to rhythm, harmony and proportion. Unfortunately this neglect of scale and human perception in buildings accelerated during the 1930s and the periods immediately after both World Wars, when builders and speculators discovered with delight that the stated objectives of the Modern movement in architecture (sunlight, vast glass walls, decent ventilation), could easily be achieved on the cheap. The results were the mean blocks of flats and dreary suburban developments that now span the globe – leaving us all impoverished.

BENIGN ARCHITECTURE

There are many dictionary definitions that attempt to address the difference between the concepts 'house', 'home', 'shelter' and 'dwelling'. I use the word

The Sathya Sai Institute of Medical Sciences, Puttaparti, India, designed by Keith Critchlow and Associates, 1991; the central dome and administrative tower from the visitors' balcony.

'dwelling' to denote a living or working space that balances life and nature; it then indicates life in an organic harmony with environment and ecology.

Most people have experienced intensely spiritual feelings in certain buildings, often specifically designed to elicit this response. This architecture goes back to the beginnings of habitation and worship, to the earliest times of humankind – possibly to life in caves like those at Altamira and Lascaux. Our remote ancestors may have watched a patch of sunlight appear on the cave wall, filtered through some opening. Over long years it was noticed that this shaft of light would move a little each day, yet always return to the same spot every year.

Much started from such early observations. Methods of counting, astronomy and mathematics arose. We made stone circles to celebrate the superior order of the heavens as a sacred fact. The walls of shelters would be penetrated to allow the sun to focus on a sacred area at the time of the solstice. Societies led by priestesses or priests learned proportions and intervals from the stars, they navigated by them across the Pacific and worshipped Brother Sun and Sister Moon. In China a 'moon window' would afford a view of the full moon at predictable times. For thousands of years, religious buildings – temples, churches, *kivas*, mosques – have filled worshipper and visitor alike with feelings of awe and spiritual awareness, and the same response can also be felt in many secular buildings.

We know that mankind is an order-making animal and can therefore assume that even when we lived in caves we impressed our personalities on the spaces we occupied. Building shelters for ourselves, we were faced with a wide choice of materials. Clay, snow, animal hides, rocks, bamboo, rammed earth, reeds, tree trunks, slate, woven textiles, desert grasses and much else. Climate, modes of food-gathering or hunting and settlement patterns influenced our choice of tools, materials and processes and – after long passages of time – building traditions began to inform the shape of our dwellings. Over tens of thousands of years, and all over the planet, people have not merely managed to build places for shelter, but have also created outstanding buildings.

Today we find that modern buildings can make people ill, sometimes fatally. We seem incapable of relating the physical and psychological discomforts we suffer to the dangerous conditions that exist in our homes and workplaces. Even when some of these hazards are identified and discussed, people seem oddly unwilling to act to improve their chances for better health and survival. Public health researchers have found that a relatively new use of water – in the central air-conditioning systems of tall buildings – causes infections and may contribute to the 'sick-building' syndrome (symptoms range from headache to sore throat, wheeziness and shortnesss of breath).

Contemporary office and residential buildings are tightly sealed structures. The integrated heating, ventilating and air-conditioning systems reduce heating and cooling costs and energy-use by recycling the same air over and over again, which may develop fungi, bacteria and gases produced by most of the man-made materials. Textiles for carpets and uholstery are increasingly made of plastics.

The mosque at the village of New Gourna, Upper Egypt, built in 1948 and designed by Hassan Fathy, who employed workmen who could construct the vaulting in the traditional way.

At dawn on midwinter's day the sun shines through the roof aperture, lighting the passage and chamber of Newgrange, the great Neolithic tomb in Ireland, constructed five thousand years ago.

These materials and the adhesives used with them, release what a medical epidemiologist calls 'a variety of volatile organic compounds', which cause eye-irritations and infections of the upper respiratory tract.[13] The fresh-air intake of one high-rise building may be so close to the cooling tower of another that the drift of fine water droplets will transmit bacteria growing in the cooling-tower water more efficiently than breathing outdoor air. One such infection, Legionnaire's disease, is already well known.[14]

There is a growing body of public evidence that prolonged exposure to fluorescent lighting can have serious effects on the health, including eye-strain, headaches, increased stress and hyperactivity, and possibly infections of the upper respiratory tract. Medical experts feel that the ideal answer is to get as much day-light into the workplace as possible.

Only since 1989 have researchers in Germany and in the United States become aware that, in ways not yet clearly identified, electro-magnetic fields can con-tribute to leukaemia, cancers and genetic damage. Some consumer and homeowner groups have been successful in preventing powerful electric compa-nies from building microwave transmission towers or installing large transformers near schools or residential neighbourhoods.

All through history people tended to build their own dwellings, frequently with the support of the community. Most people had some basic hands-on experience of how to build a house, and had participated as helpers in the mak-ing of homes since childhood. They used materials that came from close to the site, and their construction methods proved over hundreds of years to be reliable and biologically healthy. The connection between designer/builder and end-user was direct. Almost like a jazz musician extemporizing, the owner-user-builder could change things as he saw fit during construction. Now the link has become much more complex. The constellation of people involved in building a house or a block of flats is represented in the diagram on the right. Although there are many connecting flow-lines between the various parties, those con-necting the person actually living in the house to the architect and builder are almost non-existent. It is no wonder that renters and

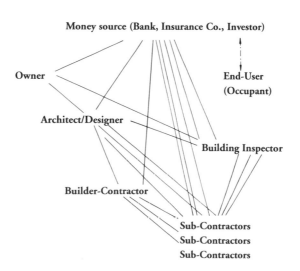

The harmonious proportions of the interior of the Church of the Redeemer, Baltimore, Maryland, designed by Pietro Belluschi (with Rodger, Taliaferro and Lamb), 1958.

purchasers feel isolated from the process of designing and building – they are. Since the entire business of building has been taken over by specialists and experts, we can expect neither health, beauty nor fitness of purpose. Building technology, and with it most architecture, is concentrated on square-foot costings, profit and the quickest return for the balance sheet – the 'bottom line'.

Yet architecture can only flourish if the dwellings built are in harmony with the people who live in them, with nature and culture. If the design profession chose the motto of the British Medical Association, 'First, do no harm!' as its credo, it would signify a giant step forward for users and towards the sustainability of the built environment.

The appreciation of architecture is multi-sensory and multi-dimensional. It becomes a do-it-yourself kit – a game played between designer and user. We derive joy from a spatial organization related in a direct manner to site, context and vegetation. A rich vocabulary of organic form and natural materials, linked to an apperception of our mythic expectations and inborn sense of harmony, will resonate and 'speak' to us if we care to really sense a dwelling, building or settlement as part of the natural and built environment. Seeing helps us to enjoy architecture, but only seeing can hinder us. We need to come to our senses again.

CHAPTER 5

The Biotechnology of Communities

The young mistakenly think that imagination is a substitute for experience; their elders are equally wrong in believing that experience can substitute for intelligence.
Arthur Koestler

Knowing is not enough; we must apply. Willing is not enough; we must do.
Goethe

W E ALL SENSE that something has gone terribly wrong with our communities. Hamlets and cities, slums and suburbs all lack a sense of cohesion. Not only is there no centre there – there is no there there. Cities, towns, villages and communities that were designed hundreds of years ago are obviously based upon some basic purpose of living that eludes the designers of our own time. Previous ages possessed one great advantage: a precise moral aim that gave meaning and direction to all planning and design. Classical antiquity sought a sense of harmony and balance, the medieval objective was mystic fulfilment, the Renaissance strove for an elegance of proportions and more recent times for enlightened humanism. Builders knew precisely what they wanted.

What then is the purpose of contemporary planners? Earlier builders knew what they were doing, because they followed the cultural imperatives of their society as their minds conceived them. Modern designers, whose purpose is the nourishing of public taste, have tried desperately hard – and with little success – to find out what that taste is. To help in this quandary, the designer uses research staffs and questionnaires, and what does he discover when at last his work is complete? That those for whom he has built move back to the old quarters of the city.

FINDING THE CENTRE ONCE MORE

Until very recently there has been no such thing as a changing purpose in planning settlements. That old towns are charming and new ones are not is due to the fact that city planners of former times – of ancient Greece, of medieval city states, of the heart of Amsterdam, London, Paris or Vienna – did not pursue *different* aims as their age changed, but instinctively always worked toward the one unchanging purpose that has always made people desire to live in urban centres in all human communities. Aristotle said that men form communities not for justice, peace, defence or traffic, but for the sake of the good life. This good life has always meant the satisfaction of man's four basic social desires: *conviviality, religion, artistic and intellectual growth, politics.*

In Salzburg, Austria, three squares flank the 17th-century cathedral and Residence.

The nucleus of cities, with all the variations in styles, therefore always included the same basic elements: inns and eating places, sports arenas and theatres to satisfy conviviality; churches or temples for the spiritual fulfilment; museums, zoos, libraries and schools for intellectual growth; city halls for politics. And, since the satisfaction of these four community-shaping desires required an economic base, these structures were naturally and organically grouped around the marketplace, creating and serving the fifth communal activity, trade and commerce.

If a new region is to be successfully developed, decentralized and open to many different possibilities, some interventions are simple. What is needed is the construction of focal points at traditional crossroads: a sidewalk café, a restaurant serving good food, a little concert hall or theatre, a charming church, a well-designed meeting hall.

Ancient planners put all their talent into the building of the communal nucleus – inns, churches, city halls. The rest of the settlement then followed by itself. Modern designers are forever concentrating on the rest of the city. But without an organic centre nothing can be held together. And we have difficulties now in conceptualizing a nucleus since we've let ourselves become convinced, falsely, that every age has a different purpose – by the time we discover our own it may have run through our hands like sand.

Model for a spiritual community founded by the teacher Aurobindo in Pondicherry, India.

PEOPLE NOT TRAFFIC

We live with traffic jams everywhere; the question is, what causes them? Narrow streets? Streets have been widened, and congestion has become worse. Too few traffic arteries? Traffic arteries have multiplied, and jams have become nearly continuous. Urban density? Cities have exploded outwards into suburbs and the surrounding countryside, reducing density, yet the gridlock has increased exponentially. Bad planning? International experts have made plans and when implemented, jams have grown. Too little thought? The reverse is true: *too much thought.* Modern planners are so concerned with traffic that they seem to think that the only function of the city is to serve as a race track for drivers between petrol pumps and hamburger stands. Los Angeles might have become an elegant city; it has instead become the first city to incorporate *rural* distances into its tormented, traffic-choked *urban sprawl.*

What most planners have overlooked in their rush to eliminate all obstacles to traffic, is that they are removing the community itself. The function of a community is to act as a goal not as a passage point, an end not a means, a stop not a flow, a place to arrive not for driving through. This is why nearly all good cities exist where traffic was bound to stop: at the base of mountains or at their top; on the bend of rivers, the shores of lakes or oceans; or – in the case of some of the most spectacular among them such as Venice, Bangkok or Manhattan – in the midst of canals or lagoons or on the tips of thin islands where any movement beyond is restricted not just in one but in all directions.

To improve the quality of modern life designers must follow two guidelines. First they must reverse their current hierarchy of values, giving less not more thought to traffic planning, and concentrating instead on trade and community planning. Secondly, they must turn to a new set of experts. Since the foremost city planners are responsible for the most glaring obscenities – Brasilia, Canberra, Ottawa and the new towns of postwar England, to mention a few – our experts will be found in the genius of the past. We must look back with humility to study not what is the latest in Los Angeles or Milan but what is oldest in Boston or Siena.

THE AESTHETICS OF SITE

One true and tried method to protect a community from turning into a speed-way is the inclusion of squares or roundabouts into the road network to act as traffic obstacles, with sculpture, music pavilions, seating, water fountains and venerable trees. Yet the paradoxical nature of communities is such that once a town becomes commercially desirable and aesthetically attractive it attracts people from other communities like a magnet. This drift toward centralization must be fought, since, once this process starts, even the most beautiful community will attract so much commerce and traffic that it will head toward crowding and eventual decay.

Received wisdom explains the selection of a site though the interplay of four determinants: distance from markets, raw material sources, situation within a transportation net and available labour. The aesthetic factor – closeness to concerts, sports, theatres, conviviality appealing to the senses – is usually ignored. This fifth possible determinant of location, the aesthetic parameter, is not just equal in strength to any of the other four but can be stronger than all combined. This can be demonstrated positively whenever a new factory opens up in the countryside. The manager is usually the first to decide to subject himself to hour-long daily commuting rather than face the dullness of the countryside. The workers follow as soon as they can afford to do so. Some indeed even prefer unem-ployment and a richly textured existence among exciting architecture, theatres, galleries, inns and a vivid nightlife.

The aesthetics of site have been overlooked, since modern location theory originated at a time during the 19th century when virtually all cities, towns and villages possessed it to such an extent that the aesthetic assets of each were cancelled out by the beauty of the others. Even the most remote western villages in Colorado boasted an opera house a hundred years ago, as well as museums and decent inns. Austria-Hungary had so many glamorous small capital cities – most of them with their own opera, palaces, theatres, courts and universities – that each had enough central force to hold beauty in balance across the land.

THE SENSE OF LOCATION

Just as birds choose the ideal location for their nests with their strongly developed siting instincts – and without the help of design consultants – so do certain human groups. Living and working in the *barrios* in Brazil, Colombia and Venezuela, I was struck by the paradox that the rich have luxury flats in high-rise towers at the base of a valley that is frequently choked by pollution, noise and traffic – whereas the poor live in slums on mountainsides overlooking the city, the ocean or the mountains. Even the large *barrio* just north of Guadalajara in Mexico is more pleasantly situated than the city. At Boroka in Papua New Guinea the slums are individual homes set on stilts in one of the most beautifully sheltered ocean bays just outside Port Moresby.

The high level of social happiness that exists in slums often surprises visitors. The slums are medically unhealthy and poverty is great, yet their inhabitants have solved many social and urban problems that bedevil designers elsewhere. There is no loneliness for the old, no lack of supervision for children. But, this high degree

The slums of Rio de Janeiro in Brazil are located high above the city and the luxury tower blocks.

of social happiness aside, what slum dwellers demonstrate from a design viewpoint is that they are one of the five lucky categories of people endowed with a wonderful sense of location. The others four are – according to Leopold Kohr[1] – the aristocrats, the innkeepers, the military and the church. And, as a direct result of their greater freedom to choose, where these favoured groups build or pitch their tents, there it is good to live. And where it is good to live it is also beautiful to live.

NATURE'S MAGIC NUMBERS

Embarking on a design for an entirely new settlement, we instinctively look for some guidelines. Nothing is as frustrating to a designer as to be given a complete *tabula rasa* without any constraints or limitations. If architects, designers and planners have neglected to use such guidelines in their work, it is because they are unaware that a body of knowledge is emerging that deals primarily with human scale, a recognition of certain magic numbers that are based on our physical, psychological and species abilities.

Our biogenetic heritage governs expectations of size, weight, distance, speed and time. 'Old' measurements like mile, pound, yard, foot, stone, reflect what we can lift or carry easily, and how we used our bodies as templates for measurement. As explained in Chapter 4, the *eidetic image* that we carry with us through life gives us another system for judging harmonious relationships and scale. 'Invented' measuring systems, like the metric system, are as meaningless to us as is the time displayed on a digital watch. Le Corbusier published two books of inaccurate mathematics, trying to fit the metric system to human perceptions, and failed. It is rather ironic that international usage of the metric system has forced us to think in these artificial terms, and to include metric measurements in this book.

Perception and *Gestalt* mechanisms provide more of our magic numbers: all that we have seen growing in nature around us since we were born reflects the Fibonacci series and thus deeply affects our concept of aesthetics. Eye-rotation and distance recognition yield us 'ideal' distances for houses from the street, house heights, and so forth. 'Experienced spaces', that is our familial and personal experiences, help us to find the ideal size for bedroom, kitchen or restaurant. This is modified by cultural constraints: rooms in traditional Japanese farmhouses tend to be smaller than, say, in England – yet the Japanese rooms are multifunctional. Single-function bathrooms in the USA are much bigger than in the Scandinavian countries, but much space is wasted.

Terrain, climate and travelling-time influence distance measurements; for instance, the distances between villages reflect how far a man could walk in a day carrying a load, how far a horse could be ridden or a cart driven; obviously in mountainous countries such as Switzerland, Papua New Guinea or Colombia towns are closer together. As far as the size of communities is concerned, here too some 'natural' magic numbers exist – they are determined by our collective unconscious regarding group size, which in turn is affected by tribal lifestyles, climate, even incest taboos that limit the number of people within an area.[2]

Assuming a height of 32 feet (9.75m), then 60 feet (18.3m) would give us a building of satisfying width in aesthetic terms. Physiological optics tell us that, in looking at others, 50 feet (15m) is the limit to the distance at which we can recognize facial expressions; we can identify gender, outlines, gait, basic colours at around 450 feet (135m). At 1000 feet (300m) we can no longer make any such identifications.[3] These numbers may seem pedantic and completely useless – unless we begin relating them to real-world situations. We find, for instance, that in plazas of many different periods, styles and cultures, the major axis of the square is almost the same length.

Acropolis, Athens	460ft	140m
St Peter's Square, Rome	435ft	133m
Place Vendôme, Paris	430ft	131m
Amalienborg, Copenhagen	450ft	137m
St Mark's Square, Venice	422ft	129m

Although the large square at the imperial city in Beijing measures nearly 9000 feet (2740m), each unbroken segment is just 470 feet (143m) long. There is some inherently pleasing and aesthetically appealing scale at work here – especially if we look at other squares, piazzas and plazas to find that almost without exception they measure just under 500 feet (152m).

To this we can relate numbers of 'commuter distances': how far office workers will walk to sit in a public plaza at lunchtime, or how far residents will walk willingly to reach a park. In the USA these distances are about three city blocks, or a three-minute walk. This not only suggests that office neighbourhoods function much as residential ones do, but also something about ideal size again. If people will walk three minutes to reach a central gathering point, then a 'neighbourhood' is, in effect, about six minutes' walking time in width – or, in linear terms, five or six blocks, which is between 1500 feet (457m) and 1625 feet (495m). Europeans and Asians will walk a little further than Americans. The city planner Konstantinos Doxiades is usually credited as 'the father of Ekistiks' (the study of human settlements). He has built many towns and, as a result of his cross-cultural studies, determined a 'kinetic field' with a ten-minute walking time of 2500 foot (760m) radius, five times the length of a typical plaza.[4]

IDEAL COMMUNITY SIZE

Professor George Murdoch of Yale University has studied more than 250 societies of different kinds and found that 'magic' numbers operate here as well. Aboriginal dialect tribes, Amazonian Indian groups, Peruvian and Tupi-Guarani hunting bands generally number between 400 and 600 individuals. Iroquois Indian long-houses accommodated 500, and excavated villages from Mesopotamia and Anatolia numbered from 400 to 600 residents. So-called 'intentional religious communities' in the United States during the 18th and 19th centuries usually had about 500 members – as did hippie 'dropout' communes in the 1960s. The average elementary school in average counties in the USA has about 500 students in some 40,000 school systems. These numbers hold steady even among some of our closer relatives: a tribe of Gelada baboons in Ethiopia will number 500 members, as will the snow monkeys of Japan. When groups of Langur monkeys in India exceed 500 in number the tribe splits up.

All this gives us a community size of around 450 to 600 individuals – it is interesting to note that in business groups working closely together some minor stresses appear only when the group exceeds 750; the 'trouble threshold' appears at 1200. Behavioural scientists consider that 250 people constitute a 'small' neighbourhood, 1500 a 'large' one', about 450 to 600 a 'social' neighbourhood.

From these numbers we can go further. With our objective a benign, neighbourly way of life, rich in interconnections and cultural stimuli, we can say that 'face-to-face' communities will consist of 400 to 1000 people (the ideal is around 500), 'common neighbourhoods' will accommodate roughly 5000 to 10,000 residents (or 10 to 20 face-to-face communities), and the 'ideal city' will house about 50,000 souls (or 10 to 20 common neighbourhoods). Special functional reasons may decrease city size to 20,000 or increase it to 120,000 – beyond that lies social chaos.

We can provide some historical underpinnings for this. The major cathedral towns of Europe, at the height of their flowering – Chartres, Avignon, Cologne, Canterbury, Siena, Padua, Rheims and Salisbury – each housed about 10,000 inhabitants. At the time of the Renaissance the major universities of Bologna, Paris, Oxford and Cambridge had a faculty and student population of 20,000 to 35,000. Florence in the time of Leonardo and Botticelli built cathedrals, theatres, palaces and public gardens with a population of 40,000, and Michelangelo's Rome held 50,000. The musically, artistically and architecturally exciting Germany of Dürer, Cranach and Holbein during the 15th century listed its 150 'large' cities, which in the first census each had about 35,000 residents.[5]

There is much more knowledge surfacing than one might suspect. It comes from many different disciplines, yet it is logical that professional architects, designers and planners should be the people to use and apply it; the designer, planner or architect works most effectively in the role of synthesist.

CHAPTER 6

The Lessons of Vernacular Architecture

Structurally and formally all the Architecture was in lovely shape, but humans were not fully understood; Design did not serve survival.
Richard Neutra

SINCE THE middle of the 20th century, architects, anthropologists and art historians have become increasingly interested in vernacular architecture, both in urban and rural settings. Many buildings, building types and settlements, never seriously studied before, have been documented through photographs and written descriptions. This trend was given strong support through the exhibition 'Architecture without Architects' organized by Bernard Rudofsky at the Museum of Modern Art in New York in 1963, as well as in his two subsequent books.[1] Sybil Moholy-Nagy, the architectural critic and historian, tackled the same topic in her *Native Genius in Anonymous Architecture*.[2]

Rudofsky's viewpoint on vernacular built form was similar to his perspective in his earlier work on an entirely different topic: the history of clothing. This field of enquiry was also documented brilliantly in his 1948 exhibition 'Are our Clothes Modern?', and accompanying book, for the New York Museum of Modern Art.[3] Rudofsky pointed out that most of our knowledge of the history of clothing and fashion, from paintings and illustrations, as well as from verbal descriptions, is primarily concerned with the dress of emperors, nobles and princes of the church. The everyday garb of peasants, artisans and other ordinary folk remains virtually unrecorded. By disregarding the portrait paintings in galleries, and instead concentrating on those modest drawings embodied in the illuminated capitals at the beginning of chapters in medieval manuscripts, or in the sketchbooks of artists like Leonardo da Vinci, Hiroshige or Hokusai, Rudofsky was able to derive much information about the simple clothing of the common people.[4]

TOO HUMBLE FOR HISTORY

This research into humble clothing can serve as an analogy to architecture. The history of architecture is well documented through the buildings of the ruling classes – palaces, castles, cathedrals and merchants' houses. Many of these buildings still survive, or have been reconstructed; plans and drawings of others have been lovingly collected and preserved. Simple, modest dwellings of the past, however, are harder to find. In the present pluralistic age, they exert a strong fascination, and offer a beguiling area for research and study.

If we look up the word 'vernacular' in a dictionary, we find definitions such as: anonymous, indigenous, naive, naïf, primitive, rude, popular, spontaneous, local or folk-based. These terms illuminate the subject no more than calling a concerto 'spirited' or a tone-poem 'deliberate' gives us the feel of a piece of music.

SIX FALLACIES ABOUT VERNACULAR ARCHITECTURE
Our views on vernacular architecture are clouded by a series of fallacies, favoured by individual architects, historians, writers or critics according to each subjective bias.

1. The Historic Fallacy
This is based on the mistaken concept that the mere passage of time somehow sanctifies built vernacular form. There is, therefore, a profound interest in such structures as Stonehenge, medieval peasant cottages, Stone Age settlements, Roman fortifications or the Guildhalls of the Hanseatic league. Neither the Congregational churches of New England nor the one-room schoolhouses of Kansas serve as vernacular examples just because of their age, but because they are templates of traditional building. The skills, methods, materials, emotions, processes and necessities that define a building as vernacular are with us today as much as 400 or 40,000 years ago.

2. The Exotic Fallacy
If distance lends enchantment to the view, then we find here a preoccupation with things whose only virtue lies in being far away. Eskimo igloos, grain receptacles in Bali or Mali, fishing villages in Thailand or the Dominican Republic, Maori houses, the longhouses of Kwakiutl or Tlingit on the north west coast of Canada, Batak villages in Sumatra, Mongolian yurts – all are equally exotic to us, and we elevate them to a specious significance in our increasing interest in the vernacular. There is a basic appeal in things that come from afar, and this emotional enchantment can be expected to become stronger as the ease of air-travel and the pervasiveness of electronic and print communication all drive the world into a drab sameness. Marshall McLuhan's 'Global Village' is being turned into a global Disneyland. In our frenzy to find appealing models, many critics voice enthusiasm and approval for Brazil's worst *favelas*, or the meanest *barrio* settlements in Venezuela – human garbage dumps no better than the dreariest slums of Detroit or Liverpool – except that they flourish with dreadful facility under a tropical sun.

3. The Romantic Fallacy
The idealization of Rousseau's 'Noble Savage' has spilled over into the concept of the 'Noble Savage's House'. Closely related as this approach is to the Exotic

Fallacy, it also speculates about the improvement in community feeling and co-operation (that German architectural and planning critics have called *Gemeinschaft und Gesellschaft*) through primitive settlement patterns and village structures. This view is a thoroughly sentimental one, and offers architects an opportunity to write a revisionist history by ascribing their own present-day systems of belief to so-called primitive societies, both past and present. In the 1930s, Le Corbusier wrote eloquently on his conviction that primitive tribes had intuitively used his *Modulor* system of dimensions and relationships, though it was based on the French metric system of the late 18th century (mathematically derived, and so not organic).[5] Richard Neutra ascribed an 'intuitive cognition of the same metric measuring systems' to Indian villages and settlements in Indonesia.[6]

By contrast, those exotic building systems that have carried over into the world of architecture and are thought of as high architecture are consciously shunned by the romantic-sentimental critics. It is difficult to find an intelligent discussion of the classic Japanese house with its sophisticated and subtle use of modular components (*tatami, shoji, fusuma*), in writing about the vernacular.[7] The history-mongering of architectural revisionists is most tellingly dissected by Joseph Rykwert in his book *On Adam's House in Paradise*.[8] Rykwert describes the painful struggles of Le Corbusier to convince the world that even our earliest ancestors used set squares, triangles and metric measurements to make sure that the earliest of mankind's mean huts formed perfect rectangles.

4. The Fallacy of Popular Culture

This theory approaches the subject from the view of 'High Culture'. Here the argument implies that *any* structure that seemingly fits certain community ideas or ideals and is repeated often enough with only minor typological variations can be called vernacular. Apologists for this view will mention McDonald's or Wendy's hamburger places, Pizza Huts or Kentucky Fried Chicken outlets as examples of late 20th-century American vernacular structures, together with their contextual relationship to 'the strip'. The 'strip' has become a shorthand expression in America for a high-traffic artery that consists largely of quick-food restaurants: in Lawrence, Kansas, where this is being written, there are forty-four such places within two and a half miles. This High Culture view shuts its eyes firmly to the fact that such quick-food places are the outward manifestations of highly centralized commercial organizations, and that design and structural decisions are made in corporate headquarters rather than on a local, autonomous level. Idiosyncratic single productions, such as the Brown Derby restaurant in Hollywood, the Los Angeles 'Super Dog' drive-in that looks like a frankfurter in a bun or the dinosaur-shaped bar and restaurant in the Arizona desert, are also sometimes called vernacular by defenders of the High Culture, since their

Certain building styles seem exotic to Western eyes because of their unfamiliarity, as, for example, the style represented by this Batak village in Sumatra, Indonesia.

The circular yurt, still used by the nomads of Central Asia and here seen in Afghanistan, is covered with felted wool, a light material that is water and wind-resistant.

The classic Japanese town house represents a sophisticated yet still vernacular architectural style.

vulgarity is equated with a rude popular wit. These structures are assertive three-dimensional statements, acting as trademarks, logos or identifiers; their reason for existence is the big sell – quite different from the unselfconscious statements of true vernacular and indigenous buildings.

5. The Fallacy of the Living Tradition

This claims that, since the majority of people in North America live in subdivisions (suburban housing developments) with picture windows, such homes and their suburban location are a true expression of vernacular striving. Here again the thinking stems from a High Culture viewpoint. The fact is that – like quick-food restaurants – these homes are the result of centralized production and design processes, and are inhabited by millions of people largely because no other meaningful choices are readily available. To choose to live in a New England saltbox with a Mexican red-tiled roof, fake Tudor beams, Greek pillars at the front door, a federal-period fanlight over the entrance and a picture window presenting an enchanting view of other picture windows across the street, bears the same relationship to the vernacular as a Cadillac El Dorado to a Pakistani oxcart, a Chinese sampan or a pickup truck.

6. The Sacred Fallacy

This assumes that any building deeply rooted in the religious beliefs of a people and signalling sacred meaning can *ipso facto* be considered a vernacular expression of faith. In this argument, a crazy-quilt collection of buildings from the cathedral of Notre Dame to the Hagia Sophia, the Stephansdom in Vienna to the Taj Mahal, the Ise Shrine in Kyoto to any Native American *kiva* are equally weighted as examples. There are vernacular aspects to most of these buildings. Others are included for their sacred meaning rather than for their representation of the profound purposefulness of vernacular processes.

PROCESS NOT PRODUCT

To think intelligently about vernacular architecture and environments, we must first rid ourselves of these fallacies. Then we must consider the various 'explanations' or 'interpretations' of vernacular architecture that are available. There seem to be six major explanations, reflecting the different preconceptions of various groups. All of them have some relevance, but each is so single-minded or monolithic, it is by its nature reductionist, reducing the complex to the simplistic. It is possible, however, to weave them together into a six-sided dynamic web which can help us to look at structures or settlements more lucidly; this is discussed later in the chapter.

It may be helpful to start from a process-oriented rather than a product-based viewpoint. Vernacular architecture is based on a knowledge of traditional practices and techniques; it is usually self-built (perhaps with help from family, clan or builders in the tribe), and reveals a high regard for craftsmanship and quality. Vernacular structures tend to be easy to learn and understand. They are made of predominantly local materials. They are ecologically apt, that is they fit in well with local climate, flora, fauna and ways of life. Vernacular buildings are never self-conscious; they recede into the environment rather than serving as self-proclaiming design statements. They are human in scale; frequently the process of building is more important than or equally important as the end product. This combination of good ecological fit, human scale, craftsmanship and striving for quality, together with a strong concern for decoration, ornamentation and embellishment, leads to a sensuous frugality that results in true elegance.

SIX EXPLANATIONS

Trying to understand the rich tradition of vernacular architecture by looking at only one aspect is like the chicken/egg or nature/nurture dilemma. Attempts have been made to explain vernacular architecture with a social Darwinist view of 'survival of the fittest', or even the biological fable of 'ontogeny recapitulates philogeny' (meaning that an organism recapitulates all the early phases of the genetic development of its species – the human embryo replicates fish and froglike phases, for example). In fact, we can't really see the subject at all unless we set aside all such individual interpretations and realize that *vernacular architecture is the result of multiple causation.*

1. The Methodological Eplanation

The writers and critics who advance this view start with the notion that method alone – used in a vernacular setting – will explain certain buildings or structures. *Method is the combination of material, tool and process.* An example is the building of a log cabin. Assuming the general availability of trees, and therefore round tree trunks, these logs are the material. An axe or hatchet is the tool. The simplest and most direct process is to chop curved saddles at the ends of the log; this is called a 'kerf-cut'. The logs then interlock, using the kerf-cuts to link together creating corners and walls as easily as the popular American toy 'Lincoln Log'. So, given round logs as material, an axe as a tool, and kerf-cuts as a process, the inevitable result will be a log cabin. This explains why log cabins have been parts of the architectural heritage of all countries that have enough trees. Historians tell us that the log cabin was first brought to the United States by Finnish and Swedish settlers in the Delaware area some three hundred years ago, and then moved westward. But the same construction can be seen in European farmhouses, early Japanese shrines or indigenous buildings at high altitudes in Kenya and Zimbabwe. This way of examining method has been more fully explored in my earlier book, *Design for the Real World.*[9]

Time brings increasing sophistication. The earliest, or most primitive log structures – like the *Yukaghir* huts of Siberian Russia – used fully rounded, untrimmed logs, as did early settlers in the USA. By the sixteenth century, Swedes, Norwegians and Finns would square off two parallel sides of the logs; in Austria, Germany and Switzerland all four sides were neatly squared, somewhat like today's six-by-fours. Moss, clay or mud were used as chinking to seal gaps between logs. As timber technology improved, the 'kerf-cuts' also became more intricate. Round logs with saddle joints developed into hewn or dressed logs with V-notches, to keep the timbers from rotting and make the structure more watertight. Later still, square and diamond notches, dovetail joints, and, in Japan, enchantingly intricate connections were developed. Increasingly specialized tools changed both process and materials so that the log hut became a wooden house. Eventually further refinement led to balloon-frame construction and other more complex wooden structures – reaching their apotheosis in the Byzantine Rococo-like splendour of Russian wooden churches. At the beginning of the 20th century, log-cabin-like buildings had become symbolic: Walter Gropius – father of the Bauhaus – built the Sommerfeld house in 1921 for a wealthy industrialist in Berlin. Middle and upper-class Germans had been seduced by over eighty historical adventure novels by the German novelist Karl May, set in an ideal Wild West replete with Native American Indians and log cabins.

It is clear that other materials, tools and processes will yield different structures. Some materials are naturally flexible and can therefore be easily bent into

An American log cabin made from round logs (above). Different joints on round and dressed logs, and a typical Austrian log house (opposite).

This traditional way of finishing earth walls in the Algerian Sahara seems to have originated from an ancient practice common in West Africa.

Russian wooden churches are among the most complex and splendid wooden structures.

Sommerfeld house in Berlin, designed by Walter Gropius and Adolf Meyer, 1921.

The structure of the tipi is influenced by the characteristics of branches and hide.

dome-like shapes. The result is a structure with a circular footprint that consists of bundles of reeds, bamboo or flexible branches that are lashed together with lianas, grasses or twine around a tension pole. These, covered with felted wool, carpets, skin, fur, leather, canvas or plastic will yield yurts, tipis, tents or geodesic domes. Snow cut into blocks will make an igloo. Tool, material and process will provide form, but before we assume that the methodological explanation gives us the key to vernacular architecture, we may have to think again, for there are many other factors that come into play.

2. The Dispersion and Convergence Explanation
This way of explaining vernacular architecture has become especially popular with social anthropologists and sociologists, as well as cultural and physical geographers. Class dispersion deals with the movement of structures or artefacts across class barriers. In many cultures such movement is unthinkable, in others it is a routine occurrence. There is no question that people on a lower social level desire to express themselves through their buildings, which often means that the mannerisms of the ruling class are copied or visually paraphrased. Ethnologists, who come into the picture somewhat later, then study the remains of such buildings and frequently celebrate them as spontaneous signs of primitive vitality.

Class dispersion works both ways. In the West in the late 20th century there has been an 'upward' movement of so-called peasant food into the area of *haute*

This Hungarian shepherd's hut is made of local reeds; structures like it can be found in many places in the world where reeds provide a plentiful and cheap building material.

A reconstruction of one of a group of round Neolithic houses with stone settings and supported by earthfast posts; they were excavated in Ireland between 1939 and 1955 at Lough Gur in Ireland.

The pointed Arabic arch (above) was brought to Europe by the Crusaders, where it became part of the Gothic style. From Venice (left) it returned to influence Lebanese architecture.

Features of the ancient adobe Pueblo of Taos in New Mexico (below) are echoed in settlements in certain regions of Africa, not through contact but because of similar climate and materials.

cuisine. The well-to-do dine by choice on such plain fare as polenta, linguini, Eintopfgericht (many leftovers cooked in one pot), collard greens with chitlins or ghoulash-like stews – once considered beneath the notice of gourmets. In architecture, design, and those areas of life directly touched by the built environment and its artefacts, the concept of 'voluntary simplicity' provides still another example of upward dispersion.[10]

Geographical dispersion is the dissemination of building features and types from one country to another, and frequently the re-importation of such features to the country of origin. Around AD 1000, returning Crusaders brought the Arabic pointed arch to Europe, where – once transplanted – it became established as part of the

Settlement in North Africa with many building details similar to the Pueblo at Taos.

European Gothic style. Much later the European pointed arch returned to Lebanon from Venice and has greatly influenced both public and domestic architecture in that country – a nine-hundred-year 'case-study' of geographical dispersion.

English settlers in Australia, New England and South Carolina originally built copies of early Victorian homes, pubs and churches. But whereas such structures still serve well in Massachusetts or New Hampshire, the hot climate of the American south or of New South Wales acted as an immediate modifier. Climate dictates style. In Australia a verandah is tacked on to the house, in the southern United States a 'sleeping porch' is wrapped around the home to provide night-time comfort in hot and humid conditions. Frank Lloyd Wright pushed the vernacular further: his two small cabins of 1940 at the Yemassee Plantation consist almost entirely of a porch that encloses a small inner core consisting of a kitchen and bathroom.[11] Meanwhile, at the turn of the century, the verandah had been exported back to England, where it now appears as a feature of holiday houses in the benign climate of the south-west coast.[12]

The modification of the Palladian style as it became dispersed in Malaysia under British colonial rule has been rigorously and sensitively described by the architect and teacher Chris Abel in his book *Living in a Hybrid World: Built Sources of Malaysian Identity.*[13] In Bandung, Indonesia, in 1989 I discovered that

Frank Lloyd Wright's Imperial Hotel (built in Tokyo in 1917) had been used – or adapted – as a master template for several hotels built in the early 1930s. Even on Bali, predominantly in the larger cities such as Denpasar or Singaradja, there are window designs and other fittings that seem to have come straight from Wright's Oak Park Studio of 1909, although these hotels were built around 1932.

I must emphasize that social and geographic dispersion supply only a partial explanation. There is also convergence: the Pueblo at Taos looks very much like the oldest housing structure at N'Djamena in Chad; the same reddish-brown adobe walls are penetrated at the top by identical horizontal beams, wooden climbing bars lead up the walls to similar roof entrances and ladders, yet there has been no contact between North Equatorial Africa and New Mexico. The sweeping gabled roofs of thatched farmhouses of the Shirakawa prefecture in Japan find their exact counterpart in the roofs of Indios' houses in the mountains of Guatemala. Why? Biomorphologists and structural botanists tell us that the 'convergence phenomenon' is found in plants and animals around the world. In Africa there are no indigenous cacti, but similar climate makes the *Euphorbia Africani* from the edge of the Kalahari desert a look-alike of the Suehero cactus of Arizona. An arid climate with little or no rainfall and a great deal of sunlight, high temperatures and chilly nights has imposed certain characteristics, such as water retention, insulation and thermal mass, shaded spots to help photosynthesis, all of which result in similar plant forms in different parts of the world.

These same climatic 'givens' shape a great deal of desert housing, as does the availability of clay or clay-like soils. But here again, other factors help to give a more complete picture, such as: living patterns, perceptions of space, culturally determined settlement structures, traditions, and so forth. To use only climatic and geographic determinants without considering these other modifiers is a reductionist fallacy.

3. The Evolutionary Explanation

There is no general agreement that vernacular form evolves over time, and in fact the architectural historian Amos Rapoport has stated that: 'Primitive and vernacular buildings are distinguished by lack of change, differing in this respect from the more "normal" historical material. These buildings are, therefore, nonchronological in nature.'[14]

Although vernacular building is deeply rooted in traditional values, symbolizing continuity within the community, we can still identify a number of changing factors. Things move more slowly in a Balinese village than in the centre of London or in a Tokyo suburb. The function of certain buildings may alter; new materials or improvements in construction techniques may be introduced; constituent parts may be rearranged – for instance, cattle may be stabled on the ground floor of the farmhouse partly to provide a source of heat, and then the adoption of separate cowsheds will lead to the installation of fireplaces. Such changes are cumulative in nature, and offer evidence of a continuing process.

This evolutionary, slow-paced development can be traced in nearly all vernacular building, but it is difficult to document. House types cannot give a true picture of the history of house-building. Vernacular structures tend to blur the differences between the dwellings of the aristocracy and the gentry, the home-workshops of artisans, the homes of the very poor, farmhouses and barns.

With the debris of non-biodegradable high-technology piling up all over the world, there has been a ready incorporation of new 'found' materials (broken concrete panels, plastic sheets, bottles, flattened tin cans, glass, and so forth) into the vernacular. This particular change, however, is so recent as to defy evolutionary classification. A historical perspective is essential to the understanding of evolutionary change, but not enough data is yet available which could provide a rigorous foundation for such a study.

4. The Social-Environmental Explanation

Vernacular buildings reflect the social and societal needs, the wants and yearnings of people more directly than structures designed by architects. To begin with, on a village level people would design and frequently build their own home and then use it within their extended family over several generations. Technological development and the division and specialization of labour has meant that the builder has developed into several different specialists. At the end of the 20th century, a six-fold disunion exists in mainstream architectural practice. The architect is commissioned by the owner – frequently no more than a speculator or front man for a banker/investor. The architect's design is carried out by a builder, who in turn employs a series of subcontractors for specialized work. The end-user, that is, the person who lives in the dwelling, labours in the factory, inhabits the prison, works in the office or attends classes in the school, stands in no direct relationship to the other five parts of this complex configuration of talent, speculation, greed, know-how and craft. The end-user's only contribution seems to lie in passively adapting to land-rights, market forces, existing structures and decisions made for and about him or her.

But the social/societal explanation relies on more than economics, or the constellation of people providing 'building delivery' and turning homes into warehousing for consumer durables. Each culture or class has its own idea of the right scale for comfort; social and environmental expectations help to determine scale. 'Rabbit hutches' is a demeaning term used to describe Japanese apartments that are for cultural and economic reasons smaller than the 'space-guzzlers' so popular with Americans. In vernacular buildings and settlements, scale enables folk to understand and 'read' the underlying concepts easily – to use Leopold Kohr's apt phrase, 'to grasp in one glance' the conceptual underpinning.[15] This is not to claim that smallness is desirable in itself, although Kohr, Fritz Schumacher, George McRobie and I myself have put this view forward strongly.[16]

Architectural education and training – at least in the United States – is skewed toward large-scale structures and big clusters of buildings (which are more profitable). Hence architects bring an enormous amount of intellectual baggage to their work, most of which ignores the social and societal patterns that are human in scale. This makes those architects who chose to work with individual homes or small settlements (notably Frank Lloyd Wright, Alvar Aalto, Bruce Goff, Arne Jacobsen, the Greene brothers in Pasadena or the early work of Herb Greene in Oklahoma) significant as professional practitioners informed by vernacular scale.[17]

Differences in the organization and meaning of spaces and rooms also arise naturally from social patterns. Local space determinants as reflected in indigenous buildings are difficult to accommodate within the framework of mainstream architecture. In Malaysia and Thailand, for example, kitchens are traditionally pavilions separated from the dwelling itself. There are hierarchical precedents, social reasons, as well as hygienic and climatic factors for this separation. Yet architect-designed or mass-produced homes in these countries cavalierly disregard these factors, building Western-style kitchen-dining alcoves into one end of the living room. As a result, pungent spices assault olfactory nerves, traditional cooking methods are arbitrarily changed; social structures are destroyed when the 'fit' between social and physical space is ignored.

Villa Mairea, Normarkku, Finland, designed by Alvar Aalto, 1938-39.

The house designed by the Greene brothers in Pasadena for David B. Gamble, 1907–8.

The typical Anatolian village house in central Turkey has been studied, analysed and described by architects and scholars for decades. Much of the information is readily available in English and Turkish.[18] Paul Oliver, the architectural critic and historian, has demonstrated brilliantly that the step from knowledge to implementation is beset by difficulties.[19] When south-central Anatolia was rocked by severe earthquakes, destroying most of the indigenous building stock, rebuilding occurred in three separate phases:

1. Initially foam-domes were built as emergency shelters; an Austrian architectural team also provided a series of winebarrel-shaped 'houses.' All were completely unacceptable within the social web of village life. Today a few remain as storage sheds for tools or grain.

2. The government developed permanent houses, similar in design and plan to low-cost suburban housing developments in the USA or Germany. Their basic houseplan violated all the social needs of the village people in terms of public versus private space, orientation, relation to street life, and so forth. This second planning disaster quickly led to the third phase.

3. The houses were re-built and re-structured by the villagers themselves. This 're-vernacularized' (if this phrase is allowable), social and societal spaces and restated the implicit meanings of house and village in Anatolia.

Foam domes, post-earthquake emergency shelters of polyurethane, 1972, Nicaragua.

We can see that mainstream architects – even when motivated by a deep social commitment – fail when faced by the needs of a society that is foreign to them. 'Foreign' in this case can refer either to another country, or to a level of society in their own country that is alien to them, since it deals with a radically different socio-economic class.

Dramatic changes have come about recently in communal housing projects in northern Europe. The malfunctions of earlier housing has led to participation-led design and construction, alternative pre-built components and/or prefabricated systems, more people-directed consultation, mixed-class communities, and radical changes in defining dwelling spaces. Much of this rethinking is a direct reaction against the megalomaniac housing developments in post-war Europe (and similar insurance-company-financed schemes in the USA), and incorporates ideas from vernacular architecture.

But it is not only social expectations that make these modifications. Environment plays an equally important role. Apologists for an environmental view try to match zones on the earth's surface with identical climatic conditions, similar local building materials and micro-environments that seem – at least superficially – to be almost mirror images of one another. It is then assumed that such resemblance of site, caused by near-identical weather patterns, will influence built form in corresponding ways. But this approach is simplistic in that it leaves out social issues, dates of construction, the differences between urban and rural, agricultural and industrial building. Any attempt at theorizing about vernacular form through environmental conditions alone can provide detailed descriptions, but it cannot explain why the structure was built in a given manner, why some materials were preferred to others, or what meanings were associated with the plan-form or the arrangement of constituent parts within the dwelling.

If we journey southward from northern Norway toward northern Africa, looking only at the roof pitch of vernacular farmhouses, we can see major differences arising from environmental differences. In the extreme north, where snowload is heavy for many months, and it remains bitterly cold, the pitch of the roof is not too steep and 'snow-catchers' will be woven into the roof in order to keep the snow as long as possible for added insulation against the cold. Only a few hundred miles further south the pitch of the roof is more abrupt so that it sheds snow quickly. In Austria, Switzerland and northern Italy, roof angles vary, reflecting both snowloads and heavy rainfall. Where strong winds prevail, boulders weight the roof to prevent it blowing away. Frequently earth will be piled on the roof and planted with grass during the growing seasons; this again adds insulation in both summer and winter. As we move still further south, roofs will become even flatter until we reach the completely flat roof-terraces of northern Africa. According to this formula, however, most modern flat-roof buildings anywhere in the world and designed between 1920 and 1960 would work ideally only in the Sahara.

Roof configuration is, of course, only a small part of the total structure, and the environment is only one of the factors which influence vernacular building. For religious, cultural and social reasons, Turkish vernacular houses have a central hallway with a raised divan-like platform, whereas a central hall with lowered living areas prevails in Nepal. Grain-storage houses and buildings in which food and ceremonial objects are stored usually stand on stilts. The reason is again often environmental; to protect the harvest from vermin, rodents or floods. But in other cases, these sacred storerooms are elevated for symbolic reasons only.

5. The Cultural Explanation

A house was made for me in Bali by the village builders. I soon found that I had to hire a local priest who determined an auspicious date for starting construction – a geomancer used his thirty-five-ring *loupan* (geomancer's compass) to align the house correctly with the river, trees, cardinal directions, and so forth.

The importance of cosmology, *feng shui*, and geomancy across Indonesia, China, Malaysia, Singapore and other parts of south-east Asia can hardly be overstated.[20] Only a few years ago, the Hong Kong and Shanghai Bank in Hong Kong, a forty-storey, high-tech structure, hired a geomancer to choose an auspicious date for the opening day. The entire high-rise building had to be changed, the V-shaped trusses had to be transformed into an 'aspiring' A-shaped design,

*Shanghai Banking Corporation building, Hong Kong, designed by Foster
Associates, 1979-84.*

several floors had to be set back on the east side of the building; altogether
several million dollars was spent to bring the building into conformity with
the dictates of *feng shui*.

Feng shui has also travelled to the West. In February 1990 work started on the
gargantuan new Denver airport, an international and intercontinental facility
with an estimated cost of 1700 million dollars. Four years later, with the actual
costs amounting to 4500 million dollars, there had been so many malfunctions
that the airport was yet to be opened, and enormous losses had been sustained
by the city and all airlines. Finally *feng shui* specialists were brought in to re-
orientate parts of the airport at a further expense of hundreds of millions of dollars in the hope that the airport could open in February 1995, three years later
than planned.[21]

Although geomancy is a fairly complex way of locating and orientating buildings, simpler cultural modifiers exist as well. In Thailand, for example, the actual
orientation of the house itself is determined only by climate and site, as long as
the residents' bedrooms are so situated that the sleepers' heads point north or
north east.[22] Speculative builders in California and western Canada have found

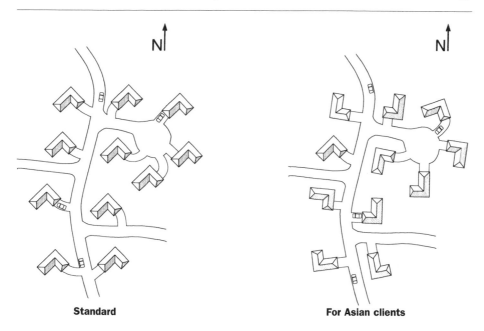

Standard   **For Asian clients**

Street plan of US housing subdivision, showing standard siting of homes, and, on the right, special siting for Asian buyers who want to sleep with heads pointing north.

that whereas the orientation of their 'cookie-cutter' houses matters little to most purchasers, recently arrived immigrants from the Far East insist that the bedrooms be so placed that they can sleep with their heads pointing north. In Islamic countries, the prime orientation must be toward Mecca – shrewd Japanese designers have recently marketed a combination compass-calculator that establishes cardinal direction anywhere in the world.

But religious beliefs are not the only reasons for house orientation. The !Kung bushmen built simple circular grass huts, closely and intimately grouped, doorless and facing toward a common centre. In a hunter-gatherer society possessions were shared and were considered a definite encumbrance to people constantly on the move. Within this small hunting group, closeness was prized; the lack of doors made visual bonding simpler; the lack of possessions made locks superfluous. This way of life, existing in the Kalahari for thousands of years, ended abruptly in the 1960s when they were offered profitable though less nomadic work herding goats for the Hererro tribes, with the result that individuals for the first time had personal possessions, which were treasured and stored in army trunks; people owned more than they could carry. This major cultural change is reflected in !Kung settlements. Wattle-and-daub huts are more than twice the size of their homes of thirty years before, are spaced much further apart, have doors that lock,and are surrounded by barbed-wire enclosures or thornbush fences. The belief that all should be commonly held and shared was replaced by a new cultural ideal; this in turn led to drastic changes in vernacular housing and settlement patterns.[23] There is no question that the !Kung are in a state of cultural (and social) flux; their vernacular concepts of a typical hut are changing accordingly.

Religion and magic, morality, and consequently sexual mores and taboos, directly influence the collective spatial images of a society. Work and leisure patterns, the relationship between wealth and status, the place of animals, all these and more are direct cultural determinants of vernacular built form.[24] We can see how the ethics of frugality and simplicity are reflected in the astringent interiors of Shaker dwellings and barns. The same religious imperatives have also moulded the furniture, stoves, carriages and other tools used by the Shakers and other religious movements such as the Inspirationist settlements of the Amana in Iowa and New Harmony in Indiana. The influx of tourists, accompanied by a renewed sense of pride, autonomous thinking and interest in historic preservation has produced an architecture of ambiguous cultural meaning. This ambiguity has its origins in the contradictions between cultural values and the purely aesthetic considerations of restoration and imitation of older architectural styles.

6. The Formal Aesthetic Explanation

There are only about a dozen or so pictures that are so instantly recognizable to popular audiences that they have become clichés. Leonardo's *Mona Lisa,* Botticelli's *The Birth of Venus,* Constable's *Hay Wain,* Van Gogh's *Sunflowers,* Picasso's *Guernica* or Hokusai's *The Great Wave off the Coast of Kanagawa* come most readily to mind. There are again only a handful of well-known 20th-century buildings that are immediately familiar: Mies van der Rohe's Barcelona Pavilion (or his later Seagram Building with Philip Johnson); Wright's Fallingwater and Guggenheim Museum; Rogers's and Piano's Pompidou Centre; Utzon's Sydney Opera House; the Empire State Building; Le Corbusier's Villa Savoye; Aalto's Villa Mairea.

The reason for listing these paintings and buildings – and both lists could be much longer – lies in their one overmastering similarity. They are all individualistic and idiosyncratic statements; the buildings no less than the pictures make explicit gestures that are only tenuously linked to their purpose. Through several centuries one view of architectural ideology has been heard more loudly than others. It is the concept of 'artistic individualism', which finds particular buildings important, or evaluates general progress in architecture on a personal basis – usually of style, fashion, fad, decoration, embellishment or ornamentation embodied in specific buildings and developed from architect to architect through history. This traditional theory (first used by Plato's disciples in evaluating all art) considers a building significant or unimportant according to how much it incorporates the 'idea of ideas' of its individual designer. The history of architecture then is seen as the interaction of such significant ideas, developed in special buildings.

This concept of architecture has only recently shown signs of losing its pre-eminence. It was and continues to be popular since it appeals both to the interests and intellects of the two groups most directly involved: architects and architectural critics. Architects find an individualized concept of architecture appealing, since it makes it possible to see themselves as heroic and romantic figures, heirs to a tradition that beckons with promises of fame and a niche in history. Critics – when not architects *manqués* – come from the scholarly, humanistic tradition which honours artistic self-expression as inherently important. They view architecture as 'poetry in steel and glass', and assign a place of pre-eminence to its creator.[25]

This critical view has also been pressed into service to 'explain' vernacular form. Much of Sybil Moholy-Nagy's and Rudofsky's work has concentrated on the decoration or the facades of buildings. During the last few years, an avalanche of photographic books from many countries has continued to describe vernacular buildings either as interpolative evidence for some formalist pet theory, or as purely visual statements, or as both.[26] Since vernacular buildings are by definition unselfconscious, no such individualistic interpretation can work. True vernacular dwellings don't loudly or aggressively proclaim themselves. Many of the simplest houses were built to display family skills and status, and sometimes individual interpretations of traditional design, but vernacular buildings don't make architectural 'statements'.

Other writers or architects have analysed vernacular architecture by the constituent parts that form the arrangement of a building; in one case at least, an enormous amount of research and study has gone into discovering and then attempting to list an underlying 'pattern language'.[27] As Paul Oliver says: 'For many societies, the symbolic significance of the part of their structures and the disposition of the buildings is fundamental to their relationship to the world of inner and conscious experience.'[28] Richard Bradfield has developed this approach with his study of settlement patterns, and his work can stand as a model for the rigorous study of relationships, origins and meanings.[29]

The aesthetic explanation is too idiosyncratic and self-serving to interpret vernacular form on its own. We must observe ornament and decoration within the context of symbolic meaning. Too often the study of vernacular buildings is used by the critical establishment to lend historic credibility to some current architectural fad or fashion.

THE DYNAMIC WEB

None of these 'explanations' can stand on its own without engaging all of the others. It is precisely because so many architectural critics have tried to fit

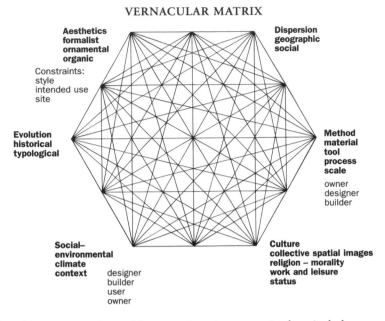

theories about vernacular architecture into just one single-minded category that few explanations have held up. I suggest that a matrix, showing the interaction between these separate modifiers can help to see and evaluate each structure as an artefact that fluctuates between these various areas of emphasis. The interaction of all of these components can help us to develop a vivid, rigorous and lively explanation of vernacular built form that is truly three-dimensional.

To come to a deeper understanding of vernacular architecture, first we need to collect as much information as possible; then all this data needs to be ordered, studied and analysed, using the six-fold matrix I have proposed. This should make comparative studies both simpler and yet more meaningful. Finally, from all this data we may gain some insight into how we can profit from some of these age-old lessons in settlements and buildings.

The thread of continuity runs through all vernacular architecture; respect for tradition, craftsmanship, the use of local materials and methods. All this, as we have seen, is modified by climate and environment, cultural and social considerations, aesthetic strivings, contextual family and settlement patterns, and much else.

But with extremely few exceptions (such as the Tassaday, a tribe with a Stone Age technology, discovered in 1978 in the Philippines), all vernacular builders are also in constant touch with technologically and technocratically developed societies. The resulting interplay is only one of several factors that lead to transformation and change in the vernacular form. Susan Kent (a professor and researcher in the cross-disciplinary areas of anthropology and buildings) has documented the spatial changes that follow the introduction of just one emblematic artefact – a television set – into three distinct cultural groups in the south west of the United States.[30] She clearly shows environmental and social changes flowing from this, even in one case demonstrating *the effects of a non-functioning TV set*. The very presence of a television set, even though it is not plugged in, forces a change in the hierarchical positioning of people and pieces of furniture in the room. Among Native Americans as well as Spanish Americans living in remote areas, the TV set is given a prominent place analogous to a fireplace or altar. In Latino homes, flowers and incense are frequently placed on the table on which the receiver rests. I myself have observed images of the painter Frida Kahlo pasted on the screen of the set. Kahlo, who has attained *de facto* sainthood among the Mexican poor, is usually depicted with a halo around her head.

We have seen how with the !Kung of the Kalahari, vernacular form has altered drastically as a direct consequence of changing from a hunting-gathering group to a goat-raising society now encumbered by possessions. The catastrophic aftermath of an earthquake, combined with a governmental insensitivity toward vernacular needs, can lead to a renaissance among the people that will lead to a strengthened indigenous building style, strongly informed by tradition. The Mexican *barrios* and Brazilian *favelas* provide examples of new materials – frequently the discards of a high-tech society – that have been readily co-opted into vernacular structures. In several pueblos in Arizona and New Mexico, it is possible actually to date structures (within ten or twelve years), just by scanning old photographs and observing window-trims, door treatments and other details that borrow decorative flourishes from Anglo houses, *but leave the spatial use and meaning of the pueblo intact*. Even the Hopi nation is building motels with souvenir shops that cater to prevailing touristic whims without sacrificing their own vernacular approach to space and place.

The creative production of new forms appears to be intrinsic to the perpetuation of many, if not all, building traditions. Whether it consists of variations on a fixed theme, elaboration towards the baroque or progressive refinement of simple geometric forms, the rate at which new forms are established rests on many factors in the builders' social and cultural milieu. Marion Wenzel's study of house decoration in Nubia in southern Egypt was carried out just before the area was flooded by the Aswan Dam. Her work clearly demonstrates the rapidity of change and the quick acceptance of innovative structural and decorative changes there.[31] Hassan Fathy's vault-making in the same area shows that sensible vernacular structural systems can be resurrected and applied to present-day settlements.[32]

The dividing line between continuity and change is imperceptible, and shifts constantly. Some cultures 'over-react', forsaking their building heritage completely whilst embracing hazardous high-tech methods, whereas other groups seem set in profound unchanging fixity like mammoths in the permafrost. But there are cultures which manage to choose wisely from their own traditional ways of build-ing, as well as from the menu of new methods or materials now available.

The learning content embedded in vernacular buildings is great, but we must find out how to discriminate and what lessons to learn and why. This is obviously not a plea to build corporate offices in the shape of fifty-storey concrete tipis, nor an invitation to erect government structures in the style of log cabins. Rather it is the hope that the single fact that sets all vernacular dwellings apart from most architect-designed dwellings has to do with comfort – visual and physical comfort that appeals directly to our senses.

The design of a house should take into consideration factors such as orienta-tion towards mountains and streams, solar direction, prevailing winds, rainfall and flooding patterns, and temperature. Research into Chinese *feng shui* or geomancy may provide new insights. We can learn from the interior gardens and fountains of Moorish architecture and the 'wind-catchers' of Iran that bring coolness and healing winds to buildings. The double-walled brick and tile structures used in the Anatolian highlands of Greece or in upland dwellings in Colombia could suggest alternatives to air-conditioning or the excess use of energy for heating. Trees and bushes can be planted as windbreaks and directors of air currents, again to save on heating and air-conditioning, and vestibules will act as air-locks both in winter and summer. Plant material close to certain outside walls, clerestory windows near the ceilings, carefully calibrated roof overhang, will provide an organically balanced interior environment.

The concept of radiant heating (called 'gravity heat' by Frank Lloyd Wright) was taken from the one room in a traditional Japanese home that was heated from below. Wright realized that comfort can be maintained with less energy expenditure if the surface of the floor is warm, because heat rises naturally. He therefore embedded pipes circulating hot water into the concrete pad on which the house sat. This system of heating is infinitely better and healthier than con-vection or central steam-heating.

Building methods should be environmentally benign. Natural and preferably local materials should be used whenever possible. A list of both structural and finishing products that 'breathe', exchanging fresh air, heat and humidity with the outside, maintaining healthy ion levels, absorbing most toxic air-borne gases, would include natural (untreated) woods, clay, rammed earth, bricks, cork, wool, bamboo, reeds, sisal, coconut fibre, rocks and slate.

As mainstream architecture itself begins to change in response to new ecological challenges, we must collect more information and start on a classi-fication of what we already have to provide a database so that the lessons of the vernacular are accessible to both architects and users. This will be an adventure of discovery to shape the forms of tomorrow through the wisdom of the old.

CHAPTER 7

Form Follows Fun

*I didn't like Europe as much as I liked Disney World. At Disney World all
the countries are much closer together, and they show you just the best of
each country. Europe is more boring. People talk strange languages and
things are dirty. Sometimes you don't see anything interesting in Europe for
days, but at Disney World something different happens all the time, and
people are happy. It's much more fun. It's well designed!*
A college graduate just back from her first trip to Europe

What do you do when the real place looks like a copy of the place where it's fake?
Another student, returning from Europe

INDUSTRIAL DESIGNERS who develop and design products, tools, and their
graphics and packaging have always found themselves in a quandary. This
dilemma is the apparent contradiction between the ephemeral and the permanent. We design things to work effectively and for a long time. At the same time,
many designs have a very short life and some are virtually ephemeral. There are
reasons for this. Industry can frequently satisfy its legitimate search for profit – or
more recently, its blind pursuit of greed – by introducing new fashions in tools
and artefacts, which will therefore be replaced more frequently by end-users.
There is now a new reason for rapid obsolescence. With the introduction
of microchips, laser-scanning techniques, digital processing and other high-
technology developments, products are frequently superseded by newer or better
– or seemingly better – inventions that demand a new shape.

From the narrow viewpoint of the end-user this is not all bad. Since the 1970s
we have all seen how certain tools and products have redefined themselves,
changed shape and – with the addition of new functions – have yet become much
less expensive. With some products, the price is literally in a free-fall situation.
Thus fully automatic, auto-focusing 'do-everything' 35mm cameras have become
smaller, more versatile, easier to use, and sell for one-fifth or less of the prices
charged for manually-controlled 35mm cameras only a few years before. A computer which in 1950 occupied eight floors of a large building at the Massachusetts
Institute of Technology and cost more than four million dollars in 1952, now has
a 'little brother' that is much faster and more powerful. It sits on my desk and
costs less than one thousandth of the earlier machine. Hand-held calculators have
dropped in price by more than 95%, some small ones are now given away free in

A used fruit-juice tin forms the casing of the tin-can radio (left) developed for Indonesia in the 1960s. Each owner participated in the design by decorating the tin can in a unique personal style (right).

large supermarkets in California to anyone spending more than a hundred dollars on groceries. Digital watches served as impressive status symbols in the late 1970s; in the 1990s they can be bought for less than twenty dollars and have completely lost their original cachet. Some minor environmental improvements have come with these cheaper models. The calculators are powered by small solar panels, replacing batteries which are among the most poisonous bits of our waste. Many of the watches also run off solar cells, and a German watchmaking firm now sells its products with an extended-life battery that is guaranteed to run for twenty to thirty years. Yet we pay a heavy price for all this 'progress' ecologically and environmentally: we destroy irreplaceable resources, waste energy and spend our lives in the pursuit of trendy trivia.

In the mid-19th century the sculptor Horatio Greenough coined the phrase 'Form Follows Function'. In the 1880s this key phrase was repeated by the American architect Louis Sullivan and in turn served as a guiding principle for the Wiener Werkstätte (the famous Viennese craft workshop led by the architect Otto Wagner), the German Werkbund (a design-orientated crafts group) and later the Bauhaus. My own teacher, Frank Lloyd Wright, redefined the slogan as 'Form and Function are One', which much later led me to develop the six-fold Function Complex[1] (p.34) comprising: *Use, Method, Association, Aesthetics, Need, Consequences.*

Having spent nearly thirty years working in many developing countries as well as in technologically sophisticated economies, I have come to the conclusion that the culture of a country shapes its forms and that these forms eventually shape us. The statement 'Form Follows Fun' is not just a pun or a facile joke, but rather one possible diagnosis of the present situation in both product design and architecture.

Elaborate designs of fruit and flowers, sweetmeats and leaves are carried to the temple in Bali. Much time and care is spent in constructing these ephemeral offerings especially for the festivals.

I suggest that we have become quite accustomed to goods and buildings that perform primary functions of *use* and *method*. The true *needs* of the consumer classes have been pushed aside to be replaced by artificially induced *wants*. The eventual *consequences* of what we invent, design, make, buy and use all centre on shrinking resources, pollution factors and global warming. In our visual boredom – constantly nudged, teased and titillated by the febrile imagination of the advertising media – a climate is created that deeply influences our *aesthetic* and *associational* expectations. Finding little of cultural value, we turn to fun, but fun that has been chewed and predigested for us by the feral image-makers of Hollywood and Madison Avenue.

Somewhere there is a soft collision between differing views of fun, of what seems desirable in a product or tool, both aesthetically and in different cultures. One of my first design assignments for UNESCO in Bali was the development of the tin-can radio, powered by a candle, wood or slow-burning dried cow dung. Since the casing for this device was a used juice-tin, I had decided not to decorate it in any way to avoid imposing a European aesthetic on the Indonesian people. Rather I hoped that local people would embellish their personal radio in their own distinctive way and thus participate in the design, which is what happened; the Balinese felt that each radio had become truly their own through their part in the act of creation.[2]

Even though designers realize that the objects they bring into life will last only briefly in the market-place, they still wish that – even in everyday use – their 'babies' might somehow remain unblemished and 'perfect'. At international conferences the design chief of a firm that made cigarette lighters would meet fellow designers who still carried their original black lighter. After years of being kept in a pocket with keys, a penknife or whatever, nicks and scratches on the black finish would cause the original brass casing to glint through. The designer would obligingly offer a free replacement then and there. I remember saying to him myself, 'No thank you, all the scratches are just beginning to give it character, making it unique!' In his search for perfection, he was never able to understand that things can't remain unchanged. In an age in which fortunes are spent on beauty creams and lotions to stretch out a semblance of youth, it is difficult to explain that material choices should be made so that objects can age gracefully once more.

DESIGNING FOR THE MOMENT

The apparent contradiction between the permanent and the ephemeral doesn't exist, except for whimsical semantic interpretations. We look at Stonehenge and are gripped by awe at the age of this sacred circle and the role it must have played in the agrarian and metaphysical life of ancestors now one with the dusky soil of

Wiltshire. At the same time we see lichens growing on the stones, and know that they release free oxygen and in so doing break down the very stones. We look at the ever-changing clouds and feel them to be gossamer constructs of the moment; yet clouds endure. We know, or think we know, that when we design for permanence, we must be exacting and careful – when our work is ephemeral, we find ourselves less engaged. But is that a preordained truth, or just sloppy thinking by architects and designers?

In Bali I came to know a people to whom permanence and the momentary were inextricably intermingled. This is reflected there in design and craftsmanship. The elaborate temple offerings that the women carry on their heads to the festivals are impressive accomplishments of design and structure. Often six to eight feet (about 2m) tall, they are arrangements of fruit, gilded decorations, hibiscus and frangipani blossoms, intermixed with sweetmeats and leaves, erected on a cylindrical, towering structure of white and coloured rice, with a bowl or basket, no wider than three feet (1m), as a base. These will be carried for miles to the temple or shrine, where they are placed as offerings to the gods. What is significant is the amount of time spent making these towers. A day or more can be spent on an offering that will have a 'useful' life of only three or four hours.

In my village I would see the little girls practising the Legong, the Balinese dance, with the Gamelan orchestra. Only after a time did I realize that all the interest of performers and spectators was closely focused on these practice sessions and rehearsals. Relatives, friends and other onlookers would crowd around every day, watching, smiling, shouting criticism and offering suggestions. But after the dress rehearsal all interest vanished – the actual performance took place largely under the uncritical eyes of tourists. 'Why watch it now?' my friend Suriati asked, obviously puzzled, 'It is too late to change anything now. The dance and the sounds are frozen!'

The gables of Toradja houses in South Sulawesi (Indonesia), are richly decorated in red, black and white, with woven rattan and bamboo and buffalo horns; the impressive prow motifs recall the boats in which these peoples sailed the Pacific more than a thousand years ago. Replicas of these houses are built as funerary cremation towers, frequently the same size as, or even larger than, the houses that serve as prototypes. Yet I was impressed when I saw that these burial towers – to be burned in thirty minutes or so – were even more carefully designed, crafted and finished than the dwellings that were destined to function a thousand times longer. The care and joyful labour expended on the festive and temporal is far greater than that used on a home that may serve a family's needs for the next hundred years.

To spend deep concentration, hours of work and a high level of craftsmanship on an object or building that is intended to give joy or fun for only a short time is not restricted to sacred or festive events. We have all spent hours on a beach, building an elaborate sandcastle. At the annual competitions along Cape Cod in Massachusetts, in southern California and on the Costa del Sol in Spain, teams of six or seven young designers will sometimes work for a whole day to build incredibly complicated sand structures of great precision and beauty, only to cheer wholeheartedly when the incoming tide reclaims it and mingles the sand with the rolling surf.

Ice castles have been built over the last three hundred years in St Petersburg, and have more recently become an annual tradition in Minneapolis St Paul, at Dartmouth University and in a number of other cities in Canada and the United States. Many of them are large enough to house concerts or exhibitions, dances and dinners, sometimes accommodating an audience of eight hundred or more. They are carefully worked in variously coloured ice, and will come equipped with towers, widows' walks, a portcullis, and other eclectic architectural snippets. This makes them into perfect examples of Post-Modern architecture – with the added advantage that with the first warm day, they deconstruct themselves! Here again, I stress the care, time and craftsmanship devoted to perfecting the ephemeral, the transitory.

The dragon festivals in Japan, and the fighting kites of Thailand and China are world famous. The kites, some of them twice the height of a man, are carefully

An ice castle (above), with towers, steps and crenellations, at the 1972 winter carnival at Dartmouth University. A replica of the prow-gabled Toradja houses is carried in a funeral procession in Indonesia (opposite).

developed and designed, beautifully painted, and often last only a few minutes. For years I have set this project for my students – to build a kite with an extra function, such as carrying a small self-designed camera that would take aerial photographs of the student, or launching a second kite from inside once it had reached altitude. The students lavished great care on the quality and appearance of these tetrahedral, tailless kites, designed and made to exist for one afternoon at most. The joy of impermanence held these young men and women in its grip. And something else. There was always an underlying sense of great optimism – at times far from justified – when it was time to fly their designs. What made flying a kite such a joyful experience was the simple principle of Occam's razor built into the exercise: the kite would fly, or not. With their imagination, labour, talent and joy they might touch the sky – or remain grounded. Their faith in being able to overcome gravity and aerodynamics was touching. Sometimes an unusually heavy kite would appear, obviously never destined to fly. Nonetheless the student might spend the afternoon tirelessly running back and forth on the field, the kite making deep furrows in the ground, its proud designer oblivious of its 'ploughing behaviour'. This is not said to mock, rather to celebrate the students' unlimited pleasure in the joy of the activity, more engaged than in the routine design of bathroom scales or a toaster.

THE FUN OBJECT

It can be argued that the greedy 1980s have left people imprinted with the idea that a part of their money should always be diverted from bread to circuses or, more simply, that they deserve more fun and should use any disposable income to get it. This will explain the accelerating, wild swings of styles, fads and trends that the market offers, and the stampede to any new venture that seems to promise novel ways of enjoyment.

This linking up of design and a fun-orientated service industry needs some exploration. We can find some insights in the world of late 1993, after the fall of the Soviet Union and its satrap states in eastern Europe. All the Communist states tried very hard to provide managerial skills and large-scale industrial planning for their young people. After seventy years, the verdict is in: Chernobyl, mass poverty, products that can't be given away, let alone marketed anywhere else, factories that had to be closed, a crazed bureaucracy and non-existent services.

Some historical background may help to fix the field of industrial design by comparing parallel developments in industry itself. The profitability of manufacturing goods is of fairly recent origin. If you manufactured something – shoes, for instance – during the 17th century in the West, your role was far from secure. Compared to the producers of raw materials or food, you were at a great disadvantage: hence the saying that 'the shoemaker's children are the last to get shod', or the tale of Gepetto who created Pinocchio to get an unpaid helper, or stories of other artisans in fairy-tales, myths and real life. By the middle of the 18th century this had begun to change, as agricultural production increased to feed a population that was moving towards the cities. A hundred years later, by 1860 say, imported foods had taken over an increasing part of the market due to refrigerated ships and rail transport. Compared to manufactured items, food was cheaper than ever before, and the producer class became very rich.

As we approach the end of the 20th century, manufacture is beginning to fall in relative profitability. With cars made in Mexico or Korea, camcorders and silk shirts in China, and microscopes and ladies' shoes in Brazil, labour costs are dropping (compared to the West and Japan), and manufacturing is beginning to redefine itself. Since product design (or industrial design, to give it its original name), is by definition involved with the design of products for some sort of industrial application, the profession is also in need of major reassessment.

The main argument running through this book is that the crucial issue for designers today concerns systems, processes and goods that protect the environment and are ecologically benign, and that the other, almost equally important areas are those that designers have frequently neglected – the elderly, the disadvantaged and all others who have special needs.

This historical resumé may explain why, with the arrival of a post-manufacturing phase in Japan and the West, the service industries have expanded at a highly accelerated rate. Viewed objectively, service industries seem to have two purposes. To provide 'convenience' (as discussed in Chapter 8), and to market 'fun'. Fun, however, as embodied in a product in Western countries – influenced by the three 'C's of Catholicism, Calvinism and Communism – must be shown to have either some social purpose connected with work, or to have a useful function. H. L. Mencken, the American satirist, said that: 'Puritanism is the haunting fear that someone, somewhere, might be happy'.[3]

Most of our fun comes neatly packaged with excuses and rationalizations. There are three ways in which we justify playing golf:

- It is an extension of work (we might meet a client)
- It will prepare us mentally for work (it relaxes us)
- It will make us fitter for work (it's good exercise)

We use these justifications for playing tennis, racquet ball, squash, and even for indulging in that most stultifying activity, jogging. Still following Mencken's acid diagnosis, we are also convinced that the more it hurts, the better it is for us.

When the object or piece of equipment we want for fun cannot be disguised as a body-building or mind-expanding tool, there is the basic pretext, 'After all the hard work I do, I deserve to be good to myself!' Manufacturers and their captive

The lines of fighting kites (above) are covered in a paste of ground glass to cut the lines of their opponents. The dragon festival (opposite) at Okunchi in Japan.

designers[4] are well aware of this, with generous help from market researchers, house-trained psychologists, and, inevitably, the advertising media.

The Japanese firm Mazda created a car to fit these guilt-ridden longings for fun. When the Mazda MX-5 (called the Mazda Miata in the United States) was designed, the marketing specialists had analysed the potential market fairly accurately and started from the romantic idea of a convertible two-seater sports car. They studied the Morgan three-wheeler 'Mog', the Mercedes SS-100 of the 1930s and later sports cars, such as the MG-TD and MGB and the Austin-Healey 3000 (marketed as 'the last angry car' as late as 1968). Knowing that their most accessible and profitable market was in the United States, they specifically studied the sports-car scene in 1989. They found that most Americans liked the interior fittings and appearance of British road cars, but had little faith in their reliability, or their own ability to repair them. They also found that according to *Consumer Reports*, a highly respected and totally impartial American periodical that evaluates consumer goods, the US public put their greatest trust in and had the lowest

The Mazda MX-5, known as the Mazda Miata in the USA, the Japanese sports car that looks like a British sports car of the 1950s, is marketed as a rewarding relaxation from hard work.

repair costs with Japanese cars. These were judged year after year to be more reliable than even the top-of-the-line German luxury imports. The design objective was therefore to develop a Japanese sports car that had the looks and feel of a British model of the 1950s, but without the idiosyncratic problems.

Next the designers considered the competition. To their surprise they found that they could virtually take over this lucrative market. There were Maseratis and Bugattis, but in the United States the nearest repair shop might be 1800 miles away, and prices were sky-high. Lotus had never attempted to meet American safety and pollution standards. Sales of the Fiat Spyder plummeted when it became known that the car was prone to rust from the salt used to prevent ice on roads.[5] By the late 1980s, a new Porsche cost three times as much as an average new two-storey family home, including fridge, stove, washer-dryer, dishwasher and land. In a class by itself was the British Morgan, with a six-year waiting period and, because of mechanical idiosyncrasies, appealing only to over-the-top fanatics. This left the field almost entirely to 'family convertibles' (from Ford, Mercedes, Saab, BMW, Chevrolet or Chrysler).

The Mazda Miata was launched in the USA with virtually no advertising, becoming known through word-of-mouth. Although it was relatively inexpensive, during the first three or four months of its début people routinely paid four thousand dollars or more above the list price. It quickly became the single most expensive consumer product ever to be a minor bestseller. It is sold as a pure fun object, yet when advertisements for it eventually appeared they all carefully stressed that it should be thought of as a 'reward to yourself' and as a stress relaxant that 'let's you see the world through new eyes'.

For once, the advertisements came after an initial sales success. On the US market I can only recall one other item that sold in amazing quantities before it was publicized. This was the 'water-gun' of the late 1980s, intended to provide fun for children at the expense of their parents. It is a toy gun, shaped like a machine-pistol and made of survival pink, green and orange plastic, holding about a gallon (nearly 4 litres) of water that shoots out like a jet to drench the victim. Its appearance on the market signalled a new and ironic twist in the gun-crazed United States: a number of states actually outlawed the water-gun (one assumes that adults were outraged by an occasional soaking), whereas genuine semi-automatic weapons and machine guns are still for sale!

Assume that 'Form Follows Fun'. As form-givers, how can designers intervene so that the form which fun assumes will be a good fit to our expectations and to our human outlook? Certain forms have an inherent appeal, and some have been repeated in a number of different variations throughout history.

FASHIONS IN FORM

At the time of the Great Exhibition of 1851 at the Crystal Palace in London, designers faced the task of giving form to entirely new objects: sewing-machines,

Stylized plant forms in cast-iron decorate the Carson, Pirie, Scott department store in Chicago, built 1899-1904, designed by Louis Sullivan.

*The Plaza dressing-table designed by Michael Graves in
1981 for Memphis, an ebullient reaction to lean asceticism.*

industrial forming presses, automatic sorting machines, domestic furniture, and
much else. The parts were predominantly cast-iron, and to lessen the impact of the
weird novelty of these new forms, they were shaped to reproduce stylized abstrac-
tions of plant-forms, acanthus leaves, lily pads, vine leaves, sheaves of wheat
or fern spirals. A few decades later the Italian Futurists waxed lyrical about 'the
beauty of a locomotive, a racing car, the staccato sound of a machine gun or an air-
plane propeller',[6] and the same anonymous machine structures that the Victorians
had taken such great pains to hide were revealed in their sparse simplicity when
Machine Art, the Bauhaus, De Stijl and some elements of Russian Suprematism
and Constructivism commingled in the jazz age. The succinct structural functions
were celebrated by artists like Ozenfant. Now the form-givers concentrated on the
clean and austere clarity of form, revealing the underlying construct.

In the hothouse atmosphere of the fine arts, the apparent beauty of machine
objects had a short run. By 1934, André Breton could dismiss mass-produced
objects by defining Surrealism as, 'The chance encounter of an umbrella and a
sewing machine on a dissecting table'.[7] The lean, ascetic simplicity of Modernism
lasted some decades, to return once more with non-functioning parts invented to

accentuate imaginary performances, as at the Centre Pompidou in Paris (designed by the architectural team of Piano and Rogers). Because of its sterile coolness it also became a target for scorn and ridicule in the furniture confections of the Memphis Movement. Though anti-design, it eventually was itself enshrined as a significant movement. This ended up as 'Post-Modern' (Modern with eclectic bits of historic trivia glued on), and finally with 'Deconstructivism', a misunderstood design adaptation of post-Marxist literary analysis; the form might be described as intentional, yet finely calculated formlessness – a revolt against the perverse precision of the Modern movement.

Industrial design, largely under the leadership of Raymond Loewy, introduced another mannerism into the melting pot of form-giving in America. This was 'streamlining', introduced with great fanfare during the early 1930s. It cut down turbulence and air-resistance, and Mr Loewy was much photographed standing next to a locomotive he had designed that 'looked as if it was moving even when standing still'.[8] One of Loewy's famous designs was a pencil-sharpener that bore the same streamlined shape and 'rush'-lines as the locomotive. When screwed firmly to a desk, it too looked as if it were rushing through the air at supersonic speeds. With the interest in energy-efficient automobiles in the early 1990s, cars have been aerodynamically styled, under the pretext that this would cut down on petrol consumption. In real terms, the energy expended on retooling the body-moulds for new car models have wasted more energy than could possibly be saved by a few minor stylish changes. This neo-streamlining seems to follow in the slip-stream of its predecessors. It is now possible to buy portable CD-players that look capable of cruising through the air at 600 mph. Both in the Depression thirties and the Recession nineties these were sales gimmicks that used motion and speed as fun determinants of form.

'ANTI-DESIGN'

It is no wonder that people who were interested in design became irritated with its increasingly meaningless contortions and convolutions. This annoyance began to make itself felt in a number of ways. There were Memphis and other neo-Dadaistic strains that attempted to violate many of the heretofore sacrosanct rules of design, relating to the function, unity with variety, predictable order, harmony, fitness for purpose, human needs, and so forth.

In the highly design-orientated Scandinavian countries, a few non-design or anti-design shops opened in the late 1960s and early 1970s. These were small boutiques run by people who had a keen nose for anonymous mass-produced objects that – in the fastidious opinion of their owners – were well designed. Hotel china, wooden bowls, French horn-handled cutlery and cotton dishcloths were among the many items for which the original form-giver was anonymous. These shops saw truth and virtue in the simple tools of everyday life, and felt no need to canonize individual designers. Many of these shops still exist in Scandinavia and there are a number now in Japan. One of the better ones has the well-chosen name 'Anti-Kitsch'. Here was simple form, celebrated by the absence of any known form-giver. Other countries do not seem to possess a large enough audience that is sophisticated about design yet wary of being manipulated.

Closely related to this was another formal aesthetic reaction against established 'good taste', propelled by the desire to extract the essence and energy from objects made by untutored farmers and by those from allegedly 'simple', peripheral societies. As a revolt against 'received design' it worked well. At the same time, however, people in their attempt to romanticize the 'primitive' (the cult of the Noble Savage has a good deal to answer for) fail to note that traditional objects hold more meaning than the routine productions of Detroit, Osaka, Düsseldorf or Singapore. Furthermore, many of these societies are enormously rich and sophisticated in ways that are integrally different from the mainstream of the West and Far East.

In my role as designer, anthropologist and teacher, I know only three peripheral societies really well, having spent years living with the people – the Balinese, the Inuit and the Navajo. Realizing the dangers of extrapolating from a sample of only three cultures, I would say that the Balinese are the most sophisticated people I have ever met, deeply committed to practise and experience all the arts. The richness of their friendship patterns and social interactions steadies a society that has astounding resilience in dealing with the menace of millions of tourists every year. Both the Inuit and the Navajo inhabit meaningful spheres of inner harmony and balance, and express this mythic being through civilized rituals, songs and dances, and a refined story-telling tradition that spans more than three millennia. Much of what Westerners see of their art is made specifically for the tourist trade – 'airport art' that has no existence beyond the souvenir bazaars. Often these souvenirs are not even related to the people but are copies of copies of copies that have never evolved and never will.

An observation by Lord Raglan may help with this dilemma:

It is a general principle that artefacts of poor quality and workmanship are degenerate rather than primitive. The reason is a simple one. New types of shelter or artefact are made for the rich and powerful and are adopted by them because they are an improvement on whatever it is that they replace. They become fashionable, everyone wants them, and to supply the demand cheap specimens of poor quality are produced in numbers. The good specimens tend to disappear because the rich and powerful come to be supplied with new types which are, or are thought to be, better, while *some of the poor specimens survive among remote rustics and are mistaken by folklore enthusiasts for the spontaneous products of folk culture.* (Italics supplied.)[9]

Much that is useful and beautiful has been preserved through this boutiquing of the developing world. Yet these folk arts have stood still and have been neither developed by their makers nor by their eager design clientele. (Balinese and North American Indian art are notable exceptions to this). The existing designs are like flies preserved in amber or, more precisely like the artificial flies encased in amber-coloured plastic that are available at Baltic souvenir shops. No new forms have resulted and the originals are frequently deformed. This is not to advocate constant, sometimes meaningless change for its own sake. At the meeting-ground of the birth of the new and timeless tradition, we have arrived back at the same intersection where the ephemeral and the eternal meet.

The reasons why 'fun' design doesn't really seem to work for most people are easy to grasp. In the West we apparently have a need to tie fun into earning a living, studying or some other serious activity. If we manage to break out of this utilitarian straightjacket, we often relapse into immature ideas of fun. In most non-Western societies fun is usually a community experience. The American concept of fun, at least the male view, by contrast seems deeply rooted in our concept of rugged individualism – we think of fun usually in highly personal terms, in that fuzzy area where sex, sport and relaxation intermingle.

When I use the word 'fun' in an almost pejorative sense here, it speaks to a passive experience, the sort of fun that has been pre-designed, pre-chewed and pre-digested by designers and corporate directors. The childlike in us is grounded in Earth and close to nature. It responds to beauty, to activities that help us use our body and mind by extending and challenging physical and mental powers, or that result in spontaneous laughter. It is when we have to rely on manufactured fun (theme parks like Disney World or Disneyland) or the specious amusement we might derive from a banana-shaped telephone that the hubris of the fake is breathing down our backs.

We seem to need excuses or alibis for having fun in the West. We tie our experience into making us more vigorous at work, to meeting people who may be important to our work, or to relaxing from work and therefore, by implication, making ourselves into better workers.

TOY OR TOOL?

Some sporting activities are treated with great seriousness. *Flow*, a psychological and anthropological enquiry into the feelings of happiness and fun, published in 1991, makes a strong case for a link between feelings of happiness and true enjoyment and taking fun activities seriously.[10] Whether playing darts in a pub or flying a kite, the more concentrated the mind and body and the more lasting the enjoyment, the more real fun will accrue. Fishing for example requires a great deal of skill and equipment that has to be well-designed and carefully crafted. Attempts

The real fun of trout fishing lies in mastering the skills. This combination fishing-reel and slingshot made in Norway in the 1970s made fly-casting too easy for the serious fisherman.

to 'enhance' dry-fly casting and other fishing tackle have not been accepted by serious anglers. In the 1970s a firm in Norway introduced a combination fishing-reel and slingshot. The idea behind this mismatch was that even a novice angler would be able to use the slingshot to skim the dry-fly across the surface of the stream at speed. By 'de-skilling' the sport and reclassifying it as a 'fun' activity, the manufacturer eliminated the real fun of mastering a new discipline. A manufacturer of shotguns and hunting rifles once approached me with the project of developing a gun-cabinet that would automatically clean sporting guns. It was necessary to point out that the act of cleaning shotguns after a shoot or rifles after a hunt was part of a process beloved by sportsmen, and that eliminating this stage would impoverish the enjoyment rather than adding to the fun. Most serious competition sports don't fit the 'fun' category at all, in spite of the strenuous attempts by manufacturers and their designers to reclassify the equipment used in these sports.

In hobby photography there have been several 35mm cameras produced in baby pink, light blue or yellow. All failed on the US and Western European market. Apparently taking a few snapshots of the family or friends in one's spare time is still intellectually and emotionally connected with the idea of photography as a serious activity that requires precision equipment – even though in reality it may be a fully automatic 'do-everything' camera selling for less than fifty dollars.

Leica in Germany produces cameras that use high-precision optics and are mechanically and electronically among the very best in the world. All the same, from time to time Leica has introduced a special gold-plated range of their finest

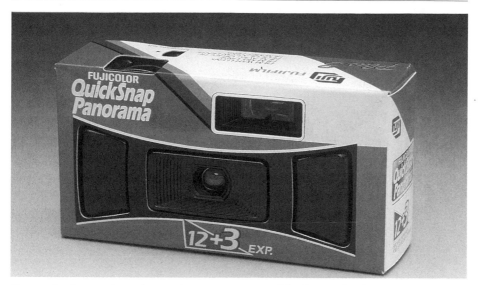

Panoramic photography used to require very expensive and highly specialized equipment.
In the 1990s, however, some of the disposable cameras are made specifically for panoramic shots.

cameras. Just as the inexpensive cameras are marketed as 'fun' objects, many of the gold-plated Leicas are sold to people who will never use them but save them in the original wrappings and boxes as investments and collection pieces. In the late 1970s Leica also marketed their top-line, single-lens reflex cameras in a so-called 'Safari' version (both camera body and lens barrels were painted in camouflage style) but this again proved to be unsuccessful on the market, always excepting camera collectors. The use of titanium on camera bodies, such as the Leica M-7, late in 1993, is another matter: this sturdy, professional range-finder camera has the advantages of a metal body without the weight.

It would be fascinating to speculate on what makes the public reclassify certain objects as design-for-fun, whereas there is deep resistance with others. These classifications seem to shift both in time and place. In Germany, for instance, even the least expensive objects that concern photography are considered to be serious and fit a sort of scientific classification, whereas in Korea and Malaysia cameras are always considered hobby equipment and intended for play-use. In Japan this stratification is much more rigid. There are serious professional and semi-professional cameras, and then there are fully automatic toys for family picture-taking, as well as those very simple disposable cameras that come with a roll of film. Towards the end of 1993 even these throw-away cameras have begun to separate into three distinct subtypes. There is the roll of film that is fronted by a disposable 'normal' camera; a second version that is intended for portrait shots; and finally a version that will take panoramic shots that can be printed 12 or 14 inches (30–35cm) wide showing, for example, the entire north rim of the Grand

Canyon, which before could only be achieved by extremely expensive and highly specialized technical cameras.

THE MEANING OF OBJECTS

Like many other designers I have been fascinated over the years with the shifting meaning of objects. This springs simultaneously from two different sources. One is the way in which a changing society accepts new tools and artefacts and how these develop semiotically over the years. The other influence comes from how things are made.

The first is clear if we look, for example, at television sets. In the early days they were firmly designated as pieces of furniture intended for the living-room. Smaller TV monitors were reclassified in the public's mind as 'technical equipment' or 'monitors', and the casing, previously carefully designed in a fake walnut-grain pattern, gave way to plain and undisguised metal or plastic boxes. As television screens increased in size, and stereophonic TV required external speakers, amplifiers and pre-amplifiers, the concept of the 'home entertainment centre' took hold. This may be a precursor of horizontally stretched 'HQ' (high-quality or high-resolution) videos and the eventual shift to three-dimensional holographic imagery. At the same time, we have seen the emergence of multimedia approaches on our home computers. With CD-ROM inputs, and speakers, and a range of software options, we can now combine music, video films, slides, text, animation and much more into a serious research or teaching tool, or else the complete works of fun (similar to the German term *Gesamtkunstwerk*).

The second influence is the way in which things are made. Historically an object bore signs of the maker's hand which formed a tactile as well as a spiritual link between the producer and the user. With contemporary production methods, this connection has been lost. It is important to regain it, yet difficult. Throughout this book the reader will find examples and suggestions on how to build the end-user back into the making of the product, to open up the process of production so that we all have a chance to participate in the creative, productive phase, and in this way build a tighter web of relations between process and product, form and content, designer and user. If fun means enjoyment and playful delight, we are all in need of regaining this lost harmony.

CHAPTER 8

Is Convenience the Enemy?

There is hope in honest error: none in the icy perfection of the mere stylist.
Charles Rennie Mackintosh

I N THE PAST, people bought things because they were necessary and useful. They were also often handsomely crafted, well made from quality materials and good to look at. These are still motivating factors when we consider a purchase. We hope that the objects we possess will reflect not just our own taste, but also the taste of our times – in other words, that they will be fashionable. We also think about what meanings and status the article will provide. Archaeologists and anthropologists tell us that humans have always needed the outward symbols that signify wealth, rank and place in the social pecking order. Even if we deliberately choose something unfashionable, archaic or strange, we are merely trying to assert our identity and ranking through a reverse-snobbery. Anti-design is one such movement that celebrates the accidental, the folk-crafted or the anonymous, as explored in the previous chapter.

LONGING AND DISSATISFACTION

Since the Industrial Revolution, and especially now, after the introduction of electronics, microchip technology and computers to the mass market, we have new concerns:

> *Can the tool or object do something that is magically new?*
> I have just sent a design from a village in Spain to a client in Nagoya
> in Japan, and received the return copy with sketched-in changes, all in a
> few minutes by fax.
> *Will it make it possible to do something differently and in a more
> desirable way?*
> The mountain bike will ride over rough terrain with muscle power alone.
> *Could it work better or less expensively than the appliance now in use?*
> The compact disc recordings will last for decades without developing
> scratches or 'hiss'.
> *Will it help the environment if I use it ?*
> The cotton string bag is preferable to a plastic carrier or paper bag.

All such considerations are rational, the only trouble is that people find that many competing choices make decisions more complicated.

Since the late 1920s, manufacturers and their industrial designers have managed to sell longing and dissatisfaction side by side. Manipulative styling creates the initial lust for the object, and then the subsequent disenchantment when it no longer looks fresh. Built-in obsolescence helps to create this dissatisfaction. The American industrial designer Bill Stumpf has spoken on this point, combining sensitivity with profound insights into design in relation to its cultural milieu. He suggested that if we know that our best friend is dying we develop a death psychology and tend subconsciously to pull away to lessen the inescapable grieving. Stumpf feels – correctly – that we have this same experience with cars: once a minor dent or scratch appears, we become aware of the car's inherent 'mortality' and tend to distance ourselves from it.[1]

People are increasingly conscious of this dissatisfaction implanted in goods, and become less willing to waste hard-earned cash during lean times. In the early 1990s, the demand for certain goods began to drop. It is difficult to persuade people to trade in their old television set for a new one when they know that 'high-definition' TV, with a completely different horizontally stretched format, is about come on to the market. The change in home computers has been so rapid that users find it hard to buy into a system that may be irrelevant in two years' time. People are keeping their cars much longer than in the past, hoping that electric automobiles, or those powered by other less polluting energy sources, might soon be available.[2]

TEN 'CONVENIENCE' TRAPS

Convenience is the new buzzword developed by the advertising brigade to help sell more goods to a jaded public. Nearly everything that could be sold was relabelled 'convenient', 'easy-to-use', or 'fool-proof'. The easy way of doing things, the increased convenience, was broken down into ten categories and sold under the banner of trouble-free, gentle, comfortable or effortless maintenance. But the end-user must analyse this so-called convenience.

1. Too small

Convenience of size is one of these apparent 'improvements' and used as a marketing ploy. Appliances and tools began shrinking unaccountably – small was not merely beautiful, but a new sales necessity. There is no question that reducing the original UNIVAC computer to a small desk model that has many more features than the earliest versions is an improvement. The microchip has now made it possible to shrink calculators to the size and thickness of credit cards, but a further reduction in size would strain the eyesight. In the 1980s a wristwatch was marketed which included a miniature calculator. It came with a minuscule silver stylus since only a baby octopus would have had the manual dexterity to work the tiny keys. The stylus was easy to misplace, and the microcalculator suffered the same fate of over-specialization as the sabre-toothed tiger – extinction. A Japanese firm makes a flat-screen television the size of a wristwatch, with an image scarcely larger than a postage stamp, which can be counted on to provide extra work for ophthalmologists, lens-grinders and opticians.

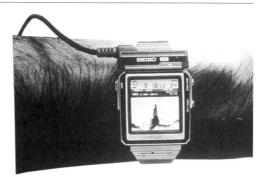

The miniaturization trend has led to this tiny television which is worn on the wrist.

Some Martian archaeologist, excavating on Earth centuries from now, might easily conclude – judging from tools found – that Earthlings had unaccountably begun to shrink in size, beginning around 1972. Quite the reverse is true. Due to improvements in health, exercise and nutrition, people have actually grown in stature. It remains for structural economists of the future to find a relationship between human size and weight on the one hand, and shipping costs between Japan and the West on the other. To avoid falling into the size convenience trap, ask yourself:

Does a smaller, more compact gizmo really make more sense than the one I already have?

Miniaturization and micro-miniaturization are – at least initially – much more expensive. The greater portability implied by smallness and its related lightness can also cause unexpected problems. Working with a German firm in consumer high-fidelity, we found that we could radically reduce the size of the AM/FM radio, tape-cassette player, CD mechanism and stereophonic pre-amplifiers to a single unit, no larger than two decks of playing cards. All that was needed was the voltage supply, powered speakers and slots for discs or tapes. The estimated price for this absurdly tiny unit, however, was nearly twelve times that of comparable full-sized high-fi components. The irony lay in the fact that the proposed equipment could be unobtrusively pocketed by a casual visitor, and a five-thousand-dollar investment would walk out of the door. Ask yourself:

Does the shrunken object really justify the higher price?

Size can obviously work both ways. One of my design clients in Japan is a subsidiary of a large automobile company. Visiting their design laboratory, I saw a photograph of former President Reagan pinned on a bulletin board. 'Reagan is one of the greatest Japanese car designers,' I was told, 'He bullied us into exporting fewer cars to America. So now we produce much larger cars for the American market. We export fewer numbers, but make a much higher profit with these over-sized models.'

'Small is Beautiful' is the maxim that Fritz Schumacher taught us in the 1970s, yet tiny is not necessarily better. Some appliances are much too large, yet the simplistic thinking that governs producers ('if you can't make it bigger, miniaturize it'), can often lead to inappropriate size.

The most ecologically responsible way to wash dishes is by hand and, preferably never under running water. If a dishwasher is really needed, then appropriate size is important for ecological, noise and space reasons. When I bought my small home, it contained a built-in standard dishwasher, large enough to wash everything for a four-course meal for twelve people. Paradoxically there is not enough space in the house to serve more than six guests comfortably. By contrast, a Japanese counter-top dishwasher exists that can cope easily with a meal for four people. This makes more sense in an age of single-parent families and one-person households, and is also slightly less harmful to the environment. Oddly, this seems to be available only on the Japanese home market and as an export to Latin America. There is an equally compact clothes-washer-cum-spindryer available in Japan, entirely adequate for a small family's needs. Both these appliances can use biologically inert liquid soaps, and are equipped with filtration systems that are claimed to cut down further on pollutants.

2. Too powerful

Another marketing tactic is powered convenience. Many tools that work extremely well manually are now rapidly multiplying in electrified or electronic versions. Starting simply, 'Dosenmeister', a can-opener made by WMF in Germany, will efficiently open standard cans and even the peskiest sardine tin because it can easily cut along small rounded corners. It is simple to clean, and it cuts the tin just below the lid, leaving a clean edge and easily disengaging itself from the top. It is muscle-powered (so saving on energy resources), will work for decades without repair and is inexpensive. By contrast, electric tin-openers have managed to substitute faults for all the virtues of the manual model. An extra 'freebie' that comes with electric can-openers is usually a built-on electric knife sharpener, and this added benefit, if used carelessly, tends to dull knives rather than to restore their edges.

The simplest and most effective way to sharpen knives is of course to use a whetstone. This requires some skill since, in inexperienced hands, there is a tendency to over-sharpen. Many years ago a client asked me to devise a 'foolproof' manual sharpener for knives. I had just spent my holiday at a beach, and had idly watched shore-birds rolling a round pebble back and forth using their beaks. It took a while before the magic penny dropped, and I realized that they were clean-

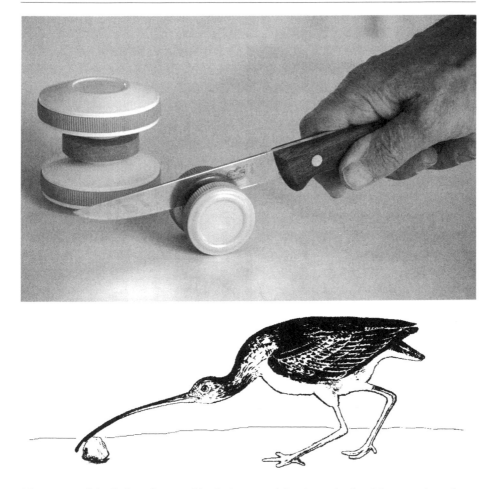

The concept of the 'foolproof' manual knife-sharpener (above) was developed from watching shore-birds sharpening and cleaning their beaks with round stones.

ing and sharpening their bills. I developed the required knife-sharpener from this biomorphic insight. It consists of two parallel discs edged with rubber (to establish friction), and two inner whetstone surfaces. The knife is then rolled back and forth a few times, and acquires a sharp edge. Later a competing firm copied this design, but enlarged it nearly five times. The curse of the big took over: the new version tends to distort the blade!

'Electronic notebooks' are another hilarious example of gadget-frenzy run amok. These are shirt-pocket sized slim battery-driven boxes that look like calculators but 'can store up to 5000 names, addresses, and phone numbers of your friends' (who has 5000 friends? Who needs their addresses on their person at all times?) and 'will also store other notes to yourself'. A notebook or address book and a pencil do the same job with greater efficiency. They cost almost nothing and are easily replaced. Entries are found more quickly in a notebook since most of us possess a visual memory for where we write things down. This is similar to the feeling for time we get from an analogue wrist watch as opposed to a digital one. The electronic pocket memo is the equivalent of the digital clock – we have no feeling, no *genius loci*, for the stored data. An address book does not rely on batteries, and discarded batteries are a major toxic hazard to the environment.

Examples of absurdities among powered consumer items are proliferating like rabbits. There is no question that many articles do a better job electrically than manually (a refrigerator stores medicines and food longer and more conveniently than an icebox, for instance), but there is always a caution and a price exacted. The fridge works well until there is a power cut, and the refrigerants now commonly in use play havoc with the ozone layer. Running a CD-player by gravity pressure (collected rainwater running down a tube and using fluid amplification, for example), might prove to be cumbersome and messy. There are obviously at least two sides to this story – yet most people when faced with powered convenience opt for it without considering alternatives, so, before investing in that electric toothbrush, ask yourself:

Is the electronic or electric model really a good choice?

3. Too many

Remember that we are talking about strategies that use the pretext of convenience to make their sales pitch. Multiple-model convenience is closely connected to the idea of powered devices. Now that you have painfully accustomed yourself to using an electric razor, wouldn't it make sense to have a battery-powered one for travel as well? And if you like the convenience of the battery model, then how about buying one that is also rechargeable? There is a large television set in the living room and a smaller one in the bedroom. The teenager has one in his room as well. Don't you deserve the convenience of a small TV set in the kitchen, so you can catch news bulletins while preparing dinner? And so the multi-gadgetry grows.

You find yourself persuaded that the high-fidelity system needs two cassette decks so that you can record cassettes for your friends – who have their own double deck in any case – or for a third player in your car. Surely a fourth cassette-player is needed – a personal stereo to listen to while jogging – and a fifth that can also record and is small enough to take to lectures and concerts. Assume that you have a sixth at the office and now multiply all these by three (two other family members). Now multiply by three again for battery-driven, rechargeable and mains-powered models, and you get to fifty-four cassette players (not counting the micro-cassette device you might use for memos or dictation). Exaggerated? Of course, but it helps draw attention to the senseless acquisition of gadgetry. I feel that the limit is reached, if not exceeded, with three cassette machines. Consider sharing (the option explored in Chapter 9) if three isn't enough, and ask:

Do I really need yet another one?

This is not a broad-based attack on specialized tools. I use every one of my nine different chef's knives, and own a plethora of drawing media and instruments. But a battery-driven, rechargeable pencil-sharpener? Never!

4. Too much

Convenience of ownership may be illusory. Most of us have grown up in societies where ownership confers both privilege and status. I challenge this idea. My friend Buckminster Fuller used to say in virtually all his talks in the late 1970s that, 'There is enough to go around,' and blame shortages on politics and bad distribution methods. We know better now. With a quickly expanding population base, and many resources irreplaceable, there is simply not enough. This is why notions such as sharing, re-using, recycling have become crucial. Philosophers and all great religious leaders have spent lifetimes warning us about the problems of possessions, telling us to do without, give up ownership, make do with less.

It is certainly true that possessions enslave us, that the things we own take on the role of sorcerers' apprentices and end up by owning us instead. There are specific anxieties hooked into owning certain objects these days that have to do with crime, theft, licences, maintenance, repair, insurance and other bureaucratic and legal procedures. All these can be avoided by leasing, as discussed in Chapter 9. The major objection to leasing and rental arrangements is, 'But you are paying all that money, and you never really get to own it!' Precisely, that's the whole point. Remember that ownership *per se* is meaningless, and ask:

How do owning and leasing compare in real costs?

5. Too complex

Added convenience can easily become a trap for the unwary user. Let us assume that the manufacturer has added extra features, controls, or buttons and dials. Once upon a time, a simple fan had a button that would turn it on at a low or high speed; now the settings read: 'on', 'high', and 'off'. Nothing has been added, except a meaningless extra marking on the switch plate. This is admittedly a trivial example, yet it is revealing of this kind of manipulation of desires.

My friend's washing-machine has a main power switch, and six control knobs, each of which has between three and six separate positions, making possible over forty-five different settings. These govern amount of water, temperatures, length of cycle, type of action, amount of laundry, type of fabric, length of spin, and so on. My friend washes only cotton textiles for table, bedding and clothes. Two or three settings at most will serve – more than forty are completely unnecessary. Also consider that micro-switches and electronic controls govern each of these extra positions and every separate control knob; inevitably the appliance will break down more often and it will be costly to have the fault diagnosed and repaired. Today's video cameras for the consumer market have such a bewildering array of switches, knobs, buttons, dials and sliding settings that it is difficult even to touch these 'handycams' without unintentionally changing several settings. All these objects have been over-designed to the point of overwhelming and intimidating the user. The questions to ask are:

> *Do the various extra features apply to my particular needs?*
>
> *Are there so many extra controls that they may interfere with smooth, long-range functioning?*
>
> *Do these add-ons improve the device at all?*

6. Too 'improved'

Sometimes the improvements are only minor, and such marginally improved convenience usually has little to commend it. A form-fitting knife for slicing, for instance, won't be easier to use, since the real discomfort and fatigue is in the wrist action. Some of my graduate students have explored the problems of the elderly in slicing meats, frozen foods or bread. A special feature of their experimental designs was that the handles were off-set in relation to the knife-blades, and a slicing guide was provided to prevent involuntary sideways movement.[3] The Swedish firm Gustavsberg have used this approach, and a selection of three knives and guide is now on sale.

An extra function-light (usually referred to as an 'idiot light'), may be helpful to show whether an appliance is on or off; however many of us have spent hours sitting in a stationary aeroplane, waiting for it to be cleared for take-off, merely because a faulty circuit caused one of these idiot lights to blink, seeming to indicate some serious mechanical failure.

Is a 'world time-zone map', too small to be deciphered on the lid of your travel alarm clock, really a needed improvement? Do you really use all four dials on your wrist watch, as well as the movable depth indicator for scuba diving? Are binoculars better when they focus themselves electronically, or can you still use the tip of your index finger to adjust them? Does a compass, mounted on the car's dashboard provide you with essential guidance whilst driving?

Does the automatic timing switch on the latest coffee maker justify paying a hundred and sixty-five dollars, and scrapping the present one? Is this 'trade-up' ecologically justifiable? Remember the metals and plastics, heating elements and glass parts inextricably combined and therefore not recyclable. Remember that the new apparatus constantly uses small amounts of electricity through its clock, warming-element and various function lights. If you decide that you really can't spare the extra six minutes in the morning, then go ahead and buy it. But remember to recycle the deposed one by giving it to the Salvation Army or some similar organization, to be reborn again rather than dissected. At this point you will have asked yourself the right question:

Does some tiny change justify your investment in the newer version?

7. Buying on impulse

When we find an article that we've always fancied in a sale, or see something in a shop window that we've just heard about, we are confronted by a highly temporary convenience. There are several possibilities to be explored. The price may be low to reflect the fact that the model has been, or is about to be, phased-out. If this is the case, the chances are that the newer version is only superficially styled to reflect some trendy notion, or else that it merely includes some minuscule improvement. The important aspect to investigate with a model that is about to be discontinued is whether replacement parts will still be readily available.

There is also the likelihood that you may be considering a poor or shoddily made copy of the original. I became so enthusiastic about the Dosenmeister tin-opener that I bought half a dozen as Christmas gifts for friends. Although my own tin-opener still operates well after many years, my friends' convenience turned out to be highly temporary. Their tin-openers had been made in another country, but were point-for-point copies of the German original, even to the prominent and illegal use of the logo. Not all foreign copies are shoddy, of course; plastic cooking utensils, designed for the firm Rosti in Denmark by Christer and Christel Holmgren of Næstved, are now produced in Thailand under franchise, and to the highest quality.

The object may be cheap because it was designed for a temporary fad. Some director's chairs are now available at a reduced price, because the fabric is printed with the camouflage pattern that so prominently figured on Allied uniforms during the Gulf War. Obviously war enthusiasts might find this a reason to buy them; others might be less interested in the visual semiotics than in the low price. The rest of us will realize that a trendy device of a few years back has made its appearance and may return some years from now as high camp or kitsch. Ask yourself:

Will replacement parts be difficult to obtain?
Is it a mean and shabby copy of the original?
Is it inspired by a short-time trend?

8. Too untested

The convenience of the new may hide defects or side-effects that are far from desirable. How much damage can flexible, plastic bumpers really prevent in a collision? Do side-beams (like those inexpensive copies of the protective body-cage that surrounds passengers in Saab and Volvo cars), really offer significant protection to passengers? Are electric plug-converters, permitting di-pole plugs to be inserted in tri-pole outlets, safe to use? How safe? Is the technology used in a tool or appliance so new that it may carry unknown hazards?

Can radiation emitted by visual display terminals and computer screens cause genetic damage? What about lap-top computers (lap-top!)? Microwave ovens or colour television sets are dangerous – none of these devices has been in use long enough for there to be a true assessment of the potential hazards – or so we are told. We know that people who work with computers for long periods complain about pains in the lower back, and tension in the shoulders, both caused by bad seating posture and stress. Carpal tunnel syndrome, a potentially crippling affliction which is now recognized in the United States by the Surgeon General and the Center for Disease Control, is also acerbated by bad posture and stress. It is only one of the conditions commonly known as RSI (repetitive strain injuries). Eye-strain is, most probably, just that, and not attributable to radiation. Physicians advise people to take frequent breaks whilst using computers, and furthermore to re-focus their eyes from time to time, breaking off from work for at least ten minutes every hour. But we know that computers emit radiation, and that the heaviest doses come from the rear of the unit. In a typical office with twenty or more computers neatly arrayed in rows, no one can presently define with any authority what witches' brew of radiation exists in the ambient mix between these machines.

Microwave ovens are shielded and carry positive locking devices whilst in operation. Gauges and meters are available to measure emissions, but few of these appliances have been tested to determine whether the seals and the shielding deteriorate with use. Exactly how a safe dosage is determined is anyone's guess. Yet, in the mid-1990s, television has been in use for more than half-a-century, desktop computers for nearly thirty years and microwave ovens for more than two decades.

Any knowledgeable product designer or engineer will point out that it may be unwise to buy any machine, tool or artefact that is either the first of its kind, or one that has been completely and radically redesigned and is presently in its initial production. With shrinking economies in most of the countries of the world and severe government cutbacks, especially in areas of consumer protection, there are often no proper evaluations available – sometimes even the awareness of a potential hazard doesn't exist as yet.

The questions to consider are:

Has it been thoroughly tested over a sufficiently long time and heavy use?

Has it been evaluated by reliable objective sources, such as 'Consumer Reports' in the United States and 'Which?' in Britain.

Has it proved itself sufficiently so that you feel that all the 'bugs' have been ironed out?

9. 'State of the Art'

'State of the Art' convenience refers to the present stage of development of any technological product. It requires an inspired guess by the user to determine whether this is the time to acquire something, or if it would be wiser to wait, knowing that major changes are on the way. An example from high-fidelity sound equipment makes this point. The impact of compact discs was immediate when they were first introduced at the beginning of the 1980s. It seemed clear that here was a sound reproduction method that finally combined extreme high fidelity with little or no reduction in quality after prolonged use. The long path that began with wax cylinders, progressed through shellac and vinyl recordings, moved from scratchy sounds to almost hiss-free long playing records seemed to be coming to its conclusion. There was also a second source of sound recording. At the start of World War II, the Gestapo began using early wire-recordings. After the war, bulky reel-to-reel tape-recorders eventually gave way to eight-track tapes and finally to the audio-cassettes pioneered by Philips. The compact disc solved the long-standing problem of bringing about a balance between quality of sound, portability and durability. CDs were virtually indestructible. They were 'read' by a laser beam, so there was no variation in sound quality, even after years of use. They became more competitive as the price of tape-cassettes and long-playing records predictably rose. Because of their inherent permanence, a flourishing market in used discs quickly developed. The greatest fear of audiophiles, that much precious recorded material would be lost, has proved unjustified. An increasing number of small and off-beat firms are re-issuing rare recordings re-mastered for the disc format.

'Never leave well enough alone' seems to be the motto of the high-fi industry, however. Now that CDs have proved their quality and established the leading market share, manufacturers in Europe and Japan are trying to 'improve' things again. There are now three new types, two of which are simply attempts to change disc size and format – Beethoven's Ninth Symphony originally determined playing time on a CD, hence its original size. The third is DAT or Digital Audio Tape. It makes it possible to dub one's own tapes from CDs, without sacrificing acoustic quality. Setting aside the moral and legal question of taping from discs, the main claim of this system is quality, yet the claim may be false. Tape stretches with use, and although it is said that this does not impair the signal with DAT tape I feel that we haven't used the system long enough to be really certain. On 14 December 1994, it was revealed on US National Public Radio that *all* videotape since 1977 is delaminating and is no longer viewable. As for taping music from discs, this is surely rather a shallow advantage when price is considered. To play DAT, one needs a DAT player; this, like blank digital tape, is very expensive.

Therefore you must ask yourself:

Is the system or device worthwhile in its present form, or is it evident that an entirely different and more sophisticated method is on its way?

10. Package as product

Many of the things we use are almost identical but for exterior appearance. This raises questions about what the appearance really means within the framework under discussion; more exactly, semiotic convenience. Does the graphic design on a box of washing-up powder make it in any way better than the near-identical powder in a box with a different design? How about breakfast cereals or soaps? Is the enormous amount of money spent on package design justified in any way? Consider that these boxes are difficult – if not impossible – to recycle because of the many coloured inks used to decorate them. The cardboard must be de-inked, a costly process at present, and one that yields a toxic runoff from the de-inking. Only about 1% of the cost of a large box of cornflakes in the USA goes to the farmer – the remaining 99% accounts for packaging, distribution and profit for an army of middlemen.

European and Japanese graphic designers who visit the States, are fascinated by the packet design of so-called 'generic foods' in supermarkets.[4] They will buy a box of generic breakfast cereal and a tin of soup to take back with them, explaining that they admire the elegant and simple design of the packaging. Often they will also buy the same foods in the garish brand-name packaging. The joke is that the generic packages owe their aesthetic elegance to the fact that they weren't officially designed at all! The box or label is of unbleached white cardboard or paper, with the contents printed in a simple black typeface. Interestingly enough, this direct approach has caught on with some top-of-the line wine and whisky labels, exclusive cosmetics and expensive books and recordings. 'Good taste' seems to be polarized between luxury and discount goods. The tawdry and flashy is reserved for the middle level, giving new meaning to the phrase that 'the baloney is the best part of the sandwich'.

The user needs to consider the relationship of package to contents. Frequently the dividing line between the goods and the wrapping is fuzzy – in some cases it

It is assumed that brand-name packaging must be assertive and brightly coloured (above),
but 'generic packaging' (below) has a direct simplicity that has influenced some manufacturers
of luxury goods.

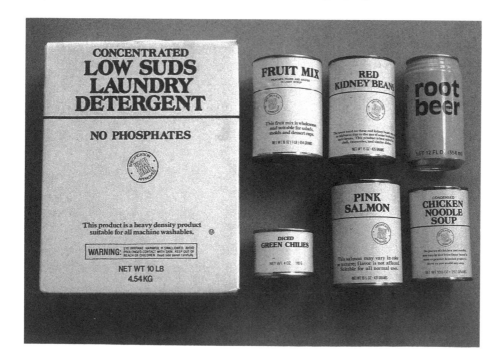

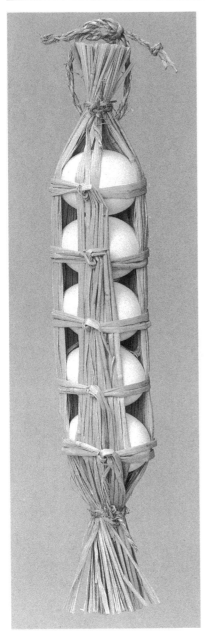

A package for five eggs. In Japan, eggs, sake cups, rice bowls and many other goods are packed in fives.

is hard to tell which is which. A whisky that sells for about twenty dollars can also be bought in a 'gift decanter' (machine-pressed glass, tatted up with ridiculous armorial bearings and encased in a fake velour-covered sarcophagus), for five times as much, with the 'value added' amounting to nil. A perfume comes in no less than six layers of packaging, to which the shop adds a seventh protective wrap and then a plastic carrier bag. It may be argued that both whisky and perfume are luxury products, yet the real difference between form and content in packaging straddles all price categories. It becomes a question of meaning.

Packaging can also be a subtle way to pre-select the number of items a customer is forced into buying at any one time.[5] Eggs come by the dozen in the US, or in a box of ten in most of Europe. It has taken energy, assertiveness and time to persuade my local supermarket to let me buy six eggs at a time. The local farmer at the outdoor market tells me that 'it isn't cost-effective' (the recently invented word that signifies mean) to let me buy two or three eggs at a time. Surely some biologically knowledgeable designer will come to the rescue soon and – through some ingenious gene-splicing – give us chickens capable of laying a dozen at once!

I fully agree with the British writer Nicholas Freeling who has observed that: 'An interest in cars is a classic sign of subnormal intelligence.'[6] This can be reflected in the difference in the performance characteristics claimed for cars. The reasonable response would be to assess these characteristics under real-world conditions and over time. The advertisement that informs us that the cars made by Volvo have a working-life of eleven years in the United States (given repair, maintenance and driving habits in the USA), provides further valuable data. The corollary, that in its native Sweden the same car lasts for sixteen years, tells still more. The information that a high-performance sports car has a top speed of 185 mph is irrelevant, since speed limits of 65 mph are strictly enforced in the USA. That the same car can reach a speed of 60 mph in less than eight seconds from a standing start is equally redundant information – who could possibly care? There are some crucial issues that count in the real world of the 1990s.

What is the fuel consumption under normal conditions?

What safety features – side bars, anti-lock brakes, double seatbelts, airbags – come as standard equipment?

Can the car be recycled easily?

How long can it last with care?

What is the average cost of routine repairs over five years?

What is the average owner's level of satisfaction with this particular car?

The American magazine *Consumer Reports* devotes one issue each year to these questions. Since the cars tested by the magazine are bought anonymously, and the editors accept no advertising, the results printed can be trusted.

Obviously there are certain existential questions that cannot be posed by a monthly magazine. Within the speciality area of sports cars alone, one can ask whether the latest Porsche is really worth fifty-eight times as much as a Mazda Miata. Should some of the cars tested exist at all? What is the meaning of a certain top-line convertible, and does that meaning change depending on the social and cultural mores of different countries? It is called a 'Grandfather's car' in its native Germany (since so many elderly gentlemen use it in their amorous pursuit of young girls) and works as the trademark of drug-dealers in Latin America; in the United States it is often a graduation gift to university students; it symbolizes the ultimate Yuppie toy in Canada, whereas it represents prestige and rank in Japan. There also exists a sort of reverse snobbery about cars in certain cultural settings. When I visited Philips Design Centre in Eindhoven shortly after the first oil shock of 1973, one of their senior vice presidents picked me up at the airport. Although a part owner and top administrator in one of the world's largest multinational electronics firms, he took evident pride in driving a Citroën 'Diane', at that time the least expensive and most modest automobile available in Europe. So you must also ask the question:

Are you buying into something trendy, or into a phoney image of quality?

DESIGN AS SIGNIFIER

Having explored these ten different categories of 'convenience' used as sales tactics, I should like to explore further the notion of semiotic content in design.

It is important to remember that architecture and design are the social arts par excellence. It is possible to avoid theatre and ballet, never to visit museums or galleries, to spurn poetry and literature and to switch off radio concerts. Buildings, settlements and the daily tools of living however, form a web of visual impressions that are inescapable. Ordinary, simple objects of daily use have been until recently always been less aesthetically demanding and less complex, than the productions of the fine arts, and so more directly satisfying. Ever since design and its products became an ideologically sacrosanct part of marketing, this has changed in profound ways. Unlike painting or sculpture, design tends to embody social meanings, or serves to make certain social meanings acceptable. We value designed objects for many different reasons, but most are no longer connected with either the use of the object or the original intentions of the designer. The intent of the designer may, in fact be uninteresting or indecipherable to us.

Some objects come to us covered with the saccharine coating of sentimentality. We enjoy them because they were gifts from someone dear, or because we inherited them and will forever associate them with, say, the magic evenings of childhood at grandmother's house. None of us is ever really free from the bondage of memories. Years after I had been apprenticed to him, Frank Lloyd Wright gave me one of his early 'Taliesin' barrel chairs. Later one of my daughters discovered that another had brought a phenomenally high price at a Sotheby's auction. Realizing that an Italian furniture company was making expensive facsimiles, though at one-twentieth of the auction price of the original, she asked why I didn't sell my chair at auction, buy six of the replicas and pocket the extra money. It was hard to explain that the replicas weren't the same because they had not been given to me personally by Mr Wright, and I didn't need six of them anyway.

The pleasure that we derive from antiques is partly because we find the lines and proportions satisfying and because materials that have aged well hold great appeal. One thinks of the honey-brown of old leather or aged oak; the silvery-grey of the boards on a weathered barn. People also treasure the idea of antiques. Something that is not mass-produced, they reason, has been crafted more carefully and with love. This may also explain the rising appreciation for the crafts over the last few decades – not only as an escape from machine precision, but also from a desire to own an article that literally bears the stamp of its maker – a visual clue to the intent of the craftsman and to handmade quality. In reaction against a rapidly rising tide of impersonal technology, we are becoming more aware of the process than the product. To this should be added the romance that we project on to anything old. The simple fact that a Phoenician coin has survived for more than three thousand years makes it precious. When we measure this against our own short lifespan, we experience three millennia as part of the pageant of history and the coin becomes talismanic.

We experience similar feelings, a strange awe, for an exotic artefact or object. Zuni fetishes, inro and netsuke (the handcarved ivory toggles of 18th and 19th-century Japan), African masks, Iranian carpets, Wayang Dollies from Java and Bali, Tibetan prayer wheels – all these carry the cachet of distance and mystery, and are consequently prized. This is nothing new. Archaeologists have found jewellery using Baltic and Icelandic amber in West African tribal burial grounds, and Zuni and Zia Indians in New Mexico were using shells from the Pacific islands in their decorative jewelry and costumes in the early 19th century. Trade routes, comparable to the ancient silk road into Asia but much older, have existed throughout tribal histories. When the object is both exotic and ancient, it is seen as doubly precious, and any mystery or strangeness attached to its function adds new dimensions of desirability. Still we must sense authenticity in the article, or at least think we do. How else to explain the great attraction of a temple mask from Thailand, and yet our curious feelings of disappointment and almost be trayal when – on idly turning over a well-produced plastic cooking spatula in our hands – we see that is was made in Thailand?

Whenever a designed object is superseded by other methods and removed from daily use, it enters a new category. Engineers' slide-rules began to be replaced by calculators in the early 1970s. One of my favourite photographs – unfortunately lost in a move – showed more than six hundred engineers' slide rules stuck into the ground around a neighbour's lawn, forming a tiny, sardonic, white picket fence. When I asked about it, my neighbour's wife said, 'We bought these slide-rules for one dollar for a barrel of them and used all six hundred.'

Even a contemporary product, when forcefully removed from its context, will go through this qualitative change. At one point I had designed a target bow, and a friend of mine who admired its lines bought one and had it mounted on a small concrete base. She said that it looked like one of Brancusi's 'Bird in Flight' abstract sculptures. Far from being flattered, I found myself deeply offended. The bow could no longer be used, in fact it could no longer even be strung. To me the true merit of the design lay in its dynamics. When strung and then drawn it went through a visually and kinaesthetically satisfying transformation. To me, as its designer, the high point came just after it had been fully drawn and the arrow released. My friend had inadvertently demonstrated that a design arbitrarily plucked from its setting, became something else. It was turned into 'art' or an 'antique', a love object. Its true content was robbed of meaning and – displaced from its utilitarian role – it entered a world of fantasy.

In the arts and design it could still be said just a few years ago that it was 'the task of the avant-garde to detect new directions in the future, as well as to explore fresh aspects of the past'.[7] But now this has all changed. We invented camp during the seventies, and made kitsch respectable for the first time. Add the nostalgia wave, and now everything, literally everything, has become 'collectable'. The past and present of the built environment, and of the objects designed to go inside it, have become one. Nostalgia has revived designs that had fallen into disuse and surrounded them with a penumbra of meanings, most of them invented by merchandisers and wide of the original mark.[8]

THE CHAIR AS DESIGN GESTURE

Consider chairs. Among the more expensive, fully one-third are anti-chairs, that is: chairs that are specifically designed to make sitting on them difficult, uncomfortable or even impossible. My favourite is an Italian chair that has knife blades and pointed hooks forming the seat. Items like these – originating from the more degenerate productions of high art – have a place in our time. They represent a flight from the formal aesthetic of the Bauhaus, the International Style, and the Modern movement in general, a reaction against the sterility and neutral boredom of the established 'good taste' that pervaded the twenties to the early sixties. Ettore Sotsass and the whole Memphis movement attempted to extract the guts and vitality from conventional bad taste, as a sort of counter-revolutionary movement against the Modern mainstream. Its real influence on the mainstream, however, went curiously astray. It is only the very rich who can afford to buy and display furniture that can't be used. Furthermore, anti-chairs have become emblematic templates for furniture designers. The mainstream sees this as an indication that all design rules and standards are now meaningless. The obvious danger is that quality will disappear.

Much upmarket furniture production these days is devoted to reproduction. So-called 'designer chairs' have been resuscitated from the past to provide dubious comfort at top prices. Most of these delectable pieces were designed by architects between 1924 and 1952. Some of the decorative upright chairs devised by Charles Rennie Mackintosh around 1900 have been lovingly recreated in Italy. It's fun to speculate on the body build of someone ideally suited to sit in one of these chairs: rather slim, approximately eleven feet tall, but with grotesquely short and bandy legs. Since the seats are flat plain hardwood, it would also help if the user was somewhat steatopygic, thus providing his or her own upholstery. For reasons entirely opaque to me, hundreds of these astonishingly expensive neo-Mackintosh copies crowd the lobbies of intercontinental hotels in South Korea, each fitted out with a tasteful velvet rope to prevent anyone actually attempting to sit in one.

Gerrit Rietveld, a leading member of the De Stijl school of design in the Netherlands which was formed at the end of World War I, designed many chairs that look like Piet Mondrian paintings translated into three dimensions and provide about the same warmth and comfort. This is especially true of his 'Rouge et Bleu' so-called easy chair of 1924. In 1935 he designed the desk chair 'Zig Zag' in solid wood whose materials and seeming defiance of the laws of gravity combine austere severity with a truly crippling lack of comfort. Visually and logically the structure 'can't possibly work', so the 'Zig Zag' may well be the accidental forerunner of much Post-Modern furniture and 'impossible' architectural details. Like the Mackintosh chair it is being revived and marketed by an Italian firm.

In 1930 Marcel Breuer designed the 'Wassily' chair, a plumber's nightmare of leather and chrome tubing, roughly cubical in shape. It is even more convoluted, albeit in straight tubing, than the original Thonet bentwood rocking chair designed in Vienna in 1862. Because of the acute angle of the seat bottom, occupants tend to slide backwards. Le Corbusier created an adjustable lounging chair in 1929 that seemed intended for the twenties 'flapper' equivalent of Mme Recamier. A half-circle of chromed steel tubing can be adjusted to various reclining angles against a dark wooden base. Although the upholstery can be leather, the original design was in black and white ponyskin (with a small round bolster for the head). One can sense the shift in attitudes over the last sixty years by observing young designers today staring in open disbelief at this piece in a shop or a museum. Was it really necessary to slaughter ponies, they seem to be wondering, just to exploit a fancied contrast between the sleek look of chrome and the soft texture of ponyskin?

Taliesin 'Barrel' chair designed by Frank Lloyd Wright around 1904.

Metal cafe chair for Wright's Midway Gardens project in Chicago 1913.

The 'Bibendum' chair, designed by Eileen Gray in 1927, combines purity of line with real comfort.

Bruno Matsson's easy chair of 1932 is designed to make sitting a pleasure.

Frank Lloyd Wright, in a rare and disarming moment of self-criticism admitted that he was 'still black and blue from sitting in my own furniture'. Mr Wright may have been too hard on himself. The Taliesin 'Barrel' chair (mentioned earlier), is quite comfortable. Possibly because I happen to be the same height as Frank Lloyd Wright, and of a similar build, I find it a wonderful chair in which to sit and develop ideas. Wright's Taliesin West 'Origami' easy chair of 1940 also provides comfort and decent support. The metal café chairs he had crafted for his Midway Gardens project in Chicago in 1913, however, must be among the most painfully uncomfortable sitting devices. Nonetheless, the same Italian firm that has revived the Mackintosh and Rietveld chairs has brought them back and they are selling steadily.

All this is not meant as a tirade against modern chair design. It must be understood that these were all attempts to 'stretch the envelope' of what a chair should or could be. One thing these chairs have in common is that they were all designed by men, and were based on their designers' egocentric wish to make a 'gesture', rather than to provide comfort. It is noteworthy that the only two well-known women furniture-designers did far better. Eileen Gray's voluptuously over-stuffed 'Cube' chair, and her 'Bibendum' chair of 1927, that enfolds one protectively among a series of two or three pneumatic half-circular bolsters, covered in industrial rubber, textiles, or – in some cases – leather, are both comfortable and comforting, without sacrificing any of Gray's purity of line or succinct vision. Ray Eames designed an occasional stool of walnut in 1957 that in its original version was a rocking stool, a really fresh idea, and pleasant and unusual occasional seating.

The 'Uchiwa' chair designed by the author in the 1960s.

A practical chair designed by Bjorn Hulten; it packs flat and is simple to assemble and take apart.

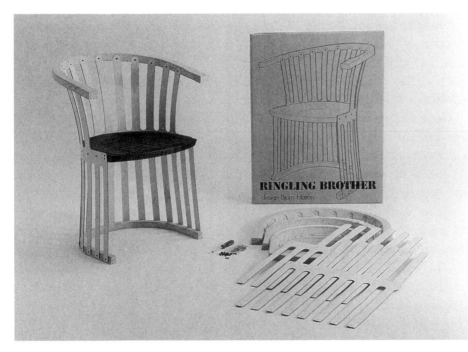

Most of the 'signature' chairs listed provide indifferent support or seating ease. All fell into disuse after their decade of glory. All have been revived as fantasy memorials to nostalgia and a world that was very different from the one artificially inseminated by the makers and purveyors of these goods today.

Unlike the fetish symbols just discussed, the chairs missing from this list never had to be revived because they have been in continuous production since they were first designed – for over seventy years in some cases. All are extremely comfortable, display unusually high levels of craftsmanship and quality control and are largely made of wood. All but one come from Denmark or Sweden. I would include Bruno Matsson's chairs with canvas webbing under the upholstery, especially his high-back chair of 1936, which has three buttons to adjust the head cushion. Hans Wegener, Finn Juhl and Poul Kjersholm have all made chairs of profound elegance that are extremely comfortable. Mogens Koch's folding 'campaign' chair, designed in 1930 – and made of beechwood, with linen slings and ox-leather arms with brass fittings – is probably the most refined re-statement of a director's chair. I should like to add the various chairs by the Danish architect Arne Jacobsen, and my own 'Samisen' and 'Uchiwa' chairs of 1960 to 1965. Many of these long-lived chairs were never mass-marketed but succeeded on their own virtues of comfort, simplicity and good form.

The exploitation of convenience in its many guises as a sales tactic has been explored in some detail. The concept of convenience has to do with leisure, in the Western world inextricably connected with the benefits and usufructs enjoyed by the traditional upper classes. It also conveys the belief that life should be made as easy as possible. Making things easy can be accompanied by negative side-effects, however. Physically (and psychologically), we need to expend effort throughout our lives, regardless of age or condition. Once we stop trying to stretch the bubble, we degenerate and atrophy spiritually as well as physically.

Greater convenience is also proffered through labour-saving devices. It is here that we must exercise caution. When machines and tools eliminate back-break-ing, mind-numbing labour, they are proper extensions of our natural powers. It is in more trivial ways that power-tools can rob us of the satisfaction of accom-plishing an exacting task with our hands. Compare the real usefulness of an overhead crane that transports sizeable metal pieces across a factory floor, to an electronically controlled reclining-chair that adjusts hydraulically, and again to an electric back-scratcher. Now take into account the amount of energy used (or needlessly wasted), in each case, and also the de-skilling of people through auto-matic tools that direct and narrow the choices open to a craftsman or artisan, whether professional or amateur.

FASHION AND CUTENESSS

'Convenience' is a powerful selling-line. Trendiness, style, fad and fashion is another strong marketing ploy to make people dissatisfied with what they have and to shop for something else. Fashion sorts through the centuries and finds an inspiration here, a notion there. It looks to foreign lands and strange peoples for hints and ideas. It metabolizes odd customs and toys with hints, fetishes and taboos. Everything is worked over and – for a brief time only – sets trends. When the gesture, the dress, or the meaning have been worn smooth with too much

Baby features arouse feelings of warmth and protectiveness.
This has been exploited in the car design on the left.

handling, they are soon discarded as irrelevant, only to be resurrected some ten or twenty years later as pastiche or – with a slight twist – as 'brand-new latest'. Fashion is driven by the old, the exotic, the unusual and the odd. By its very nature, fashion proceeds out of nostalgia to celebrate the 'body eclectic'.

The economic basis for fashion lies in the drive to make people buy things they don't need, one form of the late capitalist technique of planned obsolescence. Fashion shares the same fate as other social movements of protest that start as rejections of the dictates of a prevailing main culture. Such spontaneous, and frequently highly personal statements or group activities are almost always co-opted by the insatiably greedy mass media.

The 'cuteness' syndrome is another means of making the consumer want to buy. The word cute is imprecise. It is used in America generally in conjunction with a diminutive as in: 'What a cute little house!' It frequently has belittling or patronizing overtones. Shirley Temple, Brigitte Bardot, Helena Bonham-Carter and Tom Cruise could be considered 'cute', but for real beauty we need to look at Greta Garbo, Gong Li, the young Marlon Brando or Catherine Deneuve.

As a colloquial term in aesthetics, cute occupies an odd position, being closest to 'cheap chic', 'cornball', 'kitsch', or pleasing with a hint of vulgarity or the tawdry. In the usefully copious vocabulary of Japanese aesthetic terms, the word *hade* (brightly coloured, somewhat exuberant as in the kimono of very young women), may come close. A greeting-card firm in Kansas City uses 'cute' as a descriptive term for gaudy, oversentimental cards featuring fuzzy baby animals or slightly obese angels. Such cards are usually intended for children or the less expensive end of the market. During a design review of proposed inexpensive Christmas cards to be sold a dozen to the box, one the design supervisors – not pleased by the apparent lavishness of a cheap card – uttered the unforgettable judgment: 'Too many angels for a five-dollar "cute"!'

The Austrian ethologist Konrad Lorenz used the term 'cuteness syndrome' to explain how and why we respond warmly and protectively toward baby animals. We can even recognize 'babyness' in species that are unfamiliar to us and for which we have no image of the mature animal – a baby duck-billed platypus, for example. This recognition of babyhood (or cuteness), has to do with the pro-portion of head to body and eye-size to face, eye motions, amount and quality of fur or feathers, apparent clumsiness, and much else.[9] This may also explain the curious attraction some people feel for paintings of children with exaggeratedly large eyes. The exploitation of 'cuteness', convenience or fashion manipulates people's reactions and emotions unscrupulously; it represents the engineering of desire. To put it differently: convenience is the enemy of excellence; fashion is the enemy of integrity; cuteness is the enemy of beauty.

CHAPTER 9

Sharing not Buying

*Unless we change the direction in which we are headed, we might
end up where we are going.*
Chinese proverb

THE EASIEST way to save resources and energy and to cut down on waste is to use less. This statement is so simple as to sound banal, yet it can serve as a guide to action. Also implied is the idea of consuming less, buying less, making do with what we have already – even at times ridding ourselves of all the unnecessary gadgets and duplicates that so hideously clutter up our lives. All this is just plain common sense, yet it is an approach to living that seems to be fairly rare at the moment.

There will be immediate objections. What about the economy and – by extension – individual and company profits? Won't pay-packets shrink, millions be unemployed, corporate balance-sheets shrivel, businesses go into bankruptcy and the world economy be devastated? Possibly, *yet how can we tell?*

In the mid 1990s, millions *are* unemployed all over the world; there *are* – for the first time since the 1920s – beggars on the streets of two of the world's socially most advanced countries, Denmark and Sweden. The homeless people sleeping in the streets of Western cities are reminiscent of Calcutta in the 1950s. Corporate executives and their politician friends are universally discredited by their greed and corruption. Bankruptcies have exceeded those of the great Depression of the 1930s, and there can be little doubt that the world economy *is* already devastated.

On a different level, won't all the fun go out of life? What about all the wonderful gadgets we have been given by modern technology? Isn't there a chance that life will become increasingly drab and dingy, shabby and mean?

Before exploring some of these doom-laden scenarios, it might be wise to investigate strategies that could lead to healing our product addiction, help create an environment that is ecologically benign and sustainable, and at the same time enrich our inner lives. This chapter is about how to buy fewer things, make better decisions about what we really need, and finally to explore a whole series of alternatives to merely buying whatever strikes our fancy.

GETTING AND SPENDING

A good start might be to look at just where we stand in our own personal lives. The chances are that if we live in a developed or over-developed country and haven't recently become victims of a fire, an earthquake, flood, tornado or other 'act of God' that we are already surrounded by consumer goods that allow us to live above a reasonable level of comfort. Most of us know more people who are smothered by their possessions than those who truly suffer at the edge of disaster.

Nonetheless, we know what stunted lives people lead trying to buy more, to own more, to consume in ever greater excess and to make more money in order to continue this relentless cycle. Even if we bought goods merely to replace what had been used up, or worn out, or grown out of, the problems of over-consumption would not go away – there are so many people now living in the world and using continuously shrinking resources. With the geometric progression of world population, we can no longer afford to escalate production, consumption, waste. It will be pointed out that birth statistics clearly show a reversal – especially in Europe and the United States – but the population base itself is such that even tightly controlled increases result in millions of births. Although some of our resources are seemingly unlimited, others are non-renewable or take decades or centuries to renew, and our over-use threatens atmosphere, climate and life. Yet the jump from two-and-a-half to over five billion people is not easily understood. An anecdote may put things in perspective.

Some years ago I heard about a craftsman who hand-built mediaeval lutes, krummhorns and other antique musical instruments, and interviewed him for my arts column in a Kansas City newspaper. His answer to the inevitable question as to who bought these things will always remain with me: 'There are more people,' he said, 'playing mediaeval lutes today, than there were playing *or listening* to lute music in mediaeval Italy.' (Italics supplied).

There are approximately one-and-a-half thousand million people in the world who can be considered members of the consumer class, and many more aspiring to join it. There is no doubt that the factories, corporations, industrial cartels, transportation networks, advertising channels and most governments (the entire world economy in truth) are directed to bring the dubious benefits of the consumer lifestyle to one fourth of humanity at the expense of the rest of the world. Leading this attempt to turn everyone into a product-junkie are Japan, Korea, the United States, Taiwan and Germany.

THE CONSUMER TRIANGLE

The considerations for deciding whether to buy or not to buy seem obvious once they are listed. Yet the concept of individual ownership forms such an integral part of our world that it is difficult for people to think along different lines.

The desire to consume forms a vicious triangle. The first side represents the increasingly greed-driven, affluent society of the West, especially during the 1980s, driven by the ceaseless clamouring of the advertisers to buy, to own, to consume.

The second side of the triangle represents the people of Russia, the other splinters of the former Soviet Union and its client states in eastern Europe. They have had to live without most of the everyday goods that we have taken for granted in the West since the 1920s, products which the merchandisers have convinced us to consider absolute necessities rather than desirable luxuries. Their present buying frenzy, their craving for all the magical beeping, blinking, humming or purring electronic goodies is understandable – after two and a half generations of forced abstinence they want their share. The third side of the triangle is formed by the folk in the developing countries who – decades after the end of colonial exploitation – find themselves still in poverty and need, while being exposed by tourists and television to the shameless waste-culture of the richer countries of the globe. Here again their needs are undeniable, and one can sympathize with their wants.

There may be a curious similarity here between the obsessive lust for consumer goods in the ex-socialist states and the developing countries on the one hand, and the sudden spurt in the growth of the African-American civil rights movement in the United States in the 1950s. Television ownership expanded rapidly in the United States during the early fifties. Poorer black families in the South gained their first insight into the real – or idealized – life-styles of their white neighbours. An African-American farm wife, watching a television commercial extolling the virtues of a new automobile or washing machine would visit the shop with her husband, and drive home in the new dream-car or have the washer delivered the next day. Seeing the same television presenter suggesting dinner at a local restaurant, the couple might decide to drive there in their new car, only to be indignantly and brutally turned away; the South was at that time strictly segregated. A similar mechanism may govern the growing expectations in the southern tier of the globe as well as in eastern Europe. The virtual reality constructed from television advertisements and television dramas as well as the global reach of Cable News Network, films, magazines and the explosion of tourism, all play their part in this age of longing.

It is plain, however, that the wasteful consumption patterns of western Europe, North America and Japan won't translate to the rest of the world for environmental and ecological reasons. There can be no globalization of Barbie dolls, Kentucky Fried Chicken, Kalashnikovs, electric hair-dryers or portable fax machines. Quite the reverse is true: unless we learn to cut back dramatically and at once, and demonstrate *by example* that the industrialized world can find frugal ways out of the consumer dilemma, all will be lost.

THE QUALITY OF LIFE

The result of flooding the world with consumer goods is deep human dissatisfaction. Obviously objects alone can never fulfil real human needs and longings.

What Karl Marx in his *Letters to Ricardo* called the 'objectification of needs'[1] has become the central aim of these post-Marxist times. Yet advertising and propaganda have managed to convince the populations of both the overdeveloped and developing nations that the real meaning of our existence can be found in the simplistic notion that, *we work to make money in order to buy things that will distract us from having to work.*

Nearly all of us have been shackled to the production-consumption-discard cycle, yet the manufacture and distribution of products waste resources and energy and are environmentally catastrophic. The goods we are persuaded to consume are forcing us into new behaviour patterns, routine methods for tranquillizing our personal longings, instead of pursuing our true and deeper needs; they have debased those spiritual aspirations that provide meaning to our lives.

All known societies have used objects to identify an individual's or family's status within the pecking order and to provide beauty and delight, but true waste (except in our modern consumer society) is rare. One thinks of the potlatch ceremonies of the Kwakiutl, Tlingit, Haida, Tsimshian and other Native Americans, yet these opulent feasts were not so much wasteful signifiers of wealth as a way of redistributing the abundance of the rainforest societies of Canada's north-west coast.

Consumerism is *not* deeply ingrained in the world's cultures; it is a fairly recent and superficial phenomenon, probably arriving with the newly invented goodies of the late 19th and early 20th centuries. These made a whole series of new miracles available to all: small boxes that, with the push of a button, would make a copy of a face or a landscape; ways of storing a song, a concerto, the voice of Caruso, and repeating them at will; horseless carriages; magic ways of talking to people around the world; devices and tools that – under the guise of 'convenience' – nibbled away at our capacity to memorize and remember, imagine, make music, innovate – or even wish to do so.

In spite of such powerful manipulation to step up our 'shop-till-you-drop' behaviour, polls and surveys continue to show that people feel that their most valued pastimes are family and social get-togethers, religious worship, sports, artistic pursuits, building or repairing things around the house, gardening, cooking, conversation and travel. In practice, however, we seem to spend nearly all our time between work and shopping sprees, with several hours of tranquillizing television before we sleep.

What is needed is to re-establish our connections with nature and with our own roots. Societies that provide leisure time for activities that are not profit-directed or purely materialistic, and give ample opportunities to establish strong human relationships, tend to be less wasteful and more deeply in tune with human needs. The strength and sophistication of Balinese society, for example, rests firmly on the many rich friendship and family connections that people maintain, as well as the fact that all Balinese are active in arts, crafts, music, cooking – creative activities of many different kinds.

Having established a frame of reference from which to examine our wasteful and environmentally destructive patterns, we can now begin to survey what can be done. There are several questions that the end-user should consider before buying a new possession.

TEN QUESTIONS BEFORE BUYING

1. Do I really need it?

Before making a purchasing decision, the first – yet frequently unasked – question should be: do I really need it? Have I been persuaded to buy it because it offers some real advantages over what I use now, or because it will actually help me in my learning, working, leisure? Will it in some way bring greater enchantment to my life and those dear to me? Or will it – under the guise of offering greater convenience – make living more complicated or become a placebo for the stresses we all experience?

Yet even if we can honestly say that we *do* need the object, and are sure that we are not buying it in the forlorn hope that it will make us more powerful, wiser, or more attractive to the opposite sex, nor prompted by some temporary whim or the seductive whisperings of the advertisers, we face many further decisions.

Will something else serve the same purpose, possibly something I already own?

Can I use a different method to accomplish the same task?

Do I understand the device, or do I have a friend who can explain the advantages or disadvantages?

Is it well made and made to last?

Can faults be readily diagnosed?

Can it be repaired and will spare parts be available?

Does it have extra features that may be unnecessary, yet add to the number of things that could go wrong?

Could it atrophy some of my skills?

When these questions have been answered, we are ready to turn to a whole new area of considerations.

2. Can I buy it second-hand?

As a working product designer I must point out that the producers *really* 'don't make things the way they used to any more'. There are shops run by charity organizations such as the Salvation Army, Goodwill Industries, Oxfam, the Society for Crippled Civilians, and so forth, in most large towns in North America and Europe. Frequently many of the things they sell are in fact brand new. In many towns in the United States, for example, graduating students, leaving their flats and houses for good at the end of the academic year, frequently abandon new clothing, small appliances, furniture and books. At one university after the students had left, building services found more than a thousand shirts, scores of dresses and suits, as well as enough cosmetics to satisfy a small town, all still in the original wrappings.

During the greed-driven 1980s, shops dealing with photographic equipment virtually stopped advertising used cameras, but every dealer still sells older equipment, and so do pawn shops. In many cases these goods have barely been used before their wilful owner trades them up for the 'brand-new latest' whatever. Most of the slides I use for my professional work are taken with a Leica that was first used by my father in the mid-1930s; it is now nearly sixty years old, but works as well as ever. Admittedly the film has to be advanced manually, there is no automatic focus, and exposure has to be determined by experience or with a separate meter, yet these conveniences were also missing from the cameras of similar vintage that were used by Cartier-Bresson, Weston, Atget, Stieglitz and scores of other famous photographic artists and journalists of the past. Most communities issue a weekly *Shopping News* which advertise for sale almost all conceivable second-hand goods; there are swap-meets where often no money changes hands; and – at least in the United States and the UK – the ubiquitous garage, estate, backyard, car-boot or moving sales, through which people are desperately trying to rid themselves of the accumulation of fancied former wants.

3. Can I buy it at discount?

There may of course be an item that you really do have to buy and where a fairly new technology is involved. If the technology is electronic and therefore difficult to examine for malfunctions – a CD-player, for instance – then it is always possible to buy a leftover of the previous year or a discontinued model through a discount shop. Many technical devices can also be obtained factory-reconditioned from dealers, often with a warranty. These are the high-tech equivalents of 'factory seconds' of crockery, cookware or cutlery that bear faint imperfections in finish or colour, or discontinued or overstocked styles. These and so-called 'remaindered' books can all usually be bought at shops that specialize in such goods.

4. Can I borrow it?

If the object you need will only be used infrequently, or just once or twice, can it be borrowed? Personal experience has shown me that most people are only too pleased to be asked to help share their expertise and some specialized tool or apparatus that they own. Most of my neighbours in Lawrence have furnished their basements with a lavish collection of small electric drills, orbital sanders, circular saws, shapers and band saws, as well as an abundance of hand tools. Most of these tools are only needed for small repairs around the house, and their proud owners are happy to lend them out and see them used.

5. Can I rent it?

Renting is one step further from outright ownership. We routinely rent certain things when buying them would pose inconveniences quite apart from the cash spent on them. On a business trip we rent a car at the airport to get to our final destination. We use the local library to catch up on our reading and listening. Whilst on holiday we frequently rent a video camera, or a moped or a bicycle to get around, or a tent, beach umbrella and deckchairs. In most towns there are shops devoted to hiring out equipment for working on the car, building a garage or sundeck, or for gardening. Some places specialize in renting out furniture and major electrical appliances to students or other temporary residents; some shops rent drinking glasses, cutlery and table settings for parties and receptions.

6. Can I lease it?

Leasing is essentially a long-term rental on contract. In many countries telephones are leased rather than owned – maintenance, repair, insurance and replacement are then no longer the individual's concern. Cars are leased by companies and, increasingly, by individual owners who recognize that in their real world they never really *own* their car at all since they tend to trade it in for a new model just after – or slightly before – making the last of their sixty monthly payments.

With the ever more rapid technological changes in personal computers, and the obsolescence of entire hardware systems within years rather than decades, it is obvious that leasing a home-computer is a better idea than buying.

7. Can I share it?

In the book *How Things Don't Work* (1977)[2], written with a close friend and colleague, the designer and teacher Jim Hennessey, we explored the concept of sharing rather than owning certain products, based on our experiences of living in California, England and Ottawa. The concept is a fairly simple one. In that earlier book we used lawnmowers as examples, and I shall repeat some of the argument here.

But first I would like to take a closer look at the phenomena of lawns. In the United States alone there are between fifty-five and sixty million home lawns, covering thirty million acres. Of all the states, New Jersey is the most densely populated, but *nearly one-fifth of the entire land area is covered with turf grass, twice as much land as that used for growing crops.* Turf grass is also used for public parks, median strips on motorways and golf courses, yet most of it is planted for purely decorative, symbolic front lawns. It has been estimated that if the average home lawn were to be used for growing fruit and vegetables, the crop would be worth about two thousand dollars. In other words, decorative grass is grown instead of approximately a hundred and twenty million dollars worth of fruit and vegetables that could easily nourish the population of several countries.

The average American family spends approximately eight hundred dollars a year on equipment, fertilizer, and so forth, to keep its lawns extremely short and looking healthy and green. Besides the barrenness of these lawns as far as nourishment is concerned and the sheer financial waste of approximately five hundred and forty thousand million dollars annually, there is also an incredible waste of energy and water, and high levels of toxic pollution from the fertilizers and insect repellents leaching into the ground.

There may be an unconscious longing satisfied by lawns. Anthropologists agree that humanity has spent much of its existence roaming the grassy landscape of East Africa. Dr John Falk, who works with the educational research division of the Smithsonian Institution, is convinced that humans have a genetically encoded preference for savannah-like terrain: 'For more than 90% of human history the savannah was home. Home equals safety, and that information has to be fairly hard-wired if the animal is going to respond to danger instantaneously.'[3]

Dr Falk carried out researches with the psychologist John Balling to find out the terrain preferences of people all over the world. From photographs of six different types of landscape, the savannah was overwhelmingly the choice, even with people who had never seen a savannah. It was found that children under twelve, including those who knew only deserts or rocky mountains, were even more emphatic in selecting savannah, another clue that this preference is genetic.

It is plain, however, that the North American obsession with the perfect yet useless front lawn which conforms to some ideal of the 1950s, is neither aesthetically satisfying nor worth the time and money spent on it. There is no need for these excesses of conspicuous pollution; there is a wide choice of native groundcover available that needs little care or weeding, less water and – being local in character – thrives in an area where 'imported' flora require an enormous amount of special care. During the Middle Ages, weeds were considered beautiful; in Japan carefully tended moss gardens are the highest form of landscape aesthetics. Those who still feel that lawns fill them with pride might consider using goats as lawn-trimmers, or go all the way and investigate Permaculture.[4]

To return to the lawnmower: there are 168 hours in a week; even during the lushest summer months, the average lawn needs cutting just once a week. This

The powered riding mower is replacing the manual lawnmower, yet is in use for perhaps only 1% of the year, making it a strong candidate for shared ownership.

can usually be done within one or two hours. This means that the lawnmower is *not* in use for approximately 166 hours per week *during the summer months alone!* When averaged out over a year, taking into account the months when snow covers the lawn, this appliance is in actual working use for between 60 to 100 hours annually, lying idle for about 99% of the year! Yet manually powered mowers are now almost a thing of the past; even electric or petrol-powered mowers arc giving way to enormous riding mowers that pollute the ground with their leaks and drips, the air with petrol fumes and the neighbourhood with noise. The fact that the latest models masticate small twigs and branches as well as the newly cut grass for mulching only provides a respectably 'Green' face for a basically unsavoury tool. It is amusing to watch one of my neighbours, exercising for half an hour on an electrically powered treadmill and then mounting the tractor-like riding mower. An old-fashioned push-mower would provide healthier exercise at less cost in equipment, fuel, pollution or upkeep.

One only has to look at all the things we own and under-use to realize that lawnmowers are fairly typical examples rather than exceptions. As if to celebrate each season with an appropriate piece of gas-guzzling equipment, North Americans and increasingly the Japanese and Europeans have found ingenious applications for backyard high-tech. The falling autumn leaves call for the use of a leaf-blower. This gadget, usually electrically powered, comes in two different

*This vacuum cleaner sucks up garden rubbish, some of which could be used for compost.
It is an appliance that even the tidiest gardener will need only occasionally during the year.*

versions. One sucks up the fallen leaves, collecting them in a series of plastic bags. Most of my neighbours put out twenty or thirty of these bags; instead of the contents being recycled as compost, they are collected by the trash service and eventually become landfill. The other version, which looks like the rape of a bagpipe by a vacuum cleaner, hangs from a shoulder-strap and maliciously blows the dead leaves into the street or the adjoining garden. It is clear that for the average garden the yearly usefulness of this device must be exhausted after an hour and a half at most.

When the days become shorter and temperatures begin to fall, it is time to dust off the snow-blower which – like the lawnmowers – comes both in a riding or self-powered version. Snowfall in Canada and the Northeast and Midwest of the United States can be heavy, and shovelling out a driveway at temperatures below freezing and in a stiff breeze can be dangerous and cause heart attacks. Certainly of the seasonal tools mentioned so far, snow-blowers are the most useful and – depending on location and the severity of the winter – will see the heaviest usage. Yet even in Ottawa in Canada, during the winter of 1975 to 1976 which was remarkable for its many heavy snows, these gadgets were in use for less than six hours a week, and frequently had to give way to commercial snowploughs. From mid-October to the end of April, the snow-blower was used for a grand total of less than 160 hours and was consequently unused for about 8500 hours that year!

During late spring, electric edge-trimmers, 'weed-eaters' and gasoline-powered pesticide-sprayers greet the return of the lawnmowers, while the family considers having an automatic, in-ground water-sprinkling system installed that is governed by soil-moisture sensors, phototropic measuring devices and heat-detectors.

What is the point of all this? I am convinced that this under-use is also true of radios, slide-projectors, irons and almost everything we own. The manufacture of these items constitutes a waste of precious – frequently irreplaceable – raw materials, and wastes energy and pollutes. I suggest that some of them (the necessary tools, that is) could and ought to be shared by neighbours or within communities. Yet saying so doesn't magically make it come true. Most appliances and other tools are flashily designed and flimsily finished – all of us are aware that it is a rare tool that outlives its own warranty period, *even with only one person using it and caring for it.* If we wish to share some of these labour-saving tools, this will call for new design for sustained use by several people and will, most probably, lead to a new design aesthetic – functionally and ecologically based and long overdue.

There are a large number of gadgets that we are forced to buy if we wish to use them, that it would make more sense to own as a community or group. There are vacuum cleaners for a start. I have repeated my *ad hoc* survey of 1977[5] of my neighbourhood in Lawrence, Kansas, and discovered that things haven't changed. The street where I live consists of 23 rather small single-family homes.

Survey of vacuum cleaners in one neighbourhood
28 regular cleaners
6 'shop-vacs' in basement workshops
15 rechargeable mini-cleaners for car interiors and minor spills
1 sub-miniature cleaner for my professional equipment

We arrive at an astounding total of 50 cleaners for 23 households! Considering frequency of actual use, there is no question that these appliances could be shared. Assuming cleaners that are well designed for several different functions, made to last and then eventually to be taken apart and recycled, one can envisage a sort of community library where such items could be borrowed. Simple calculations convince me that six cleaners and one shop-vac could easily handle all the needs of the neighbourhood, a net saving of more than 80% of the units now in use.

Assume then the existence of a neighbourhood or community centre. Here one could share not only vacuum cleaners, lawnmowers, snow-blowers and snowploughs, but other items that could be communally owned. There might be sewing machines; computers and computer printers; a large area of wall-mounted lockers, each of which is one household's bulk frozen-food storage. There could also be workshop and gardening tools – possibly even a small crafts workshop – and it might also be feasible to share cameras, camcorders, slide projectors and even bicycles, shopping carts and some types of sports equipment. Such a 'Sharing Library' could also stock goods that folk in the neighbourhood

In the Netherlands the white bicycle scheme encouraged sharing instead of buying, and a free, healthy and unpolluting means of transport. The bikes could be borrowed by anyone who needed them.

have discarded as no longer suited to their needs, or left behind when moving away – a sort of revival of the 'free stores' of the hippies in the late 1960s. There is no question that this place would also serve as the local recycling centre.

'If you design a neighbourhood playground, don't forget the washing machines!' This is a motto that also comes from *How Things Don't Work.*[6] A beautiful playground, designed and built by my students in collaboration with the parents and children of a low-income area in the American Midwest, had one drawback: the children did not play in it. We discovered that many of the mothers were reluctant to let their children go there unsupervised. A neighbour with a bulldozer created an artificial central mound on which we built a sort of greenhouse, equipped with four second-hand washing-machines and a dryer, all funded by a neighbourhood party, and the problem was solved. Mothers gathered there to do their washing and watch over the children.

> From here on the playground was in constant use, serving the neighbourhood in several socially valuable ways. The greenhouse became a natural centre where the mothers would gather, exchange community gossip, do their laundry, and at the same time be able to supervise their children at play. There were two further positive spin-offs: a neighbourhood bulletin board soon made its appearance in the green-house-laundry, listing things to be swapped, shared rides needed to another town, services, baby-sitters and things for sale. The use of a nearby commercial laundromat (demanding exorbitant prices from this captive audience of slum dwellers), declined until it was finally forced out of business.

Revisiting the area twenty years later, I was delighted that it still existed and had become a focal point for other activities. There were notices for conversational English classes (all this had been located in a Hispanic-American area), announcements of a free clinic offering X-rays and children's immunization programmes, a number of bins for recycling, and the nucleus of a free clothing exchange. The greenhouse gossip group had turned itself into an active women's gathering that explored issues of feminine status and identity, problems of child-bearing and breast cancer, and even invited occasional guest speakers from similar communities.

8. Can we own it as a group?

Sharing to cut down on waste, to make things more affordable or just to reduce the amount of raw materials locked up in goods can operate on many different levels. One of my passions has been flying gliders and sailplanes. I have rarely met a glider pilot who owned his own rig, whether in Elmira in New York, in England or at Narrowmine in Australia. Gliders are just too expensive and are not flown often enough by an individual for personal ownership to make sense. Flyers therefore tend to form syndicates in which each member pays in a share, a fraction of the total cost, to become a co-owner. The group shares both flying hours and the cost of maintenance.

I was favourably impressed to notice that in Denmark designers and architects often share subscriptions to expensive international professional magazines. A copy of, say, *Domus* or *Bau-Biologie* will have a list of ten or twelve participating members of the reading circle clipped to it, and it is forwarded in turn to each on the list, finally ending up in the local library for the public at large. Clearly this

Children didn't play in the new playground until washing-machines were installed. Parents and children then all spent time there, and it became an important focus for the community.

not only reduces subscription costs for each individual by nine-tenths or more, but – which is even more important – it cuts down on the wastefulness of paper and printing inks as well as transport. Many people in the Scandinavian countries subscribe to ordinary consumer magazines in the same way.

It is obvious that these two examples could serve as templates for sharing in many other fields. There are small but costly diagnostic instruments coming into use that, because of their limited yet important use, can only be sensibly acquired through co-operative small groups. These would include air-quality monitors (to be used in a small area with feedback to a central authority), decibel meters to assess ambient noise levels, radon and radiation meters, as well as devices that measure rays emitted from microwave cookers, television sets, computer terminals, high voltage transmission lines, transformers and much else.

9. Can I build it myself?

The so-called average person, anywhere in the world, is better informed and more aware of his or her needs than any designer or architect. It is therefore plain that the design needs of most people can best be served by the users themselves working in close collaboration with a designer. The next step is to suggest that people should be empowered to design their own solutions to their own specific requirements.

These observations are not in any way startlingly new, but draw on precedent. Vernacular architecture is not only usually self-built, but also self-designed. Throughout many centuries end-users would work directly with a local builder or craftsman to add rooms to a house, have a desk made, build a carriage or have a cool-space dug for food storage. Yet these remarks are not intended to suggest a regression towards a Luddite attack on the machine age and our Post-Modern existence. The emphasis is rather that the close relationship between using and making, being and becoming, needs to be strengthened once again. Even today large groups take pleasure in re-inventing, changing, modifying and building their own tools and environments. I base this in part on the surprising interest shown both in North America and Italy for two earlier books written in collaboration with James Hennessey – *Nomadic Furniture* (1973) and *Nomadic Furniture 2* (1974)[7] – and, more tellingly, the photographs and letters sent to me from Germany, Croatia, Italy and the United States, describing self-built furniture.

10. Can I buy a kit?

With this in mind, I would like to turn to an additional group of options. On the most basic level, we are all becoming used to the fact that many of the goods we buy now come to us in somewhat unfinished form. Mail-order catalogues frequently carry the phrase 'Some self-assembly required' in small print at the bottom of the page. We realize that the wine-rack or bookshelf we buy will be delivered as a flat package. The bicycle we buy for our child, even the pram for the baby, will not arrive ready for use. The reason for making the users into – frequently unwilling – participants in completing the construction lies in the savings the manufacturer makes in shipping charges. Generally the costs reflect bulk more than weight. There is of course a small additional profit for the manufacturer in having the final bits sorted out by the customer.

This new assumption on the part of manufacturers, that people will finish the assembly of a product themselves, has beneficial side-effects. When building things from a kit, there is a good learning experience for the customer. It becomes simpler to understand how and why the gadget works.

More importantly to my mind, the design of objects that must be completed by the customer is beginning to influence how goods look. If self-assembly were to be combined with Design for Disassembly, the aesthetic results would be radical and fresh. How such a new aesthetic would emerge is discussed in Chapter 12.

THREE FURTHER QUESTIONS

Having considered all these possibilities, we must now ask the vital questions:

   1. *Will it harm the environment?*
   2. *Does it use composite materials?*
   3. *Does it waste energy?*

These are all issues that have to do with a tool or device operating at optimum efficiency at the edge of survival, or at least to its maximum potential. Some things that embody ideal form in our society are precisely those objects that also need to perform superbly under marginal conditions.

Competition sports equipment, professional cooking tools, premium gardening equipment, rock-climbing and sailing gear, fishing-tackle and hunting weapons, high-altitude expedition tents – all these possess great beauty because in these fields the appropriateness of form for function is of high importance. It will be noticed that changes in appearance occur infrequently in most of these goods, and they are usually due only to the introduction of new materials, tools or processes. The introduction of carbon-fibre plastics, for instance, has changed the configuration of glider wings, hunting bows and tennis rackets.

When I first began flying gliders in the late 1950s, most gliders, including those for high-altitude competitions or aerobatics, had been built by their owners and this frequently led to new and experimental wing configurations. Since the 1960s a number of firms in Florida and southern California have sold replicas of classic sports cars (the Mercedes SS-100 of 1938, the 1954 MG-TD, for example), in kits from which enthusiasts can then assemble the bodies, do their own upholstery,

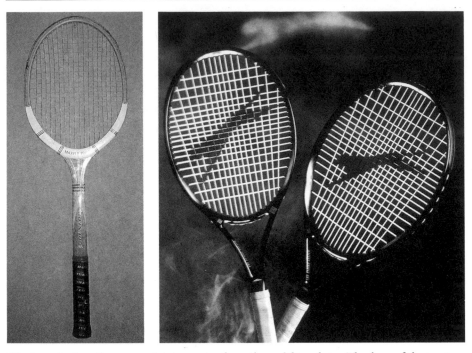

The introduction of new materials is a major factor in modifying design. The shape of the tennis rackets made from carbon-fibre plastics (right) is radically different from the old wooden racket.

and use an existing chassis and engine, to finish up with the wiring cradle, the 'plumbing' and painting the bodywork.[8]

Compare the care and quality control an individual can exert in building his or her own car, with its mass-produced equivalent. If you were to put together an automobile from a kit, quite apart from whatever hands-on experience you might bring to the work, the end-product would be of higher craftsmanship, quality and therefore safety than some production car built by assembly-line workers who hate their meaningless and repetitious small tasks and the end-product itself. The so-called 'Monday' or 'Friday' cars could reflect weekend hangovers, end-of-the-week doldrums and social anomie. Through the influence of the Korean and Japanese automobile industry, more robots are used in car production that ever before. This has had the unfortunate side-effect of increasing worker hostility leading to small acts of sabotage, such as welding small steel pockets containing loose bolts into obscure places in the car, ensuring permanent rattles and consequent customer dissatisfaction.

If cars were available in the form of build-it-yourself kits, four distinct advantages would follow, as with so many other things made in this way:

1. The owner-builder would develop an understanding of how the thing works, making trouble-shooting, repair and replacement of parts easier.

2. In cases of damage from collisions or wear extra replacement parts would be readily available and could be easily fitted.

3. Extra parts would be low in price. At present all the parts that make up a car if bought separately cost up to four times as much as the fully assembled automobile.

4. Building from kits would enable people to improvise, conceive alternative solutions and become both more inventive and creative in fitting the car to their own needs rather than the other way around, even substituting alternative or hybrid power plants.

I hold no special brief for automobiles – my convictions lie in the opposite direction. Yet the idea of anyone being able to build their own car has a certain dramatic appeal in a society hung up on cars. Nearly all 'ultra-light' aeroplanes come as kits and are user-built. They tend to be extremely carefully put together for the same reason that flyers prefer to pack their own parachutes – it's safer.

Some of the really exacting top-of-the-line devices we use are frequently only available in kit-form, or are preferred that way by fastidious users. The relatively small market for harpsichords, claviers and pianofortes is virtually dominated by precision kits made by Dolmetsch, Frank Hubbard and a few others. The reasons for this lie in climatic changes and acoustic function. An upright or grand piano requires tuning only every year or two. Concert grand pianos by Bösendorfer or

Build-it-yourself kits, like this car kit from Denmark, will demand a different approach to design, and will also increase end-users' understanding of how their machines and appliances work.

Bechstein are so delicate that, as they are moved from city to city with the performing artist, re-tuning is needed before each performance.

Harpsichords with their all-wood construction are even more sensitive to changes in humidity and should ideally be tuned before every use and also 'voiced' from time to time. Yet it is impossible to tune a harpsichord (or voice it) unless its workings are clearly understood. Therefore the knowledge brought about through the building process is the necessary prelude to being able to play it. Since building a harpsichord is profoundly labour-intensive, there are sizeable savings in building one yourself. In addition, the instructions and building manuals have been written with an knowledgeable audience in mind and are therefore forgiving enough to permit the builder to alter the acoustics by experimenting with the form of the sound chamber, and to explore the use of different woods. Lately many musical instruments, such as Southern Appalachian mountain dulcimers, flamenco guitars, harps, lutes and violas, have been added to the list that gives the owner a choice between self-building or buying ready-made.

Until the early 1980s, when Japan, Taiwan and Hong Kong began to dominate consumer electronics, exporting low-cost products and accelerating the trend towards extreme micro-miniaturization and microchip techniques, an American firm called Heathkit sold many advanced electronic devices for kit-builders:

Musical instruments, like this harpsichord, are increasingly available in kit-form – much cheaper than buying ready made.

sophisticated, large-screen, colour television sets; amplifiers; short-wave radios; radar fish-spotting gear. There are still hundreds of firms catering for those who wish to learn and understand by making things themselves. Some of the finest optical and radio telescopes available to individuals come in kits, frequently even the most critical aspect – lens-grinding – is left to the enthusiasts.

POSSIBLE ANSWERS

Before closing this chapter, I should like to sort out what may be possible right now, and how all this may play itself out in the future. It is certainly possible to make intelligent choices as to whether to buy or not to buy. Swapping, bartering and borrowing things probably preceded commercial trading by thousands of years. Similarly people have bought used merchandise for generations – it is only recently that it has become almost respectable once more.

Renting and leasing are also tried and true ways of having access to goods, although many people rarely consider them as alternatives to outright ownership. The apparent novelty of leasing may be the reason why recent advertisements for leasing cars in the USA suggest this as a clever way to avoid paying some taxes.

The concept of a small group of users sharing some expensive consumer durables has been pioneered in Europe by the co-housing movement in Denmark and Sweden, and subsequently by some communes in the United States and Canada under the slogan 'have more, own less'. It is also no new and startling idea to make something for oneself, self-designed or from plans, or assembled from a manufacturer's kit. Entire homes were cobbled together from parts such as bay windows, towers, entryways, and so forth, featured in Victorian builders' hand-books and catalogues. Both conserving resources through sharing, and building or assembling things from kits, were strongly advocated by Jim Hennessey and myself in the book cited earlier, *How Things Don't Work*.[9]

What is new is the emergence of take-apart technology, also known as Design for Disassembly, which should make some of these suggestions for alternative styles of use easier to put into practice. It will also bring about a profound change in design and consequently in the way things work and look. Creating things from kits makes sense and offers a whole new option, and the coming of take-apart technology will make this easier and more logical.

Some words of caution are needed at this point. Not everyone is interested, willing or able to build things. Using one's hands constructively is a basic human need, yet people working all day on assembly lines might groan at the idea of spending a number of weekends assembling a motorcycle, or two nights making a camcorder. Others may feel themselves too cack-handed to make much sense out of a box of parts and a manual of building instructions. Yet this doesn't invalidate the basic concept. Someone could buy a kit for building a tool-shed, drafting-table or library steps, and then might commission someone else to do the actual work or to help with the building process. It would help to decentralize production, lead to a broader and greater understanding of how things work, and usher in all manner of innovations and customized one-off productions. On an important human level, such procedures will also provide strong and satisfying feelings of participation for the user-makers which – from my design experience in several developing countries – leads to self-esteem and and makes the user not only more knowledgeable about the appliance, but also more critical about what is necessary and what is superficial.

Finally I should mention that in 'building a case' for this approach, I have chosen everyday consumer products that are familiar to most people. This is in no way meant to endorse the continuing use of these appliances in the future in their present form. The products that make sense environmentally and ecologically are explored in other chapters.

CHAPTER 10

Generations to Come

*The creation of something new is not accomplished by the intellect
alone, but by the play instinct, from inner necessity. The creative
mind plays with the object it loves.*
Carl Jung

*Education must begin with the solution of the teacher-student
contradiction, by reconciling the poles of the contradiction so that
both are simultaneously teachers and students.*
Paulo Freire

WE FACE ANOTHER *fin-de-siècle* or, as I prefer to think of it, we stand at the
cusp of the 21st century. Young people starting to study design or architecture in 1995 will begin to exercise decision-making powers in these professions by
the year 2012. Children born as this is being written will come into their own as
users and workers, and the question of how to educate designers and architects is
becoming ever more important and urgent. More crucial, how do we educate the
end-users of these public arts, those who will work with the tools and objects that
are available, live and work in the dwellings and spaces? The importance of this
question is made even more vital by the ecological and environmental context of
all our diverse futures. To mediate the increasing dissonance between a robust high
technology and a fragile milieu, new disciplines and new methods are brought into
the process of design and must also be included in the education of designers.

DRAWING FROM DIFFERENT DISCIPLINES
As discussed in Chapter 3, we designers and architects are encouraged to think of
ourselves as artists, with the result that a good deal of design and architecture
seems to be created for the personal glory of its creator; the desire to 'shock the
bourgeoisie' (which is no longer shockable) still lingers, and the wish to be
different for the sake of difference. Some designers seek inspiration by trying to
see the future through a rear-view mirror. (In architecture specifically this used
to be called plagiarism, and was considered shabby and *declassé* – it is now
respectable and is called 'historicism'.) To a large extent these sources have
become exhausted and sterile. As I have said throughout this book, only a
multi-disciplinary approach can yield new insights, and the main thrust will come
from the natural sciences.

The research into the swimming behaviour of trout and pike made by Dr Heinrich Hertel in Germany during the 1930s resulted in significant improvements in ship design. Radar was invented from studying the way in which bats navigate, and *Tursiops truncatus* (the bottle-nosed dolphin) has provided a model for the development of sonar-location methods. Commercial aircraft now use a ground-speed recognition system in landing that was first discovered in a South American beetle. By studying crystallography I have found the ideal angle for a twelve-speaker cluster in high-fidelity reproduction. At present I am developing a highly reflective paint-like substance for making hazard signs clearly visible at night; it is based on the refractive characteristics of the colour nodules found on the wings of butterflies. With the increasing importance of avoiding the disruption of the biological web of life, an ecological view must be part of any multi-disciplinary team.

Such advisory groups should continuously study not only the introduction of new tools and materials but also what might be called the 'mythology and folklore of post-technological society'. To cite one example: in the study of Alzheimer's Disease, doctors have found small deposits of aluminum in the brains of victims. As far as can be determined at this time, Alzheimer's disease results from a genetic predisposition, and the use of aluminum cookware can now be dismissed as a triggering factor. There is, however, some evidence to suggest that aluminum used in cookery may have an adverse effect on the immune system.

Patients are increasingly required to take several different prescriptions which has led to the realization that the interaction between various drugs can be hazardous or fatal. It is safe to assume that the combination of paints, finishes and other chemicals might pose similar dangers, making it another important area of interdisciplinary investigation relevant to design.

Researches in chemistry, physics, anthropology and human ecology will frequently help to determine a saner approach to design, manufacture, marketing and distribution. Biology for instance can show us the way to make the object and package into one unit – in many cases saving materials and energy wasted on packaging. A link between science and aesthetics is demonstrated best by the fact that Watson and Crick chose the spiral for the model of the DNA chain since in the final analysis they judged it to be the most beautiful.

The study of ethics is of even greater importance to designers at a time when environmental and ecological responsibility are crucial, since any design decision involves an ethical dilemma. The world-wide ban on the use of ivory is a dilemma that has been resolved through a good linkage between design, botany and chemistry. Inuit and other indigenous carvers now can choose a 'vegetable ivory' in the form of a nut from Latin America that has characteristics similar to ivory, and a synthetic ivory has also recently come into use.

My first book bore the subtitle *Human Ecology and Social Change*. It would be inappropriate to repeat the arguments of 1969 here. What has changed is that we have more knowledge about the relationship of the goods we use and our environment, and realize some of the profound connections between community and social values on one hand and a sustainable environment on the other. We understand now how the holes in the ozone layer are caused. We realize that most of our increasing social pathology (serial killings, suicide, rape and other acts of aggression, drug addiction, anomie, and so forth), are directly linked to over-population, crowding and a loss of human scale, and that these in turn are hooked into the 20th-century marketing ideals that 'bigger is better' and 'newest is best'.

Much education in architecture and design is still based on the idea that as much 'good design' (whatever that means) as possible needs to be decanted into the students' heads within three, four or five years – not counting additional years spent in post-graduate studies.

Several questions need to be asked at the start of this chapter:

Is there some innate sense or senses that we share, and which we tap into for aesthetic satisfaction?

To which group should design education ideally address itself?

At what age should education, rather than narrow vocational training, for design begin?

Can design education be helpful to anyone apart from designers and architects?

THE SEARCH FOR GOOD FORM

I would like to turn first to the question of an underlying matrix of perception. In Chapter 4 we discussed such magic numbers as the Fibonacci series, the 'golden section' and 'divine proportion', as well as such concepts as the eidetic image. Now I draw the link between simplicity and our search for ideal, iconic forms.

Simplification leads to elegance. Simplification also implies common sense, a quality that seems to get rarer as the world becomes bureaucratized. Elegance as I use the word here means that a problem has been solved directly, unself-consciously, with minimal effort and in such a way that the object or product can be understood easily and is a good fit with its environment. Designers, architects, and planners seek order. They try to make sense out of chaos, to bring direction to what is not yet formed. This implies a *search for good form*, the basic pattern-seeking, pattern-generating need that lies at the base of all human thought and action. Some experiments may make this point more clearly.

The psychological mechanism at the base of our search for form is called *closure*. When presented with a diagram of three dots in space, or with three

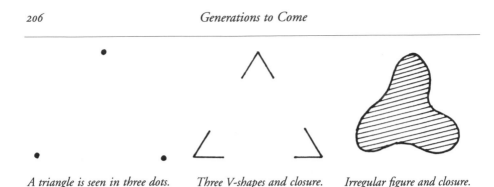

A triangle is seen in three dots.   *Three V-shapes and closure.*   *Irregular figure and closure.*

V-shaped figures, most people will establish closure between the three groups and manage to see a triangle. When presented with a senseless blob, most people will again pull this shape into a triangular form that 'makes sense'. This has been established by psychologists. The psychological mechanism has been called 'the search for good form'.

With this in mind, in 1970 I developed two experiments to prove to my students and myself that the search for good form is a reality for all of us. I have carried out this experiment twice a year ever since, testing between thirty and sixty subjects each time, which means that nearly 3000 students from eleven countries have participated in this experiment.[1]

The students were shown two simple designs. In the second drawing the figure is intentionally labelled A-B-M-D. After presenting the two designs to the group, the drawings were wiped off the board and each student was asked to draw both pictures, making no notes and handing in the results immediately. The students' drawings were then destroyed. A week later, the students were asked to produce the figures from memory, and to hand them in at once, whereupon the drawings were once again destroyed. This process was repeated once a week for fifteen weeks.

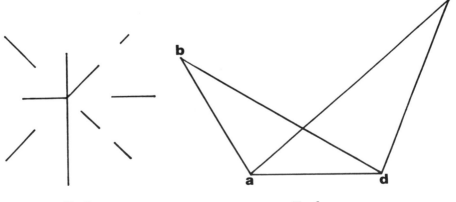

Test figure 1   *Test figure 2*

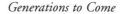

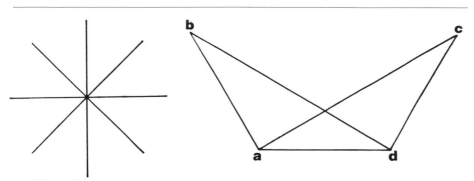

Test figure 1 becomes an asterisk.   *Changes to test figure 2 by 54% of the students.*

At the end of the fifteen-week period, 91% of the drawings of the first figure looked like a large asterisk. In 54% of the drawings of the second figure the design had been evened out and had been relabelled A-B-C-D, and in 41% the right leg had been even further exaggerated than in the original and had also been relabelled, this time A-B-X-D.

The basic drawing and thinking mechanisms are easy to explain. Tiny mistakes crept in week by week, caused by 'misremembering' the original design. These errors were cumulative and finally resulted in the drawings shown. It will be noted, however, that all the drawing mistakes, all the memory lapses and all the cumulative errors moved towards identical images in more than 90% of the cases.

What do the new figures have in common? The first design, the asterisk, is probably the only sensible form that can emerge from the scattered hen tracks

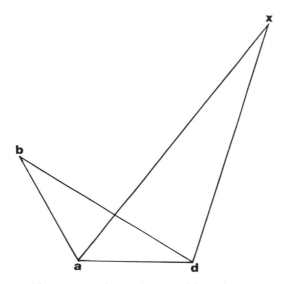

Changes to test figure 2 by 41% of the students.

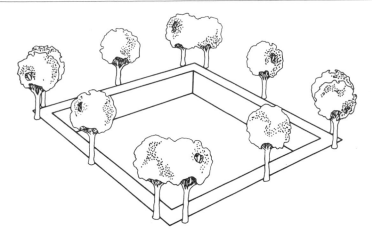

Perspective drawing of a square swimming pool and surrounding trees.

that formed the starting image. In the second original image, the intent of the designer is unclear. The design seems out of balance and the labelling is nonsense. In this case, more than half of the students have decided (on an unconscious level) to regularize the picture and relabel it the way it 'ought to be'.

Slightly less than half the students chose (again unconsciously) to remember the original visual imbalance, resulting in a wildly exaggerated right leg. Although they remembered that the odd leg was marked differently, they have chosen to relabel it X, because X stands for the unknown in most equations, and because M does not make sense mathematically or geometrically in the context. In all three cases, the participants have unknowingly pursued a search for good form, for something that makes sense, something that is easy to remember – an emblematic device.

This basic experiment comes to grips with perceptual factors in terms of Gestalt psychology and should influence designers' search for consistent form. Common sense must prevail when a design is planned.

The design profession is beset with professional jargon and working procedures that are confusing to the uninitiated. For example, assume that we are building a 30 foot square (9m square) swimming pool, edged with a 2 foot (0.7m) concrete walk. On each of the four sides, three poplars, about 12 feet (3.5m), are planted at precise intervals. To communicate the appearance of all this visually usually calls for a perspective sketch. But looking at the sketch we see that it does not provide any information about relative sizes, the position of the trees and other important details. Either this information must be dimensioned in separately or specifications must accompany the drawing. Many laypeople will not understand the drawing at all, and to some it may communicate chaos. Some people when shown the sketch said, 'But I thought all the trees were supposed to be the same height – the ones at the back look shorter,' or, 'Look – the trees are

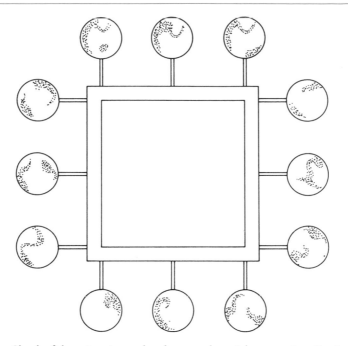

Sketch of the swimming pool and trees as they might appear in a Coptic drawing, that is without the conventions of drawn perspective.

growing into each other!' Some said with alarm, 'I thought the pool was square, not that funny rhomboid shape!'

It is easy to say that people do not understand because they do not know how to look at perspective drawings. Or that people are not used to seeing perspectives that show things the way they really are. Yet nothing could be further from the truth. The rendering shows the pool and the trees as they might look to a person in a helicopter, hovering 45 feet (14m) above ground, 50 feet (15m) from the front edge of the pool. Perspective is just one version of reality. It is an artistic convention and no more.

When the same pool and trees are shown as they might appear in a Coptic manuscript, everything is measurable. All the relationships are precise and to scale. The pool is the right size and shape, and the trees are equidistant and the right height. If you argue that the trees seem to be lying down, you are merely showing that you are accustomed to the conventions of perspective drawings.

Of course, designers and architects use a number of supplemental drawings – sections, details, call-outs, exploded views, and straight orthographic projections. But in the case of the swimming pool the modest Coptic drawing communicates everything, and is easiest to understand by those who are not accustomed to designer shorthand. This is not an argument for doing away with perspective but a plea for fitting the message to the audience.

One of the basic functions of good graphic design is to make words and images understandable. Graphic design students frequently fail to understand that the business cards that they design for themselves will largely be seen by people in their late forties to late fifties at an age when the accommodation range of the eye has been diminished. I have watched executives helplessly turning these 'well-designed' cards sideways and upside-down, desperately trying to read the print, which is too small and too fine.

The print on most charts, maps, technical literature, and packaging is frequently difficult to read for anyone with less than perfect vision. Remarkably, medicine labels usually show the name of the pharmaceutical company and drugstore in large bright letters, while the side-effects and cautionary warnings are in minuscule type. One item in my collection has yellow typeface on a white background, making the words virtually invisible.

Simplicity and common sense seem to be curiously absent in design. One of the tasks of architects and designers is to make things simple without making them simplistic. In an increasingly complex world, cluttered by enigmatic messages, perplexing tools, and cryptic objects, the designer's task is to unravel the Gordian knot of confusion and help express things clearly and simply.

DESIGN EDUCATION FOR ALL

The questions as to how design should be taught, to whom, and at what age such education should start, are all closely linked. Design can bring great benefit to education, not just with the education of designers, but with the education of everyone – specifically children from kindergarten and nursery school all the way through secondary education and beyond.

There are four distinct ways in which design can be beneficial in education. There is the traditional role which is to educate design students at universities, polytechnics and technical institutes. Then there is the education of young children and teenagers, a new and vital area. Thirdly, the physical structure of schools from both an architectural and environmental viewpoint is, and will continue to be, the proper concern of architects and environmental designers. School curricula and teaching methods can be greatly aided by systems design. Finally, there is educational software – seats, desks, tables, teaching aids, wall-charts, teaching machines and audiovisual materials – which is in desperate need of creative innovation and redesign.

In the final analysis, man shapes society and his future by what is taught to the young, how it is taught and why. Design education should be introduced into nursery, primary, and secondary schools instead of limiting it to vocational and occupational studies at a post-secondary level. It could easily take the place of the art eduction and art appreciation courses now being taught. Although many strides have already been made in this direction, primarily in places such as Britain and Scandinavia, this view will undoubtedly be criticized as philistine. But instead of viewing this as an attack on the arts, examine the positive results that can come from design education. Design is a conscious and intuitive effort to impose significant order. This need lies at the base of all meaningful art. In addition, it is one of the most basic human drives – both intellectual and emotional – to order, arrange, organize, and discipline a seemingly chaotic environment. This statement is based on thirty-five years of design experience and half a century of living experience. The search for good form clarifies a latent sense of harmony and order in most people. To bring order out of chaos is a deep-rooted desire in all people with a sane view of the world. Design is both the underlying matrix of order and the tool that creates it.

Enough polemics. There are examples and case-histories that will support this argument. Most generalizations can mislead. Nonetheless, if we compare different societies, it can be argued that expectations for elegant and simple design are most widely shared in Denmark and Finland. Having lived and worked in Scandinavian countries and elsewhere, I have come to the conclusion that the main difference lies in design education.

In Denmark, design education forms an important part of day-to-day lessons in kindergarten and nursery school. This is equally true in Finland. Compare the restrained and pure tile designs brought home by kindergarten children in Copenhagen to the mawkish puppets made of used orange-juice containers, tinsel, and mint-wrappers in England, or the Thanksgiving turkeys made of pie plates and cotton wool in the United States with the simple and austere cutting-boards made by children of the same age in Finland. What keeps these children's design products from looking sterile is the use of natural and organic materials – the earthy glazes or the woodgrain form their own decoration.

Little can justify the cultural phenomenon known as art education. The British and American students have taken rubbish, turned it into ornamental rubbish, and then been told that they have created art. Of course we need art. Painting, poetry, music, dance and sculpture give us great joy, and recent psychological studies have shown clearly that babies and small children exposed to music and painting, to bright colours and a well-modulated environment develop perceptual skills far more quickly than children who are not.

We are all involved in design. As end-users we are both consumers and victims of the environment, buildings, tools and artefacts that make up our world. If design is a conscious and intuitive effort to impose a meaningful order, then the how and why of this should be taught.

For many years I have felt that what is routinely taught as 'foundation design' and 'basic design' in Western Europe and North America is for the wrong people at the wrong time. These courses are generally taught at post-secondary design and architectural schools to young people between the ages of seventeen and twenty-one. The projects in these courses offer splendid opportunities for discovery and self-knowledge. Such basic exercises as supporting a standard brick 16 inches (40 cm) above a table top with the least number of toothpicks forming a tower; designing and making a spinning-top that will continue to spin for four or five minutes; arranging squares of textured material according to roughness and smoothness; packaging an uncooked egg in such a way that it can be dropped six feet without damage; making visual comparisons between boats and fish, birds and aircraft – these and many other basic design exercises are splendid nudges to the imagination. But they are wasted on eighteen-year old design students. The same exercises could be taught to six-year-olds, when basic design studies should begin. I have taught standard university-level design courses to six and seven-year-olds – the results have in many cases exceeded my expectations from university students.

Except for the biological exercises and biomorphic transformations, the examples just given have been used for decades in design education for young adults. Some were first initiated at the Bauhaus in Germany three-quarters of a century ago. But the world has changed since 1919, and so have the acquired cognitive skills of young children.

With the popular 'Transformer' toys of the mid-1980s, a child of four was able to change an aggressive cast-metal robot into a sleek sports car through a few simple turns. Could this same child, in playschool or nursery, gain some hands-on insight into biomorphic design and the link between nature and human-made by making the connection between a mechanical butterfly and an ornicopter? Assuming that such didactic fun-toys were to be designed and made, might not this eventually lead right back to 'grown-up' design? To a 'transformer bicycle' that accommodates a pregnant woman in her eighth month? To a 'transformer cooker' that can use different power sources, as well as 'kneeling' like an obedient camel for short-statured people, those in wheelchairs or the elderly?

And even these pseudo-bionic examples still beg the question of using present-day technology. Teaching in the American Midwest I frequently work with young university students who, at eighteen years of age, untravelled and 6000 miles away from Europe or Asia, find it difficult to break out of their mindset. I invented a design project that would force them to come to grips with the outside world. Selecting a postcard of a different city in the world for each student, I would arbitrarily pick a building and punch a hole through one of the windows. The student would then be asked, say, to discover in the shortest possible time if the people living in the flat kept a pet, and, if so, to find out its name. The student was also required to record how many links it took to communicate with the

A tank that can be transformed into a robot and back again with a few simple turns can teach a very young child the elements of versatile design for more useful purposes.

tenants. A few years ago it took about a week to ten days, and five to seven human links. Now students can do it in a few hours, usually with only three 'connectors'. The technology explored uses fax machines, modems and computers. Through the international student office, the student will usually be able to find someone at this university who comes from the place in question and can then 'solve' the problem through electronic means. It is great fun, good learning-content for culturally isolated students and has worked with ten-year-olds as well.

To get in touch with other aspects of late 20th-century technology, we rework the simple microchips used in talking greeting cards, or build simple wheeled toys that are phototropic (that is, they will follow a flashlight like a dog on a leash), and thermophobic (they avoid heaters, fireplaces and stoves) as they roll across the floor.

I mentioned the design for a spinning top that would continue turning for five minutes. Just to design and build it is a wonderful learning experience for young people or children. Since there are almost no reference materials available, it calls for invention, creativity, problem-solving behaviour. Yet even so, the young designer soon realizes that *a top that spins for five minutes is supremely boring* and won't hold the attention of a child. So the exercise changes: should it also play a song while spinning? Tell a story? Spin a series of 'virtual colour' discs (black and white) into startling colour or flicker displays? Become part of a game like skittles? Furthermore, the very technology changes the project. Although it is hard enough to make a top that rotates in a stable fashion for five minutes, one of my students from Vietnam used electro-magnets, a tube filled with quicksilver (fulminate of mercury) and various other devices to make a top that would spin for more than ten hours.

Examining what makes a teacup work, why a certain chair is uncomfortable, why one screwdriver raises blisters while another does not, what is good quality and what is not, why some cars are safe and comfortable while others are 'unsafe at any speed', what makes one room soothing and another distressing – all this can be explored in secondary schools. I was invited to an English secondary school at Bramhall in Cheshire to work with their twelve and thirteen-year-olds on a major design exercise – to look at a product, evaluate and criticize it, then design and build a better version. The children's solutions were amazingly apt, as good or better than those that might have been produced by students at a poly-technic or art college. One of the finest courses in industrial design in the world was taught to fifteen and sixteen-year-olds at a secondary school in Belgrade, in the former Yugoslavia; now very young students from Croatia do extremely well at a new school in Zagreb.

A stretcher that can be operated by one person, designed and made by Renson Seow Kian Hoch, a thirteen-year-old student at the Victoria School in Singapore.

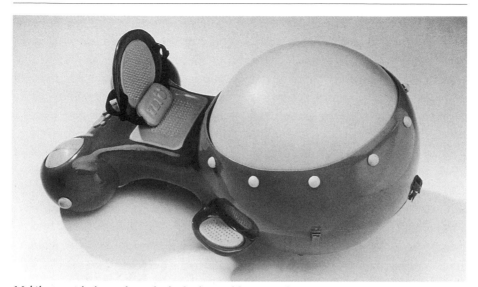

Mobile toy with three spherical wheels, designed by Pixie Tham Mei Lan, aged twenty, from Singapore. Its main objective is to improve the psychomotor skills of the disabled.

Applied product design is also taught at the Victoria School in Singapore to the equivalent of seventh-grade students. Renson Seow Kian Hoch, a student at the school, has imaginatively created a 'one-man stretcher' that can be operated by a single person. As he explains, it is designed to 'ensure speedy care and treatment as well as comfort for the injured, particularly on the way to hospital. It can be used in civil and military applications.' What makes the innovative nature of the design, the drawings, model-building skill and craftsmanship remarkable is that Renson Seow is only just thirteen years old.

Pixie Tham Mei Lam, also from Singapore, has designed the 'Trio-Mobile' toy for disabled children, and this is her description: 'This toy is designed to allow handicap children to exercise their hands and waist. Through play it helps to boost their confidence and develop psychomotor skills. It has three spherical wheels. Hanicap children move and steer the front wheel with their hands, arms and waist instead of pedalling.' The Trio-Mobile is brightly coloured and has a great appeal for children. It is an *inclusive* toy since it can be used by all children, whether disabled or not.

While teaching design to young men and women in Denmark, I was often worried at the thought of their entry into the profession during a deepening economic depression. Many of these young people ended up filling beer bottles or driving taxis around Copenhagen, but it was amazing how their design training helped them while they carried out these temporary jobs. For one thing, it raised their public conscience, and, for another, it increased their insistence on quality. Because they had been taught to evaluate, they did not unquestioningly accept work procedures. At the brewery, for instance, a student pointed out to the management that they did not need to wear uncomfortable earphones; the machines could be soundproofed instead. The students' design education also meant that they took greater care in choosing their homes, in buying things to furnish them and in selecting the tools they used. They noticed and commented on the quality of public spaces, street furniture, and anything else that increased the sense of a cohesive community.

I have no idea why we think of design or architecture as strictly vocational study areas. The training that is called the 'studio system', consisting as it does of hands-on performance, verbal and non-verbal communication, critiques, and self-criticism, is a superb preparation for almost any area of human endeavour.

Frank Lloyd Wright was once asked by a reporter which of his students he considered to have been most successful. Mr Wright, who had trained young architects in his studios for about forty years, thought about it briefly and then said, 'Why that's easy: Wes Peters; he's the best damn dairy farmer in the state of Wisconsin!'.

On any given Saturday morning in America, millions of children spend an hour or two learning ballet. No one ever worries over the fact that out of these millions, only about four hundred will ever support themselves through modern dance or ballet. The payoff is in fun; training mind, body and eye; *and in creating a stable and informed audience for dance.* This sort of cultural growth is also created through the study of design and architecture, and always has been.

WORLD INFORMATION NETWORK
One critical issue is the nearly total lack of horizontal crossover of information on a world-wide basis. There is a vital need for an information network that will encourage success, and prevent obvious mistakes from being repeated. This is of particular importance in developing countries, who may repeat the same mistakes that we have made in the technologically overdeveloped world. There is no simple answer to this dilemma. We are neatly caught between our own wasteful habits and the temptation to patronize the Third World by preaching discipline and modest habits which we ourselves have never followed. The developing world is frequently eager to share all the 'goodies' that they have seen in our films and on television. It is their right to follow in our footsteps, and we have no business asking them to follow a different path. Yet there are signs of hope.

The Industrial Revolution devastated the countryside of Britain. In the USA we repeated most of these mistakes in strip-mining and cutting down primal forests – yet we learned from the British example and our ravages of nature did not last nearly as long. The Scandinavian countries did even less harm, since they were in a position to learn from many earlier mistakes in America, Britain and south-western Europe. The Eastern bloc countries, however, especially Bulgaria,

Romania, Slovakia and the Czech Republic, were unable to learn these lessons under an arrogant leadership that differed from their capitalist counterparts in the West only in having substituted 'production quotas' for profit and greed. Right now many Western countries are exporting their dirtiest manufacturing processes to the developing world.

The bright spot lies in the fact that a number of recent treaties – such as NAFTA in 1994 (the North American Free Trade Act that binds Mexico, Canada and the United States together) – tie manufacturing performance to strict environmental laws. Furthermore, many so-called developing countries have shown a profound preoccupation with keeping their environment clean and safe – Papua New Guinea and Nigeria are examples. To some degree, this is based on the experiences of their own young people who study in the industrialized world and learn about social responsibility and environmental care along with their regular subjects. There are also frequently cultural, spiritual and religious reasons for a much deeper link to nature, that makes stewardship of the land an important part of life. One thinks of the powerful unity between humans, animals, plants, landscape and climate among native Americans and Inuit; the reverence for the land among the Ainu on Hokkaido – later translated into aspects of Zen – and *feng shui* in China; the love for Amazonia among indigenous peoples of Brazil; or the spiritual joy and awe that binds Haida, Kwakiutl, Tsimshian, Tlingit and Bella Coola to the Canadian rainforests.

Many developing countries may go through the same stages of pollution that we have, but they will leapfrog some of our worst mistakes, and the time spent on this phase of industrialization should be much shorter. Cleaner technologies are coming into use, and several countries, such as Japan, Sweden and Germany, are busy exporting environmental cleaning and scrubbing devices along with technologies and consumer goods.

A word of caution needs to be added. As designers we must be conscious of the whole mix that goes into the making and the real world consequences of the things we design. At the same time our talent lies in design rather than political action. Although designers are frequently activists, anxious to intervene in human and social ecology, we are really at our best if we intervene through design. The creep of dirty factories and polluted workplaces from the rich and powerful countries to the poor is a systemic political failure that cannot be solved through design alone but will need political remedies.

THE QUALITY OF LEARNING

The physical structure of schools, classroom environments, and the conceptual structuring of schools are all important issues. They are being explored by architects, environmental designers and systems designers in many parts of the world.

It is vital that there should be more direct feedback from users – schoolchildren, teachers and administrators.

Children are naturally active. If they are to be kept in classrooms for many hours a day with limited exercise periods, the classrooms should at least be visually exciting to compete with discos, amusement parks, video arcades and other stimulating public spaces. If their home environment is unstimulating, the classroom may also be the most exciting place the child visits all day. Dull classrooms represent a kind of sensory deprivation not conducive to learning.

Finally, there is the software used in schools. A few examples from recent practice will demonstrate how and where design can have its greatest impact in this area. In 1981, one of my classes was asked to consider the problems of educating young children. The ensuing discussions lasted for several weeks. To re-establish some link with the real world, the students were asked to visit schools, talk to teachers, and interview and play with schoolchildren. The students were shocked by what they learned. With only a few exceptions, the teachers they encountered could be divided into two groups – the old and tired who had long since given up, and the young and tired who were just on the point of giving up. Both groups seemed bereft of new ideas and were unwilling to give new approaches a chance. The schoolchildren considered going to school an unpleasant chore.

I repeated this project twelve years later, in 1993. Little had changed, except that more computers were available to the children and most of their younger teachers were computer-literate. This makes studying more fun. Whether it makes it more worthwhile remains to be seen. We have to look further than the propaganda of hardware and software manufacturers and industry's obvious need for computer operators; there are also some disturbing medical and psychological assessments and the findings by Jerry Mander.[2]

In 1981, as in the 1990s, there were many educational toys, teaching machines, and language-learning laboratories that did a superb job, but other teaching aids had become highly commercialized. Classroom teachers and administrators had a difficult choice selecting from catalogues bursting with meaningless puzzles, silly mathematical quizzes and trashy plastic learning-toys trivializing the act of learning. A typical catalogue was twice the size of the Manhattan telephone book and all the items listed were extraordinarily expensive.

Meeting and playing with children and spending all night in discussion with those teachers who still dared to care, we realized that it was possible to design simple things on a small scale that would improve the quality of learning and participation on many levels. The design group found no panacea that would radically change the structure of schools. That change must (and will inevitably) come directly from children, parents and committed classroom teachers. Instead, a few small gadgets were presented.

'Floppy Math' introduces children to many mathematical concepts, and the game is simple and cheap to make.

Many children dread mathematics. Mathematical concepts are often difficult for children to grasp. Lectures and demonstrations can be boring and textbooks are either remote or make dismal attempts at humour. The introduction of computers has brought about new teaching methods and has transformed mathematics and geometry into a challenge for many more children, but computers cost money.

One of my students designed a combination toy and game for learning mathematics by the sense of touch through the fingertips. The Chinese saying, 'I look and I see; I listen and I hear; I do and I understand', is given new meaning when children learn about numbers through hands-on experience.

'Floppy Math', like so many brilliant ideas, was disarmingly simple. A set consists of a comparison square, sixteen inches square and subdivided into a grid of 4 x 4 squares; an activity square, the same size as the comparison square; several smaller squares; and a number of right-angled triangles in various sizes. All the squares were made of bright cotton, each side printed in contrasting colours. The comparison square was also double-sided, with a contrasting grid of sixteen squares on each surface.

The comparison square was like a games board or matrix, to count off quarters, eighths and sixteenths. A number of games were possible with the activity square. It could be folded diagonally or vertically to demonstrate the areas of triangles or, by merely counting the layers of fabric, that two halves make one. Fold it once more, and four quarters make a whole, and so on. By selecting a right-angled triangle and making two squares, each consisting of two triangles joined at the base, and a third square on the hypotenuse, the children could see in front of them a visual proof of Pythagoras's theorem: $a^2 + b^2 = c^2$ (the square on the hypotenuse of a right-angled triangle is equal to the sum of the squares on the other two sides).

The icosahedral dice, which have twenty equilateral faces, were designed in the 1970s for engineering students to generate random numbers.

Many other manipulations are possible. What makes the solution truly elegant, however, is the fact that it is an open-ended game. Only the imagination of the children and teachers sets limits to what can be done with the squares and the triangles, and they can also be used to explore topological transformations, space warps and harmonic theory by more advanced students. The outlay for materials is minimal, and the different game boards can be sewn by children or their parents. Decentralized design and entrepreneurial manufacturing can make the game available to schools everywhere. Because of the low cost of materials and minimal equipment needed (a sewing-machine), small manufacturers or even cottage or village-level groups could make such a product.

CREATIVE PROBLEM-SOLVING

In the 1970s, when work with computers was a more laborious process than today, I saw my engineering design students struggling with the task of generating random numbers. Random numbers, as used in the computer sciences, are two sets of three random digits from zero to nine. Since it is psychologically impossible for anyone to generate numbers that are truly random, students and people working with computers had to buy books consisting entirely of thousands of listings of random numbers. Proof-reading and printing these volumes was expensive, and so they cost a lot; they were also tedious to use. Trying to develop a simpler, less expensive and more pleasant way to generate such numbers, I designed icosahedral dice.

Since normal gaming-dice generate a limited set of random numbers (from one to six) I experimented with a series of ten-sided geometric constructions

Large wooden icosahedral dice for learning games, designed by Bernie Rosen and Beckie Wilson as students at the Kansas City Art Institute.

(deltahedra) that would accommodate ten digits. Because they did not roll easily, a survey was made of all polyhedra (the five Platonic solids: cube, tetrahedron, octahedron, dodecahedron and icosahedron) as well as the seventeen semi-regular Archimedian solids and their duals. It was plain that no easy-rolling ten-sided solid could be developed that was not also geometrically loaded.

The icosahedron, with twenty equilateral faces, was the most spherelike, rolled easily, and permitted the digits zero to nine to be displayed twice on each die. Two rolls of three dice (their digital order was colour coded so that red meant the first digit in a three-digit number, yellow the second and blue the third) would give a six-digit random number. The set was sold for one-tenth of the price of the random-number book.

Two students used my concept of icosahedral dice for a whole series of learning games. Their wooden dice are about the size of a small apple and are made of walnut or birch. They feel pleasant, roll easily, and are extraordinarily good looking. Each of the twenty faces of these icosahedral dice bears a word, number, concept or colour. Two or more dice are needed for a game. Dice sets have been made for teaching geography, plot development, history, biology and other subjects. In a typical geography game, three dice are rolled, yielding a country, a political, economic or social feature and a time scale, which, taken in combination, might inspire a wide-ranging and very interesting classroom discussion.

In another game, three dice from geography and three from biology gave:

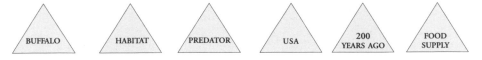

Three dice with twenty faces each can result in 8000 possible combinations. From time to time the dice may produce combinations such as:

Everyone can have a good laugh, and then an interesting discussion may arise from this seemingly nonsensical throw, including the making of building components, weapons and jewelry by the First Nations.

It has also been suggested that the dice could also be used as a psychological testing tool in such diverse areas as Family Profile Preference (FPP) and Thematic Apperception Tests (TAT). I have now taken these icosa-dice a step further. Using a method I developed in the early 1960s for creative problem-solving called 'bisociation technique',[3] I have used the tetrahedral dice to expand this to 'trisociation'. Instead of bringing a design project into random collision with one of seven stimulus words (resulting in seven different free-association solutions), in trisociation, played with seven dice, 1,280,000,000 solutions are possible. Even in a trisociation game using only four dice, there are 64,000 possible choices. The system is elegant, because it performs a type of solution-seeking of which even computers are incapable. Until a random hunting circuit is developed for computers the icosahedral dice are the only simple, effective way of doing the job. Several years ago, a successful American mystery writer began using these icosa-dice for constructing his elaborate plots. He seems pleased with the results.

Children are physically active bundles of stored energy, often so frustrated at school that their inborn need to acquire knowledge is stifled. The continuing assault on a child's sensibilities by beguiling advertisements – the frequently decerebrating programme served up to children on television, the underlying capitalistic concept of 'you are what you buy' and that you express yourself through objects – has made the task of education even more difficult. But committed designers working closely with children, parents and teachers as part of a multi-disclinary team could help to turn things around.

CHAPTER 11

The Best Designers in the World?

Author's note: Most of the observations in this chapter are based on living with, or visiting, certain Inuit tribes during the 1940s. (Inuit, meaning 'The People', is their own name for themselves: Eskimo is a derogatory Algonquin word meaning 'eater of raw flesh'). I encountered the central Yupik and other Inuit tribes of western and northern Alaska, the Tchin in the Black River region and the Iglulinmiut west of the Foxe Basin, as well as settlements on the eastern shore of Hudson Bay in Canada. My only experience in coastal Greenland, where the most Westernized Inuit are to be found, was of very short duration during the early 1970s.

'WHO ARE THE best designers in the world?' I am astonished at how often that question is asked. Usually the questioners offer their own multiple-choice answers: 'Is it the Finns, the Danes? Where does Italian or German design fit in? And what about the Japanese or Americans?' From the viewpoint of a working designer, dealing with new materials and changing technologies, as well as the influence of market forces, the question is simplistic to the point of absurdity. Yet if we define design as finding working solutions that are immediately applicable to problems in the real world, the answer – or my answer at least – is readily apparent: Inuit are the best designers. They are forced into excellence by climate, environment and their space concepts. At least equally important is the cultural baggage they carry with them.

Survival is the keyword to the existence of mankind; how survival is achieved will vary with cultures, peoples, climate, environment and resources. Except for the threats posed by thermonuclear accidents and an increasingly poisoned environment, so-called civilized peoples enjoy so many built-in protections, and are so lost in the routine preoccupations of daily life, that the survival question is ignored. But to folk living on a more 'primitive' level survival is an everyday issue. It has the immediacy of essentials: food, clothing, shelter against the elements, and tools for fishing, hunting, protection or defensive and offensive action against wild beasts and – all too often – other humans. To this we can add objects and artefacts with ritualistic meaning, for personal adornment and for storage.

THE EDGE OF SURVIVAL

Inuit survival is forced to operate under even more restrictive conditions. Unlike people in moderate climates, their existence rests on continuous confrontation

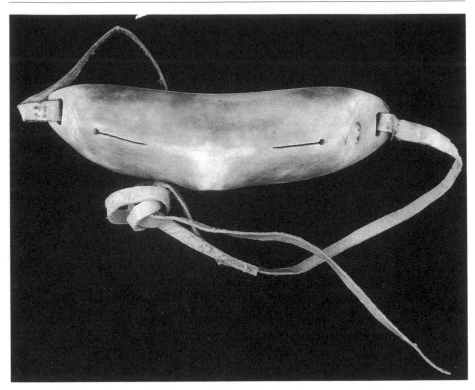

Snow-goggles from Northern Alaska carved from fossilized walrus ivory and with rawhide straps.

with, and accommodation to, nature. They depend on co-operative interaction with the environment because nature itself is too harsh to overcome.

It is not just climate that delimits. The materials available to the Inuit until the mid-20th century were modest and frugal: ivory, bone, driftwood, rawhide, fur pelts and skins, small pieces of wood and, lately, metal. As designers we know that tight limits and tough constraints help force innovative design into being.

Inuit clothing shows how, in dressing for the hunt in an extremely inhospitable climate, clothing takes on the characteristics of architecture. There are insulation spaces; closures and outer layers that act like vestibules or airlocks; and the inner-most layer worn next to the skin consisting of bird-skins with down feathers to create a hefty 'loft' layer. The outermost layer is carefully designed to shed snow, ice and water, and works much like a roof and a series of drainpipes with well-defined seams carrying the water run-off. I draw attention to the exclusive use of natural materials. Recently Inuit have experimented with plastic substitutes and artifical fur, and found the results quite literally deadly. Only natural skins and Arctic fox fur works in snow, ice and extreme cold. The fibres of artificial fur will actually cut into the facial skin and freeze into the cheeks, and man-made underclothing will increase sweating and so pose major health hazards to the wearer. The expression *sagluyok nuya* ('hair that tells lies') describes the dangers posed by plastics as well as disillusionment with such inorganic materials.

Snow-goggles are usually carved from driftwood or, preferably, fossilized walrus ivory. Sunglasses or European ski goggles can't be used – the plastic frames shatter in the extreme cold, whereas metal frames pose obvious dangers at -75°F (-59°C). The eye-slits are extremely narrow to prevent snow blindness, but terminate in rounded holes to provide for greater peripheral vision. The fluid carving will produce a sensuous fit to the brow of the wearer and snow-goggles are kept extremely slim, so that the cheeks are fully exposed: this is how even the slightest changes in wind direction and moisture are sensed – important navigational aids when crossing snow-covered terrain.

From Greenland, where wind-chill can be even fiercer than in the Canadian Arctic, comes the face-protector. It looks like a mask but it serves only as a protective shield against extreme cold. It is made entirely of natural hide and fur.

The Inuit mask illustrates three points: the multi-directionality of the carver's vision: the narrative, story-telling quality of the images; and the simultaneity and non-hierarchical order of the parts that contribute to a harmonious whole.

Greenland face-protector of caribou hide and fox fur.

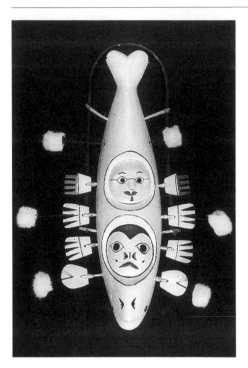

Inuit mask combining whale, kayak and sky.

The mask is carved to represent the spirit of *Kelalugak*, the white whale. The 'canvas' on which the narrative is told is the entire mask. The body of the whale is a double image that can also be read as the kayak itself. Inset at the top is the face of a hooded Inuit hunter wearing snow-goggles; below appears the face of the seal peering through a breathing hole in the ice. Surrounding this whale-shape are the hands of the hunter, the flippers of the seal, and the paddles of the kayak. A third layer (both of meaning, and of the mask) is the large 'U'-shape that completes the composition and represents the heavens. It is a deep bottle-green, the precise colour of the Arctic autumn sky. Finally six tufts of Polar bear fur suggest clouds. The mask is designed to be hand-held as a visual aid for story-telling rather than to be used in rituals.

Inuit drills and drill bows, sculpting tools for working ivory and bone, spears, harpoons, and bird traps are superbly designed for maximum efficiency. Containers and food dippers are made of steam-bent thin-profile wood, and are reminiscent of bentwood boxes made by Shakers in 19th-century America or farmers in 17th-century Finland, (or the furniture of Alvar Aalto of the 1930s).[1]

INUIT DESIGN SKILLS

Inuit design skill is directly connected to a number of abilities and perceptions:

1. Acute powers of observation.

2. A highly retentive memory.

3. The omni-directional nature of their traditional winter home, the igloo.

4. A different system of orientation from that of Europeans or Americans.

5. Sensitive reactions to changes in moisture, wind direction, sound and other minuscule stimuli.

6. An amazing mechanical aptitude allied to great empathy or *Einfühlung* for things electronic or mechanical .

7. The absence of concepts for 'art' or 'artist' in daily life.

Many times among the Inuit I was amazed by their powers of observation in both detail and precision. They continually saw things I did not. They would spot a seal on the ice, and even when they pointed to it, I was unable to see it until we were much closer. They would see a sled or boat approaching long before I could do so, and when it left, the children would continue to watch it long after it had gone from my visual field. This is not to suggest that their eyes are better optically than mine, they are not. It is only that such experiences are important and meaningful to them, and that they have become excellent observers through years of unconscious practice and training.

Connected to these strong powers of observation is a highly retentive and detailed memory. This may be related to their great ability as mimics: imitating a seal or bear was part of the routine hunting lore. After listening to an unfamiliar song on the radio, they could instantly reproduce it with near perfection. Since the late 19th century, the concertina or accordion have become favourite musical instruments, and many Inuit can repeat a tune exactly after hearing it only once.

Even when the time in which to observe something is quite brief, details will be absorbed and remembered for an extremely long time. Kazingnuk, an elderly hunter, could guide a hunting group efficiently through an area he had not seen since he was a youth in his teens, and then only once. When we travelled by sled through unfamiliar country, Kazingnuk would constantly glance backwards. Each of these brief looks would familiarize him with how the environment would look on our return. And even years later the route would be firmly established in his mind and instantly retrievable.

Until the 1960s, Western notions of rectangular enclosed space were still fairly unfamiliar to most Inuit. Summer tents of sealskin or caribou hide are circular and dome-shaped, as are winter igloos. There are no vertical walls, parallel planes, right angles or even straight lines. Most significantly, an Inuit doesn't mould an igloo from the outside (as Canadian children 'playing Eskimo' do), but from the inside looking outwards. He will begin by using his snow-knife to cut and dress a great many snow-blocks that are chamfered to lean inwards and at the same time are angled upwards. Because of the angle and the chamfering, the result will be a series of concentric circles that diminish in diameter as they rise upwards and form a spiral-generated dome. When the final piece at the top has been put into place, like a hemispherical keystone, structure and builder have become one. Only now will he cut a small crawl-hole as a door, at the base.[2]

Among the Igluligarjumiut of the Keewatin district, skins are stretched on sinews against the interior snow wall. This creates a cold-air insulation space, and makes it possible to maintain an interior temperature of 59°F (15°C), without damaging the structure. When we think of Inuit, we see them usually as heavily dressed, yet inside the igloo only a minimal amount of clothing is frequently

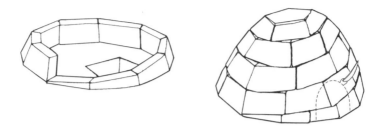

The igloo is built from the inside, a spiral formed from chamfered snow blocks.

worn. More recently, newspapers have been used to create even greater insulation areas and thermal barriers, and I have been in igloos where the temperature was nearly 80°F (27°C), with an outdoor wind-chill of -55°F (-48°C).

Contrary to Hollywood-induced popular notions, most igloos that are more than temporary overnight shelters for a hunting party have a number of rooms. Usually an airlock-like vestibule goes past storerooms for dead seal, then through a 'hall' from which several rooms are accessible, with a seal-oil lamp burning in each room and a snow sleeping-platform. The igloo creates an omni-directional space from which Western concepts of linear or hierarchical order, sequence and series are curiously absent. The igloo provides a metaphor and a scale-model of the Inuit world.

SPACE CONCEPTS

In winter the horizon will recede far into the distance and there is no distinguishable difference between earth and sky. Without perspective (except when the sun is close to the horizon and briefly sidelights the ground), there is no middle distance, no features except wind-devils. When snow fills the air, concepts of up and down, near and far, lose all meaning, and one is blinded by whiteness: *aputakuyuitok.* The bowl of the ground and sky are one with the igloo. The Inuit system of orientation rests equally on this featureless multi-directional home and the surrounding landscape.

The walls of homes are often decorated with pictures or photos from magazines. In the snow-house these also reduce dripping. To a newcomer it is startling that little effort has been made to place these images 'right-side-up'; they seem placed haphazardly. Yet the relationship between viewer and image is so active that the spectator is drawn into the images, moving in and about in a *haptic* manner, so that considerations of 'up' or 'down', 'left', or 'right' are of little importance. Whenever a magazine arrived for me, my Inuit friends would gather around me in a circle to look at the illustrations, with the younger ones reading the text. Never was there the slightest jostling for position – it wouldn't occur to Inuit that reading something upside-down or sideways is harder or different in any way. The children would sometimes make fun of my turning and twisting my neck to see pictures displayed on the walls 'correctly'.

This radically different orientation system has been cited by both Marshall McLuhan and Edmund Carpenter as a result of Inuit living in an aural, acoustic, non-linear bubble of space – in a society that is moving directly from a pre-literate to a post-literate (electronic) mode, and has not been moulded by linear thinking.[3] It is a fact that Inuit, when asked to draw a map of a coastline, will do so with their eyes closed whilst listening to the sound of waves lapping against the shore – frequently such maps drawn a hundred and fifty years ago are as accurate as modern ones prepared from aerial photographs. Even Inuit children can solve the 'nine-dot problem' on their first try, whereas most Westerners are frustrated by an inability to violate the logic of right-angled space.

An understanding of one's own locale requires a different cognitive skill than that for drawing an accurate and detailed map. The anthropologist Franz Boas[4] tells us of Inuit drawing maps where linear distances of 1000 miles are involved, and accurately drawing charts of areas of 150,000 square miles, all in proper scale. Some large Inuit maps, surviving for a hundred and seventy years, could only be exactly verified through the use of satellite-mapping techniques. Comparing two maps of the same region, one drawn by Inuit and relying on non-visual cues and the other traced from satellite observations, it is interesting to compare the points of difference. The map drawn from memory by an Inuit named Sunapignanq shows much greater detail of inlets and small islands in the Cumberland Sound and the north and east shorelines of the Hall peninsula. This is important, as the best fishing grounds are found there. The land mass has been shown smaller in proportion; it is of little interest to fishermen. The southern shore of the peninsula as well as the lower half of Frobisher Bay are shown as virtually featureless in the Inuit chart. The ComSat map by comparison is amazingly similar but emphasizes inshore navigational features much less.

Three-dimensional maps of coastlines were carved of wood as long as three hundred years ago. These Inuit charts are usually carved from driftwood and are

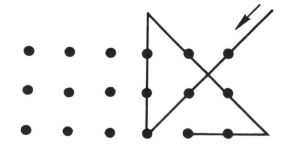

The Inuit system of orientation means that even children can rapidly solve the nine-dot problem.

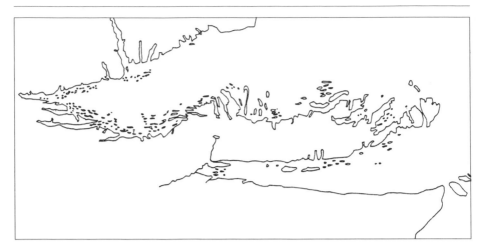

Maps of the Cumberland Sound–Frobisher Bay region, drawn from memory by Inuit Sunapignanq (above), and generated with modern cartographic techniques (below).

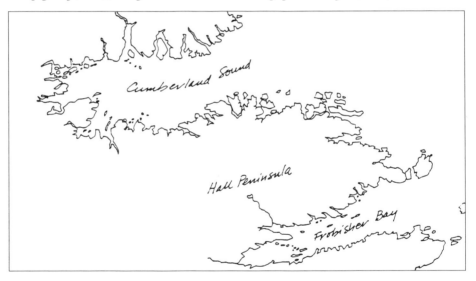

made to be *felt*, rather than looked at. Usually the actual landmass has been highly abstracted – it is the *edges* that can be 'fingered' on a dark night in a kayak. Since they are made of wood rather than paper, they are impervious to the weather, and will float if they are accidentally dropped overboard; being three-dimensional they are more functional in terms of accurately rendering shorelines to people in boats or kayaks.

To me the land at first seemed monotonous and without detail. But this was only indicative of my own insensitivity. To my Inuit friends, the environment was full of meaningful reference points and was extremely varied. When I drive through New York City – a place which seems to be total chaos to an Inuit –

Inuit carved wooden maps from Greenland were made to be read by the fingers. They are weatherproof, and will float if dropped overboard.

I assume that a rectangular grid overlays the city's streets, and that certain buildings, markers and street signs will delineate my route. Inuit use natural signifiers; these are not markers or points but rather contextual relationships. These relationships will include wind, salinity of the air, slight contour changes, type and moisture and hardness of snow, moisture content of the air, distance to shore, and 'ice-crack'. Returning from the hunt with neither moon nor stars visible, when even the lead dog could barely be seen, we were unable to find snow suitable for building an igloo for the night. We continued, twisting and turning over sea ice, until we arrived at the unlit settlement some five hours later. Had we missed the white igloos on equally white ground by even a hundred yards (90m) in the dark, we would have perished.[5]

The orientation of Inuit – as miraculous to Westerners as the homing instinct of birds – is a necessity for survival honed to perfection by a lifetime of experience. It has to do with abstracting essentials from landscape and climate, which is a strong basis for all art and design, not just in the far north. A hunter will notice even the slightest change in the wind from the direction in which the fur on his parka blows: an organic sextant. In contradiction to much published research, my Inuit friends told how amused they were by stories about hunters or fishermen who tried to use the stars as guides, their unanswerable point being that much night-time travel often has to be done on overcast nights.

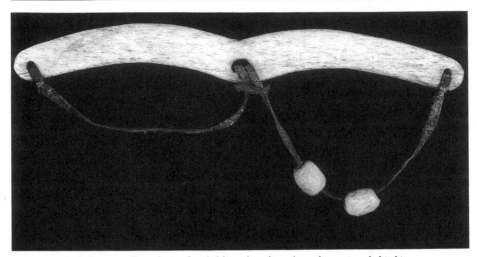

Inuit puzzle and story-telling device for children, based on three-dimensional thinking.

THINKING IN THREE DIMENSIONS

The Inuit puzzle is used as a story-telling device for children and as mnemonic tool. To separate the two bone beads from one another *without untying the rawhide string,* and then to bring them together again, calls for topological transformations of a very high order. It is another example of three-dimensional design thinking. This is one of the oldest folk puzzles, known in the United Kingdom and North America under such names as 'Camel and Needle', 'Ox Yoke', or 'Washer-and-Loop Puzzle'. The point is that Inuit don't find it frustrating or particularly puzzling, whereas Westerners do. It is based on a different way of conceptualizing spatial relationships, rather like the Inuit nine-dot problem.

The Inuit posess amazing abilities to understand and master intricate mechanical mechanisms quickly. Marshall McLuhan writes: '*Eskimo have proved to be wizard jet mechanics without benefit of any training whatever. These mechanisms they grasp by ear, inclusively, not by eye, analytically.*'[6] Most Inuit are top-rate intuitive mechanics. They enjoy taking apart and reassembling watches, jet engines, electric and electronic tools, all machinery. They will correctly repair instruments that Canadian or American mechanics, flown in to fix, have been unable to do. Working frequently with handmade tools, they make replacement parts of metal or ivory. Piluardjuk used the rear axle of a US Army truck and, finding it too large for his jeep, reduced the diameter by nearly half, using only handtools. At a lecture in Toronto, Edmund Carpenter told how, on being asked by a missionary to fix a complex machine that had stopped working, he had removed the inspection panel and immediately realized that it was far too intricate to repair or even to understand. An Inuit who was watching, slipped his hand in, made some quick adjustments and it was fixed.

The explanation of these abilities comes from various parts of the culture. First there is great manual dexterity, learned through the actual making of small objects that must work. Then there is Inuit time-space orientation; conceptually space and time are never separated, but any situation, tool, artefact or machine is seen as a dynamic process. Then Inuit are keen observers of details with a profound ability of recall. Finally their space concept is not one of static enclosure (such as a room with walls and boundaries) but as multi-directional in process.

ART IS LIFE

As among the Balinese of Indonesia, I found that there is no word for 'art' or 'artists' in Inuit. Where the Balinese say: 'We have no art, we just do the best we can,'[7] the Inuit phrase is: 'A man should do all things properly.'[8] There is no distinction made between decorative or utilitarian goods. All men are carvers, all Inuit sing and dance. 'When a song rises within you, you sing; when you feel a form emerging from ivory, you let it fulfil itself.' Similarly the language really has no words that mean the same as our 'create' or 'make', which both imply an individualistic, personal act. 'To work with' is the nearest Inuit term, which signifies that the material itself, perhaps driftwood or ivory, has a role equal to that of the carver in developing the process. Again, like the Balinese, Inuit are more

Tupilak, 'harmful ghost', is an exquisite carving tossed away with the angry feelings it represents.

interested in the activity of creating in partnership with the material than in the end-product. In the West we think of the end-products of design (or the arts) as possessions; to them these are transitory acts, relationships. All *authentic* Inuit sculpture is quite small, usually under four inches (10cm) long, and without a base to rest on. Figures are carved in the round, with great detail even to the animal's sex organs, but never with a favoured side for viewing. It is carried in the clothing, passed from hand to hand for viewing, and then negligently dropped in a bag or toolbox, or simply lost. Design to the Inuit is an act, not an object; a ritual, not a possession. A distinctive sign of traditional art is that the ivory sculptures roll about clumsily, since they lack a base. Again, Inuit view their work dynamically and omni-directionally, the pieces are to be turned this way and that, explored by the hand in a continuation of the way in which the carver originally explored the piece of ivory, asking it: 'What do you want to become?'

The truly ephemeral nature of Inuit art and design (another similarity between Inuit and Balinese) is best shown through the carving and traditional disposal of *tupilak* by the coast Inuit of Greenland. *Tupilak*, which means 'harmful ghost' in most Canadian Inuit languages and dialects, describes small ivory carvings. They fit the hand easily like all true Inuit carvings, and, lacking a base, can't stand 'properly'. Their function was originally to absorb all the bad and violent feelings and emotions of the carver. Once completed and beautifully finished, the carver would toss the *tupilak* in the ocean or a brook. This would externalize and get rid of rage and hostilities, and leave the carver and his family cleansed of aggression and hatred. More recently the Danish government and Greenland tourist organizations have touted *tupilak* as precious sculptures for collectors.[9] It is ironic that Inuit rage or aggression should be turned into a commodity that tourists are encouraged to buy.

LEARNING FROM THE INUIT

Without engaging in polemics, it is safe to say that design in the West suffers from too much 'easy living', meaningless comfort and so-called labour-saving devices. This is no plea for Puritan or Calvinist harshness. But the reason why competition sports equipment, camping and rock-climbing gear, gliders, gourmet cooking-pots and chef's knives, and – sad to say – weapons for hunting and war, work so well and look so well-designed, may lie in the need for optimum performance under marginal conditions. Design for the very elderly or for severely handicapped people also sets the stage for tools that must work well in demanding situations. Many of these designs serve superbly well, but when we look at the mind-blinding displays of everyday consumer goods flooding the market in the West, we see that we still have a great deal to learn from other peoples. My belief is that a good starting-point is the Inuit – the best designers in the world.

CHAPTER 12

The New Aesthetic: Making the Future Work

We cannot remain moral in any recognizable sense of the word,
nor can our projects and creations – including tools, homes, cities
and landscapes – retain any sort of moral earnestness, without
somewhere in the background the support of a deeply felt
mythopoeic or religious model of reality.
Yi-Fu Tuan

Throughout this book, many ideas and approaches to architecture and design have been explored. If we now attempt to weave them together, we realize that inevitably a new aesthetic must emerge out of the web of necessities, solutions and concepts.

1. The sustainability of life on this planet – not only for humankind but for all our fellow species – is paramount.

2. Sustainability can be helped or hindered by design. The impact of petrol-powered automobiles on the environment, wars, foreign policy, economics, morals and jobs is profound enough to serve as a chilling example.

3. Ethical design must also be environmentally sound and ecologically benign. It needs to be human in scale, humane and embedded in social responsibility.

4. Such design requires the help of governments, industry, entrepreneurs and laws,[1] and the support of ordinary people through local user groups and individual decisions to shop intelligently and invest ethically.

5. Designers and architects all seem to be waiting for some fresh style or direction that will provide new meaning and new forms for the objects we create, based more on real requirements than on an arbitrarily invented style.

6. All objects, tools, graphics and dwellings must work towards the needs of the end-user on a more basic level than mere appearance, flamboyant 'gesture', or semiotic 'statements'. Nevertheless, the lack of any spiritual basis for design will make ethical and environmental considerations mere well-intentioned afterthoughts.

7. Design, when nourished by a deep spiritual concern for planet, environment, and people, results in a moral and ethical viewpoint. Starting from this point of departure will provide the new forms and expressions – the new aesthetic – we are all desperately trying to find.

Anyone with even a speck of sensitivity will agree that in the 1990s most dwellings, public buildings, means of transport are disturbingly ugly. Everyday objects look shoddy, mean and self-assertive. They need to look assertive; at the point of purchase every item on display must, visually speaking, screech for attention. This visual dominance is needed to distinguish it from its near-identical neighbours. Allowance is seldom made for the fact that this design assault will continue when the appliance is installed in one's home.

This dismaying visual pollution signals the imminent emergence of a new aesthetic, and most designers and architects will readily agree that, after Modernism, Memphis, Post-Modernism, Deconstructivism, Neo-Classicism, Object-Semiotics, and Post-Deconstructivism, a new direction – transcending fad, trend or fashionable styling – is long overdue. New directions in design and architecture don't occur accidentally, but always arise out of real changes in society, cultures and concepts.

We are still, metaphorically speaking, treading water. We are still looking for a new reality-based aesthetic. Ecology and concern for the environment, which includes recycling, Design Diversification or adaptive re-use, Design-for-Disassembly, the use of non-compound materials, and – most importantly – using less, are the most profound and powerful forces, and may indeed develop the new directions that are so desperately needed in both design and architecture.

I would remind the reader of some cautions and suggestions in earlier chapters. In Chapter 7 I applauded the idea that form could be fun, yet tried to point out the narrow division between style and fad, fake and authenticity. The seeming chasm between the momentary and the permanent is an illusion maintained by projecting our own life-span on to objects. The questions and checklists in Chapter 8 may empower the end-user to find alternatives to the market-driven frou-frous served up by the advertisers. Some of the alternatives mentioned in Chapter 9 – buying used, building and modifying, re-use and recycling – exist already. Others – sharing, ridding ourselves of the pretentious, managing with less – we need to bring back to maintain a sustainable society. It is through individual action, as well as through user-iniatives that we can make a great U-turn and find harmony and balance once more in our lives.

Powerful industries, corrupt governments, persuasive lobbies and special interest groups form a cabal to persuade us that things are going to be all right. Claims that there is something awry with the health of the world are viewed as alarmist, if not worse. [2] 'No direct link has been established between factory emissions and acid rain,' they tell us. 'Scientists are bitterly divided about the warming of the earth.' 'Green thinking will put millions out of work.' All nonsense, of course, but what can we do? The sheer magnitude of the problem makes us feel impotent. Can anything be done? Does the voice of an individual still count? Local groups have stopped the building of high-voltage transmission towers, unwanted hyper-markets and ring roads, and have saved threatened buildings, wetlands and meadows. It was a people's initiative that levelled the Berlin Wall; groups of neighbours voted to prevent the Austrian government from building an atomic power plant. Surely it must also be in people's power to get toasters made that last and can be recycled, to demand a land that is fair and green, buildings that foster a sense of harmony and well-being?

It is not difficult to find buildings that evoke the spiritual in us. What stirs this recognition of the spiritual and fills us with awe works on deep levels of our psyche. The eidetic image is constructed from the harmonic relationships between various parts of our bodies. Our biogenetic heritage also shapes our satisfaction from a preconscious recognition of the Fibonacci series, the golden rectangle, spirals, and rhythms connected to our heartbeat and the seasonal cycles.

Design is different. At first sight, there is no such thing as a piece of industrial design that carries spiritual values. We may intuitively sense beauty in objects, particularly those that have been formed to operate in survival situations. Gliders and sailplanes must maintain altitude without engines as long as possible, and at the same time exploit the slightest thermal updraught to rise; their form is shaped by the winds and temperature currents. Somehow we sense this and call the result beautiful or meaningful within the Function Matrix. A Swedish hand-axe is so beautifully fitted to the human hand, the handle retro-curved to add power and the blade formed into a long arc of cutting power, that the tool is a pleasure to use. But it is the *intent* of the designer, *the intended use*, the *fulfilled need* that can endow even the humblest object with deep spiritual values. A chair that is designed for the ease of a severely disabled child gains a moral dimension – with the designer reaching an inner state of grace through the act of helping others. A graphic design that enables a sick person to communicate symbolically with doctor or nurse, or that empowers Inuit people to read books in their own language – all these become spiritual through their ennobled function and help to enrich the designer's soul.

Beginning in the mid-1960s, technological innovations, especially in consumer electronics, created improvements in the performance of many tools and devices and ushered in entirely new gadgetry. We are in the middle of an accelerating period of technological obsolescence, when the latest

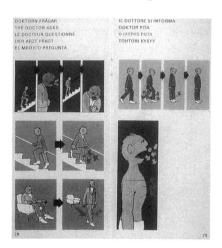

A page from a Swedish book for describing medical symptoms with pictures.

device frequently incorporates real advantages. The number of electronic devices as well as the pace of marketing them has increased enormously during the profit-and-greed propelled 1980s – and the number of useless, trivial and vulgar new products has swelled. Now, in the 1990s, designers, profoundly schooled in the design of the artefacts of a throw-away culture, find themselves facing a complete paradox: *to design things that will last, yet come apart easily to be recycled and re-used.*

Yet the design profession – driven by new laws as well as necessity – is responding to the challenge. Most consumer durables have become ever more complex aggregates of many different materials, especially plastic – great amounts of it. There are growing social and political demands to recycle these materials. What can be done? The question demands a new approach from designers, and is sure eventually to have far-reaching structural and aesthetic influences, changing the way things are conceived, built, used and look.

Europe is decades ahead of the United States when it comes to concern for the ecology, and is also way ahead on Design for Disassembly. The Electrolux Corporation of Sweden already has a design-to-take-apart dishwasher, sold through Zanussi, their Italian subsidiary. But the leader of the disassembly initiative is BMW. The Z-1 two-seater has an all-plastic skin that can be taken from the metal chassis in less than twenty minutes. This limited-production sports car, currently sold only in Europe, has doors, bumpers and front rear and side panels made of a recyclable thermoplastic. BMW also uses a pilot disassembly plant where it cuts apart five standard automobiles a day to learn new take-apart technologies. Some new lessons are learned, such as substituting rivets

Take-apart technology can revive methods from previous successes, such as the Citroën 2-CV (this one dates from 1939); the body is fixed together with bolts, with no need for screws or glues.

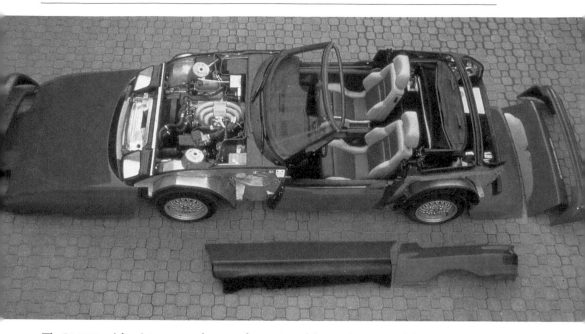

The BMW Z-1 (above) is easy to take apart for repair and for recycling. One of the new BMW 3 series (below): the parts that can be recycled are coloured green and the recycled parts blue.

and dowel-like connectors for glue or screws. Other approaches may be resuscitated from the past. The Citroën 2-CV of 1936 and 1948, and its many later descendants, was *bolted* together, without screws or glues. Using scores of different types of plastic in manufacturing defeats attempts at sorting, and consequently prevents cost-effective re-use. 'We have twenty different sorts of plastics in a typical car,' explains Arno Eisenhofer, BMW's disassembly director in Bavaria. 'Five kinds would be better and three should be possible.'[3]

One interesting insight from disassembly by BMW is the rediscovery of repairability. In a seeming throwback to early Fords and other early 20th-century cars (when everything was built to be repaired), take-apart design makes it both faster and easier to work on cars once again. Trunk-lids, bumpers or doors can be removed without hours of labour-intensive and hence costly time. David Thompkins is Director of Industrial Design for a US manufacturer of engineering plastics, which is owned by Montedison, a chemical supercorporation in Italy; he says: 'When labour costs went up and material costs dropped, with injection moulding, automation and one-way fasteners we became a throw-away society. DFD is a way of re-thinking all that now.'[4] The German government has introduced new laws that will require its car manufacturers – Mercedes Benz, BMW, Porsche, Volkswagen and Audi – to repurchase or take back, disassemble and recycle *all* German cars. Cars will be required to be made from non-compound materials, and specifically developed for easy take-apart.[5]

This design-to-take-apart technology has also been adapted to large and small appliances and tools, down to the 'U-Kettle' made by the Great British Teakettle Company. By contrast, another kettle, also from the UK, was distributed to half-a-dozen people for their comments by *Design* magazine.[6] This kettle looks like a bullet lampshade of 1939, violated by a steel truncheon, and sells for around £130 in the UK. Most of the testers found it difficult to fill, hot to handle and little use from a functional point of view. This is a valuable study in social irresponsibility, the contempt for a social contract which has become the trademark of Post-Modernism. To design durable goods for disassembly may sound like an oxymoron, but it is a profoundly important issue for a sustainable society.

'Design Diversification' is the development of a new application for a part that has been over-manufactured, requiring a product designer's innovative thinking. During the Korean War, clear plastic blisters were used on combat aircraft fuselages to provide a broad view for rear-gunners. Thousands of these plastic half-spheres, thirty-three inches (84cm) in diameter, were still on the manufacturer's shelves in 1957, and the design staff managed to develop them – or recycle them – into skylights for homes and offices, decorative plant stands, and dome-topped display tables for galleries and shops. Others ended up as free-standing street-furniture and kiosk roofs in Curitiba in Brazil.

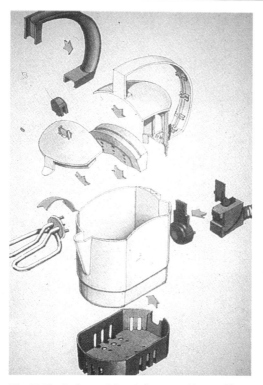

The U-Kettle design (above) for easy self-assembly.
The Hot Bertaa (below) designed by Philippe Starck.

Plastic half-spheres, over-manufactured for aircraft during the Korean war in the 1950s, have been transformed into these market kiosks in Brazil. Design Diversification requires imagination.

When the craze for Hula-Hoops ended in the mid-fifties, I was commissioned to recycle (or 'diversify') some five hundred thousand of them for a large mail-order firm. I designed a collapsible textile tunnel for children to crawl through. When unfolded it was twenty-four feet long (7.3m) and had eight hoops as vertical stabilizers. It was about thirty inches wide (76cm) and collapsed to less than twelve inches (30cm) high. It gave great enjoyment to small children, and the fabric when worn could be replaced to vary the 'ghost-train' crawl.

Although there is a great deal of emphasis on the twin areas of re-use and recycling, another strategy is frequently neglected. This is the imaginative design exploitation of waste falloffs from primary manufacturing processes, as in the bookweight made from small leather scraps described in Chapter 3.

The salient point of Design for Disassembly is evident: *if the tool, appliance, object, whatever, has been initially designed for take-apart technology, then it should also be easier to assemble.* Designing and making durable goods that can easily be disassembled, requires closer tolerances in connectors and joints, and less 'forgiving' parts. Satisfying both of these requirements, the British 'U-Kettle' is for these reasons easy to assemble. Again we can recognize that this approach will move design toward a new aesthetic. It is interesting to speculate about this new – yet unpredictable – look of things. Throughout history the appearance of built or made goods has been determined by the six interlinked aspects of what I have described as the Function Complex. To some degree the final appearance of a product or a dwelling has always reflected the personal gesture, whim, or self-indulgence of the designer, as well as the stylistic mannerisms of the time.

The rise of a new aesthetic that is formed by environmental and ecological considerations will be unpredictable in its shapes, forms, colours, textures and varieties and – at the same time – enormously exciting. Exciting since, unlike all new styles of the last hundred and twenty years, it will not be a manipulative re-statement of what has gone before. What after all was Post-Modernism if not modern architecture with eclectic bits of kitsch added to hide the essential bankruptcy of both design and structure?

I am not making a case for aesthetic transformation by extrapolating from a kettle put together by someone in an evening. Industrial assembly procedures for most consumer products have become so simplified that assembly work can be performed by workers with little or no experience and training. Sophisticated Macintosh lap-top computers or 'Powerbooks' are hand-assembled in Ireland for the world market by previously untrained workers. Complex Honda automobiles are built by previously inexperienced ex-farmers and service personnel in Canada and the USA, while complicated video recorders are put together by ex-fruitpickers in Mexico.

We can therefore expect that the number of products that people will be able to build for themselves will rise dramatically under the twin influences of take-apart design, and the manufacturers' need to save on the cost of shipping and their own final assembly work. None of this is really new – only the broad range and scale of goods will change. Washers, toasters, stoves, refrigerators, furniture, coffee makers, wheelchairs, television sets, radios, bath tubs, lamps, microscopes, even computers,[7] will need to be redesigned for disassembly and could therefore also be available as kits. A recent book that deals with kit-based products, lists a score of high-performance sports cars, regular automobiles, a dozen different aircraft

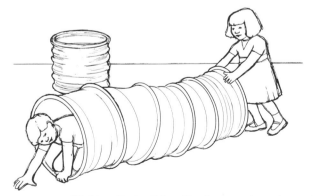

When Hula Hoops went out of fashion, Design Diversification came into play, and stacks of unwanted hoops were used to make collapsible play-tunnels for small children.

(including a five-passenger plane), a helicopter, motor boats and hundreds of other items. Included in the list of arcane musical instruments are spinets, Irish and concert-size harps, clavichords, cembalinos, citterns, violins, lutes and bagpipes. Houses and geodesic domes are also available for self-building.[8]

If one of the most important tasks of design lies in extending new options to the user, then it would be useful to make it possible to buy a product in one of three ways:

- In its fully assembled state
- In kit-form, to be completed by the user
- In kit-form, to be assembled by someone on behalf of the user who feels inadequate or unwilling to do it himself or herself

This is already happening in many parts of the world. It is no longer possible to buy a bicycle without assembling parts of it oneself. Most furniture is sold with the label, 'Some assembly required'.

It is likely that the customer will learn more about the product, and be able to make simple repairs after having put it together; this will also lessen the alienation between tool and user, and allow improvisation and improvements on the workings and aesthetics. The third option, hiring someone to construct it, may give rise to a return of repair shops and 'Mr Fixits', certainly an ecologically friendly development, and retaining a tradition of 'hands-on' experience.

Finally we arrive at a paradox in both architecture and design. It is the seeming conflict between the permanent and the ephemeral, things that last and things that are meant to be discarded quickly. We find enjoyment and beauty in the evanescent: the changing sky, water in all its forms, the fragile colours of flowers or a butterfly's wing, and *for enjoyment only* we spend a great deal of artistic and creative effort in designing and making things for short-time pleasures. We build and fly brightly coloured balloons, send carefully constructed kites into the sky and create colourful banners for the pure joy of seeing them flutter in the breeze. We get satisfaction from building elaborate sandcastles and ice palaces, *and doesn't much of our enchantment lie in the fact that the sea will reclaim the sandcastles with the incoming tide – that in the end our beautiful ice palaces will ultimately melt?* It mirrors our own path from birth to death to rebirth again. We take pleasure in this natural cycle of recycling – designers need to learn from this marriage of the transient with high aesthetic quality.

When I started as a first-year student of architecture and design in 1952, our professors told us that any building we designed only needed to last twenty-five to thirty years – after that it would have to be torn down. 'Heating and air-conditioning ducts, electric wiring, elevators and much else,' we were told, 'will be completely old-fashioned and obsolete by then, and it will be simpler and more efficient to tear the building down and build anew.' Possibly this may have been partially true then (at least true for those who earned their income from making buildings); it is certainly obscene to think along such lines in a world that is running out of energy and has its back to the wall ecologically and environmentally. We must build and design for the long haul.

At the same time we must resolve the seeming contradiction between the transitory and the lasting, the ephemeral and the permanent. If we view these apparent opposites in a holistic way, we soon recognize that any dwelling or building, any tool, object or artefact is no more than a fleeting episode in an ongoing, enduring stream of development that is timeless. This permits Paul Oliver to declare correctly that, 'The Eskimo igloo is the oldest known shelter known to mankind',[9] even though no Inuit snow house will last more than one long winter season. The point is of course that the material, shape, spatial and ritual expectations are all embedded in the concept of igloo and have lasted unchanged for some fifty thousand years.

Possibly the perfect metaphor for this 'fleeting permanence' is found in the Ise Shrine in Japan. The buildings that form Ise are both very old, yet simultaneously extremely new. They owe their extreme age to the fact that they are identical with the ones that stood there since the year 686. They are archaically and aesthetically pure. They are clean – they are Shinto. At the same time they are very

Fenced enclosures surround the old Ise Shrine (top) and the new buildings. The shrine is rebuilt in the same way and with the same rituals every twenty years.

Craftsmen have created the calm elegance of the Ise Shrine.

new since they are ceremonially rebuilt every twenty years. Carpenters wearing spotless white clothes go to the sacred forests on the Kiso Mountains to cut the new timbers. They take frequent baths, maintain constant cleansing ceremonies both for themselves as well as the materials and their tools; should a single drop of blood fall on any piece of wood, it would be rejected.

Two fenced enclosures stand side by side and are used alternately. In the empty enclosure the new group of buildings is made in the exact image of the previous shrine. During the night of the changeover, the few sacred symbols are transferred to the new shrine. The old buildings are then carefully dismantled and their materials – sanctified by twenty years of spiritual use – are put to good work elsewhere. The buildings are made primarily of cypress with some cedar, unpainted and finished with natural palm oil. All parts are dowelled, no nails, screws or glue are used. The roofs are thatched and there are a few metal ornaments. In 1993 the new Shrine was starting its sixty-first 'incarnation'.[10] There is nothing spectacular about these buildings and spaces, just great refinement, elegance and subtlety based on a profoundly high level of craftsmanship. It is precisely this high level of quality that is apparent in objects or dwellings that were never intended to be permanent that is now becoming of interest to designers and architects.

The temple offerings of Bali, the Toradja cremation towers, the Thai dancers' paper headdresses which are gilded, painted and embellished with blossoms and tiny mirrors and beads, are ephemeral structures that demonstrate a profound mindfulness on the part of their creators, a striving for perfection. This mindfulness, springing from deep roots of aesthetic experience and spiritual awareness, will enrich the work of design, and – by recognizing the proper place of what we do in terms of the ever-present now as well as the lasting – help to ensure a future of fleeting episodes that will form a rich web of permanence through continuity.

NOTES

The place and date of publication are given only the first time they appear in the notes, and not for sources listed in the Select Bibliography.

Introduction: The Power of Design pp.7–14

1. 'Time-binding', through language, writing and memory, was a term first coined by A. Korzybski in *Science and Sanity,* Chicago, 1948.
2. Roszak, *The Voice of the Earth,* New York, 1992; London, 1993.
3. From James Wines's lecture at the Canadian Design Conference in Vancouver, February 1994.
4. Lovelock, *Gaia, The Ages of Gaia* and *Healing Gaia.*
5. The California Institute of the Arts, where I taught and was Dean of Design, is a huge structure so designed and sited that half of it almost always needs air-conditioning, the other has to be heated.
6. Frank Lloyd Wright, *An Autobiography,* New York, 1932; London 1945.
7. Orr, *Ecological Literacy,* New York, 1992.
8. Lewis Mumford, *The City in History: Its Origins, Its Transformations, and Its Prospects,* London and New York, 1961.
9. Lena E. Johnson-Davis, *Defining Sustainable Architecture,* Lawrence, Kansas, 1994.
10. Ibid.
11. The life of this remarkable Balinese is documented in *Lempad of Bali,* videotape by John Darling for the Australian Broadcasting Company, in co-operation with the BBC, Dutch television and WGBH Boston, 1980.

1 Here Today, Gone Tomorrow? pp.17–28

1. A.B. Appleby, 'Epidemics and Famine in the Little Ice Age', in *Climate and History: Studies in Interdisciplinary History,* 1981. My thoughts are in part adapted from Donald Worster, Putting Nature into History', Dept. of History, Univ. of Kansas, April 1991. I am indebted to Professor Worster for the citation of several papers and books.
2. I.G. Simmons, *Changing the Face of the Earth: Culture, Environment, History,* Oxford, 1989; and J.U. Nef, 'An Early Crisis and its Consequences', in *Scientific American,* No.237, 1977.
3. Vaclav Smil, *The Bad Earth: Environmental Degradation in China,* New York, 1984.
4. Mark Elvin, 'The Environmental History of China', *Asian Studies Review,* Nov. 1990.
5. B.L. Turner, et al, (ed), *The Earth as Transformed by Human Action,* Cambridge, 1990.
6. Information from news documentaries and news reports since 1988.
7. These findings are based in part on two articles by Tony Hiss, *New Yorker,* June 1987, since incorporated in his book, *The Experience of Place.*
8. D'Arcy Thompson, *On Growth and Form,* first published Cambridge, 1917.
9. 'Notes and Comments', *New Yorker,* 9 Oct. 1989.
10. L. Eisley, *The Immense Journey,* New York, 1957.
11. These observations are based in part on the introductory paragraphs to Bill McKibben's essay, 'Reflections', *New Yorker,* 11 Sept. 1989.

2 Designing for a Safer Future pp.29–48

1. V. Papanek, 'Seeing the World Whole: Interaction Between Ecology and Design', Fifth Inaugural Lecture , University of Kansas, 1982.
2. As given in White, *Green Pages.*
3. A. Leonard, 'The Myth of Recycled Plastics', *Greenpeace Toxic Trade Update,* No. 5.2, Washington D.C., 1992. See also, *Toxic Trade Update,* Nos. 6.1 and 6.2, 1993.
4. Developed by Floyd Wallace from Lansing, Michigan, with research grants from Sandia National Laboratories. In a stainless-steel chamber, 200ft (60m) long, tyre chips react with seven proprietary metallic and inorganic catalysts, forming hydrocarbon vapours, which are condensed to produce oils for home heating or to lighten heavier oils. During a test, each 20lb (9kg) car tyre yielded: 1 gallon of oil (3.8l); 6lbs carbon black (2.7kg); 3lbs steel (1.4kg); ½lb ash (363gm); 25 cu ft methane (0.7 cu m). The process is marketed by Titan Technologies of Albuquerque, New Mexico; the first two Titan plants opened in Korea in June 1994.
5. The Texaco Company is researching this process.
6. *Sumoto,* Japan (AP), 22 Jan. 1992.
7. Tetra (four), kai (and), deca (ten) describes a 14-sided, semi-regular, Archimedean polyhedron, also known as the truncated octahedron, with 6 squares and 8 hexagons making up the 14 faces. The only semi-regular polyhedron whose modules will close-pack in space (due to the many angles of adherence inherent to its structure), it fills space truly three-dimensionally. In biology, the tetrakaidecahedron is a schematic form of the human fat cell, and is also related to the spiral arrangement of the DNA chain.
8. Papanek, *Design For The Real World,* (rev. edn).
9. R. Ingersoll, 'The Ecological Question', *Journal of Architectural Education,* Feb. 1992.
10. 'A Look at Eco-Design' in *Oeko-Architektur, bauen mit der Natur,* Darmstadt, 1979.

3 Towards the Spiritual in Design pp. 49–74

1. The first poster for the Bauhaus in 1919 carried Gropius's invitation to prospective students to help build the Bauhaus as 'the new cathedral of socialism'.
2. This useful coinage by Kirkpatrick Sale describes the results when we judge the past using only the standards of our own period and culture.
3. 'All beauty that has not a foundation in use, soon grows distasteful, and needs continual replacement with something new. That which has itself the highest use, possesses the greatest beauty.' From the *Shaker Millennial Laws,* 1795.
4. Freud wrote of the relationship between horror and beauty in *Civilization and its Discontents* (New York, 1961 edn); 'terrible beauty' is in Siva as both creator and destroyer. A fighter-bomber, however, has no such ambivalence.

5. Maria Benktzon (Swedish designer and founder of RFSU Rehab) and the Institute for Social Design in Vienna have carried out ergonomic research on the hand configurations of the disabled; see also the guidelines published in 1991 by Nils Diffrient and the Massachusetts Institute of Technology.

6. See note 10 to Chapter 2.

7. Categories: newspaper; cardboard and other paper products; metals; flattened aluminium tins; white glassware; coloured glassware; plastic; organic waste for mulching; wood; highly toxic materials such as batteries, engine oil and chemicals.

8. For a more detailed discussion, see Papanek, *Design for Human Scale.*

9. Ibid.

10. Nietzsche's idea of 'self-overcoming'– that the repeated process of overcoming baser drives will, by itself, yield ethical experience – is closely tied to his conviction that 'immediate gratification invariably is self-destructive over time'. (*The Will to Power,* New York, 1968). This is repeated by Freud's, 'Every fresh renunciation increases the superego's attack on the ego and thereby creates increased moral thinking. The more ethical we are, the more ethical we become.' (*Civilization and its Discontents.*)

13 A. Maslow, *Motivation and Personality,* New York, 1954; 2nd ed., New York and London, 1970; and *The Farther Reaches of Human Nature,* New York, 1971; Harmondsworth, 1973.

4 Sensing a Dwelling pp.75–104

1. Dr R. Wurtman as quoted by Hiss in *The Experience of Place.*

2. R. Ornstein, *The Healing Brain,* New York, 1987.

3. I am obliged to my friend and colleague Dr Fritz von Foerster for the description of the experiment, first published in A.H. Maslow and N.L. Mintz: 'Effects of Esthetic Surroundings, I', *Journal of Psychology,* 1956, 41, Provincetown, Mass.; and N.L. Mintz: 'Effects of Esthetic Surroundings, II', *Journal of Psychology,* 41, 1956.

4. Lewis Mumford, *The Culture of Cities,* London and New York, 1938. Since Taliesin West was completed in the late 1930s, glass clerestories and more permanent roof coverings have been installed because of major climatic changes.

5. Ke Guo, Master's Thesis (unpublished), Univ. of Kansas, 1993.

6. G. Nitschke, 'A Place, Space, Void', *Kyoto Journal,* Fall 1988.

7. V.S. Ramachandran, 'Perceptual Correlates of Massive Cortical Reorganization', *Neuro-Report,* July 1992. See also J. Shreeve, 'Touching the Phantom', *Discover,* Vol. 14, No. 6, June 1993.

8. A simple design solution: to turn up the volume beyond 90 decibels, two different knobs would have to be twisted simultaneously, a warning light would pulsate, and the plastic lead connecting the earphones with the player would also light up, running down the batteries more rapidly.

9. As discussed with Zen Buddhists at the Tassajara monastery and shrines in Kyoto.

10. *The Renewing of a Vision – Frank Lloyd Wright and the Meyer May House,* (videotape) Grand Rapids, Michigan, 1987, describing sensitive restoration by Steelcase Inc.

11. For a study combining rigorous architectural criticism with Jungian psychology, see F. Grosspietsch, *Carl Jung's Tower at Bollingen,* Master's Thesis (unpublished), Univ. of Kansas, 1987.

12. Even Christopher Alexander, architect and architectural theorist, has done little to explore the 'Square-versus-Round Plan' puzzle in his seminal books, *A Pattern Language* and *A Timeless Way of Building.*

13. Cited by Johnson-Davis, *Defining Sustainable Architecture.*

14. From my notes taken at the Third International Conference on Indoor Air Quality and Climate, Stockholm, 1986, it seems that most sealed buildings are in a sick condition at least part of the time, and should be written off as 'failures'.

5 The Biotechnology of Communities pp.105–112

1. The material in this chapter is based on experiences in many countries, interviews, reading and observation. Besides the sources cited in the text and in the notes that follow, see: C. Alexander, et al., *A Pattern Language,* and *The Production of Houses,* New York, 1982; Kohr, *The Overdeveloped Nations;* K. Lynch, *The Image of the City,* Cambridge, Mass., 1960; Lord Raglan, *The Temple and the House,* London and New York, 1964; Yi-Fu Tuan, *Landscapes of Fear,* New York, 1979; W.H. Whyte, *The Social Life of Small Urban Spaces,* Washington D.C., 1980, and *City.* I have also drawn on two articles by Hiss, *New Yorker,* June 1987, incorporated in *The Experience of Place.* These writers are in no way responsible for any conclusions I have reached.

2. The foregoing material is also explored in Papanek, 'Seeing the World Whole: Interaction Between Ecology and Design', University of Kansas, Fifth Inaugural Lecture, 1982.

3. The material in this section is largely developed from Maertens, *Der Optische Maassstab.*

4. Many of these figures are from Sale, *Human Scale.*

5. Much of this section is based on Konrad Lorenz, *Der Abbau des Menschlichen,* Munich, 1950; and L. Kohr, *Die Kranken Riesen: Krise des Zentralismus,* Vienna 1981.

6 Lessons of Vernacular Architecture pp.113–38

1. Rudofsky, *Architecture without Architects; Streets for People;* and *The Prodigious Builders.*

2. S. Moholy-Nagy, *Native Genius in Anonymous Architecture,* New York, 1957. For a more idiosyncratic view, see also, A. Van Dine, *Unconventional Builders,* Chicago, 1977.

3. Rudofsky, *Are Our Clothes Modern?* For Rudofsky's recent views, see, *Sparta/Sybaris: Keine neue Bauweise, eine neue Lebensweise tut Not,* Vienna, 1987.

4. Rudofsky, *The Unfashionable Human Body.*

5. Le Corbusier, *The Modulor,* London, 1954; and *Modulor 2,* London, 1958.

6. R. Neutra, *Life and Shape*, New York, 1962.

7. An exception is the classic work on the traditional roots of Japanese contemporary architecture, Engel's *The Japanese House*. Tatami are the reed-covered modular mats, 30" x 60" (76cm x 152cm), 4" (10cm) thick; rooms are still defined as four-mat rooms, seven-mat rooms, etc.

8. Rykwert, *On Adam's House in Paradise*.

9. Papanek, *Design for the Real World*, (rev. edn).

10. D. Elgin, *Voluntary Simplicity*, New York, 1981. For the dietary metaphor, I am indebted to R. Lawrence's 'The Interpretation of Vernacular Architecture', *Vernacular Architecture*, Vol. 14, 1982.

11. W. Allen Storrer, *The Architecture of Frank Lloyd Wright*, Cambridge Mass., 1978.

12. J. Larkins and B. Howard, *Australian Pubs*, Adelaide, 1980.

13. C. Abel, 'Living in a Hybrid World: Built Sources of Malaysian Identity', *Design and Society*, 1984.

14. Rapoport, *House, Form and Culture*.

15. Kohr, *The Over-Developed Nations*. See also, L. Kohr, *The Breakdown of Nations*, London, 1957; *Is Wales Viable?*, Llandybie, 1971; and *Development Without Aid*, Llandybie, 1973, and New York, 1977.

16. For Kohr, see above; other works dealing with this question are: G. McRobie, *Small is Possible*, New York, 1981; Papanek, *Design for Human Scale*; Schumacher, *Small is Beautiful*.

17. 'The true basis for the more serious study of the art and architecture lies with those indigenous more humble buildings everywhere that are to architecture what folklore is to literature or folk song to music and with which academic architects are seldom concerned....Although often slight, their virtue is intimately related to the environment, to the heart life of the people. Functions are usually truthfully conceived and rendered invariably with natural feeling. Results are often beautiful and always instructive.' Frank Lloyd Wright, *The Sovereignty of the Individual*, Chicago, 1911.

18. *M.E.T.U., Journal of the Faculty of Architecture*, 1976 to date, published by the Middle East Technical Univ., Ankara.

19. P. Oliver, *Shelter and Society*, London, 1969.

20. How geomancy and cosmology influence the location, building and orientating of a house has been described in C. McPhee, *A House in Bali*, New York, 1946. For more detailed studies, see: Lip, *Chinese Geomancy*; Rossbach, *Feng Shui*; Too, *Feng Shui*, and *Practical Applications of Feng Shui*.

21. Associated Press, 8 Dec. 1994.

22. Smit Vajaranant, *Student Housing and Study Centre in the Historic Site of Sukhothai, Thailand*, Master's Thesis (unpublished), Univ. of Kansas, 1983.

23. R.B. Lee, *!Kung San: Men, Women and Work in a Foraging Society*, Cambridge and New York, 1979; D.E. Gelburd, *Indications of Culture Change Among the Dobe !Kung San*, (Master's Thesis), George Washington Univ., 1974; John Yellen, 'Bushmen', *Science 85*, Vol. 6, No. 4, May 1985; M. Sahlins, *Tribesmen*, Englewood, N. J., 1968.

24. Claude Lévi-Strauss, *Tristes Tropiques* (trans. J. and D. Weightman), London 1973; *The View from Afar* (trans. J. Neugroscher and P. Hoss), Oxford, 1985.

25. See especially, Andrew Saint, *The Image of the Architect*, New Haven, 1983.

26. See, for instance, J.-L. Bourgeois, *Spectacular Vernacular*, Salt Lake City, 1983; J. Dethier, *Down to Earth: Adobe Architecture*, New York, 1983.

27. Alexander, et al., *A Pattern Language*.

28. P. Oliver, *Dwellings: The House Across the World*, London, 1987; *Shelter and Society*, London, 1969; and 'Cultural Factors in the Acceptance of Resettlement Housing', paper for the First International and Interdisciplinary Conference on Built Form and Culture, Univ. of Kansas, Oct. 1984.

29. R. M. Bradfield, *A Natural History of Associations: A Study in the Meaning of Community*, (2 vols.), London, 1973.

30. Kent, 'The Effects of Television Viewing: A Cross-Cultural Perspective', *Current Anthropology*, Vol. 26, No. 1, Feb. 1985.

31. M. Wenzel, *House Decoration in Nubia*, London, 1972.

32. Fathy, *Architecture for the Poor*. See also: Fathy, *Natural Energy and Vernacular Architecture*, Chicago, 1986; J. M. Richards, *Architects in the Third World: Hassan Fathy, J.M. Richards, Ismail Serageldin and Darl Rastorfer*, London and Singapore, 1985.

7 Form Follows Fun pp.139–58

1. Papanek, *Design for the Real World* (rev. edn).

2. Ibid.

3. H. L. Mencken, *A Choice of Days: Essays from Happy Days, Newspaper Days and Heathen Days*, New York, 1980.

4. Designers who work in a studio within an industrial enterprise are known as 'captive designers'.

5. *Consumer Reports: Annual Buying Guide*, Dec. 1992, New York.

6. From the *Futurist Manifesto*, Paris, 1909.

7. Breton, quoted by Sir Herbert Read in *Surrealism*, London, 1936.

8. R. Loewy, *Never Leave Well Enough Alone*, New York, 1950.

9. Raglan, *The Temple and the House*.

10. Csikszentihalyi, *Flow: The Psychology of Optimal Experience*.

8 Is Convenience the Enemy? pp.159–82

1. Stumpf, *Are Metaphors Enough to See you Warm on a Cold Winter's Night?*, (audiotape), Utrecht and Amsterrdam, 1987.

2. In the USA, this hope is based in part on laws passed in California in 1989 requiring that 2% of all cars driven after 1 Jan. 1999 should be emission-free; rising to 10% in 2003, and 50% by 2010. In France, electric cars are already being used in experimental studies.

3. See Papanek, *Design for Human Scale*.

4. Generic foods, washing powders, etc, have been sold in North American supermarkets since the 1970s. They cost less than so-called prime brands,

but the contents are almost identical, often from the same suppliers, though the olives, say, may not be of uniform size nor the macaroni of equal length.

5. In Japan the tradition is to pack in fives. For beautiful packages made of natural and entirely biodegenerable material, see Oka Hideyuki, *How To Wrap Five Eggs*, New York, 1967, and *How To Wrap Five More Eggs*, New York, 1975.

6. N. Freeling, *Castang's City*, London, 1980.

7. Henry Miller, in a discussion with the author, Big Sur, California, 1968.

8. Dr Leopold Auenbrugger diagnosed nostalgia as a disease in 1788. During the American Civil War, nostalgia was described as 'a mild type of insanity caused by disappointment and a continuous longing for home'. Of 5000 cases in the ranks which required hospitalization, 58 were fatal. From A. Broyard's review, *New York Sunday Times*, 16 Feb. 1986, of D.W. Goodwin, *Anxiety*, New York, 1986.

9. See Konrad Lorenz, *Über Tierisches und Menschliches Verhalten*, Munich, 1966; and *On Aggression*, London, 1967. This topic was also explored by Thompson in *On Growth and Form*.

9 Sharing Not Buying pp.183–202

1. *The Letters of Karl Marx*, Englewood, N.J., 1979.

2. V. Papanek and J. Hennessey, *How Things Don't Work*, New York, 1977.

3. J. H. Falk and J.B. Balling, 'Development of Visual Preference for Natural Environments', *Environment and Behaviour*, Vol. 14, No.1, Thousand Oaks, Calif., Jan. 1982.

4. Bill Mollison, *Permaculture: A Practical Guide for a Sustainable Future*, Covelo, Calif., 1990. Mollison developed the concept of Permaculture, an elegant way of letting growth take care of itself, in Tasmania in the 1960s.

5. Papanek and Hennessey, *How Things Don't Work*.

6. Ibid.

7. J. Hennessey and V. Papanek, *Nomadic Furniture: Where to Buy and How to Build Lightweight Furniture that folds, collapses, stacks, knocks down, inflates or can be thrown away and recycled*, New York, 1973; London, 1974; and *Nomadic Furniture 2*, New York, 1974. Also published as *L'Arredantento Mobile*, Milan, 1977; *L'Arredantento Mobile No.2*, Milan, 1978.

8. A car designed for disassembly would also be easier to assemble. It would divide naturally into: body and engine; electronic and hydraulic black-box components; solderless wiring and connectors.

9. Papanek and Hennessey, *How Things Don't Work*.

10 Generations to Come pp.203–22

1. Experiments 1954–80 with first-year design students; also with graduate students at: Ontario Coll. of Art; State Univ. of New York at Buffalo; Rhode Island Sch. of Design; Sch. of Design of North Carolina State Coll., Raleigh; Purdue Univ.; California Inst. of the Arts; Royal Academy of Architecture, Copenhagen; Architectural Association, London; Carleton Univ., Ottawa;

Kansas City Art Inst. I also worked with students at Konstfackskolan in Sweden, and in Vienna, Nigeria, Brazil and Australia.

2. Mander, *In the Absence of the Sacred*, and *Four Arguments for the Elimination of Television*.

3. I developed bisociation technique as a problem-solving tool in the early 1960s. The word derives from 'bi-association', coined by Arthur Koestler in *Insight and Outlook*, New York, 1949, discussed further in Koestler, *The Act of Creation*. He describes the result of collisons of two opposite ideas in humour, scientific discovery and peak religious experiences as the 'Ha Ha', 'Ha!' and 'Ah…' reactions respectively. Trisociation is here presented for the first time. It is possible systematically to engineer these collisions, resulting in new insights and often new discoveries, a method described in *By Accident or Design?*, my PBS radio design commentary, and in Papanek, *Design for the Real World*.

4. F. Boas, *General Anthropology*, New York, 1948.

11 The Best Designers in the World? pp.223–34

1. See especially: C. Burland, *Eskimo Art*, London, 1973; I. Christie Clark, *Arte Indio y Esquimal del Canada*, Barcelona, 1970; W. Fagg (ed.), *Eskimo Art in the British Museum*, London, 1972; Lopez, *Arctic Dreams*; D.J. Ray, *Eskimo Masks: Art and Ceremony*, Seattle, 1967, and *Artists of the Tundra and the Sea*, Seattle, 1961; P. and M. Thiry, *Eskimo Artifacts Designed for Use*, Seattle, 1977.

2. This method was redesigned for Dow 'self-generating' plastic foam domes. See Papanek, *Design for the Real World* (rev. edn).

3. Marshall McLuhan, 'No Upside Down in Eskimo Art', McLuhan and Papanek (ed.), *Verbi-Voco-Visual Explorations*, New York, 1967.

4. E. Carpenter, in *Oh, what a blow that phantom gave me!*, New York, 1972, tells a nearly identical story, as did Peter Freuchen in *The Arctic Year*, New York, 1958. We can conclude from this that the experiences described are far from unique.

5. McLuhan, 'No Upside Down in Eskimo Art'.

7. Cited by Sister Corita Kent in her lecture at the California Inst. of the Arts, Nov. 1970.

8. E. Carpenter, *Eskimo Realities*, New York, 1973.

9. J. Meldgaard, *Eskimo Skulptur*, Copenhagen, 1959. See also *Greenland Tupilak*, Royal Greenland Trade Department, c.1976.

12 The New Aesthetic pp.235–46

1. Many who are prominent in environmental and ecological matters are labelled 'crypto-fascists' or 'eco-nazis'; some receive death threats or are physically assaulted. See D. Helvarg, *The War Against the Greens*, San Francisco, 1995.

2. V. Papanek, 'Areas of Attack for Product Designers', *Journal of the Industrial Design Education Association*, New York, April 1963, published in expanded form as *Miljön och Miljonerna*, Stockholm, 1968, and as *Design for the Real World: Human Ecology and Social Change*, New York, 1971; London, 1972.

3. Quoted in the article 'Built to Last – Until it's Time to Take it Apart', by B. Nussbaum and J. Templeman, *Business Week*, 17 Sept. 1990.
4. Ibid.
5. As given in White, *Green Pages*.
6. C. Gardner, 'Starck Reality', *Design*, June 1993.
7. It is clear that self-assembly, especially of sophisticated devices, will require diagnostic and built-in autodiagnostic devices, such as the virus-detection and cleansing programmes already in use with Apple Macintosh computers.
8. F. Coffee, *The Best Kits Catalog*, New York, 1993.
9. Oliver, *Dwellings: The House Across the World*.
10. These observations are based on discussions with priests and designers at Ise. I am also indebted to Kenzo Tange and Noboru Kawazoe and their monumental book *Ise: Prototype of Japanese Architecture*, Cambridge, Mass, 1965.

SELECT BIBLIOGRAPHY

Ackerman, Diane, *A Natural History of the Senses*, London, 1990; New York, 1991

Alexander, Christopher, *A Timeless Way of Building*, New York, 1979

—, et al, *A Pattern Language*, New York and Oxford, 1977

Anderson, R.F., 'Divining the Spirit of Place', *Yoga Journal*, San Francisco, Sept./Oct. 1986

Appel, Alfred, *Signs of Life*, New York, 1983

Badimer, A.H., (ed.), *Dharma Gaia, A Harvest of Essays in Buddhism and Ecology*, Berkeley, Calif., 1990

Baer, Steve, *Sunspots: An Exploration of Solar Energy through Fact and Fiction*, Seattle, 1979

Beck, P. V., A. L. Walters and N. Francisco, *The Sacred: Ways of Knowledge*, Tsaile, Arizona, 1992

Bell, A.D., *Plant Form: An Illustrated Guide to Flowering Plant Morphology*, New York and Oxford, 1991

Beng, Tan Hock, *Tropical Architecture and Interiors: Tradition-Based Design of Indonesia, Malaysia, Singapore, Thailand*, Singapore, 1994

Berdel, Dieter (ed.), *Soziales Design*, Vienna, 1985

Bernsen, Jens, *Design: The Problem Comes First*, Copenhagen, 1983

Berry, W., *Sex, Economy, Freedom and Community*, New York, 1993

Blake, Peter, *Form Follows Fiasco: Why Modern Architecture Hasn't Worked*, Boston, 1977

Bootzin, D., and H.C. Muffley, (ed.), *Biomechanics*, New York, 1969

Boys, C.V., *Soap-Bubbles and the Forces which Mould Them*, enlarged edn, London, 1920

Bradfield, Richard Maitland, *A Natural History of Associations: A Study in the Meaning of Community* (2 vols.), London, 1973

Bruchac, Joseph, *The Native American Sweat Lodge*, Freedom, Calif., 1993

Brunskill, R.W., *Illustrated Handbook of Vernacular Architecture*, New York, 1971

Burall, Paul, *Green Design*, London, 1990

Callenbach, Ernest, *Ecotopia*, Berkeley, Calif., 1975; London, 1978 (a novel)

Campbell, Joseph, *The Way of the Animal Powers* (Part I, Vols. 1 and 2; Part II, Vols. 1, 2 and 3), New York, 1983–90; London, 1984–90

Caplan, Ralph, *On Design*, New York, 1982

Carper, Jean, *The Food Pharmacy*, New York, 1989

Castile, Rand, *The Way of Tea*, Tokyo and New York, 1979.

Caston, Don, *Eighty-Eight Easy-to-Make Aids For Older People and For Special Needs*, Point Roberts, Washington, 1985

Clausen, M.L., *Spiritual Space: The Religious Architecture of Pietro Belluschi*, London and Seattle, 1992

Collani, Luigi, *Design 1,2,3* (*3* vols.), Solingen, 1986

Cook, Theodore Andrea, *The Curves of Life*, London, 1914

Covello, Vincent T. and Yuji Yoshimura, *The Japanese Art of Stone Appreciation: Suiseki and its Uses with Bonsai*, Rutland, Vermont, and Tokyo, 1984

Critchlow, Keith, *Time Stands Still: New Light on Megalithic Science*, London, 1979

Crowther, Richard L., *Ecologic Architecture*, London, 1991; Boston, 1992

Csikszentmihalyi, Mihaly, *Flow: The Psychology of Optimal Experience*, New York, 1980

—, *Flow: The Psychology of Happiness*, London 1992

Dalby, Liza, *Kimono: Fashioning Culture*, New Haven and London, 1993

Davidson, A. K., *The Art of Zen Gardens*, New York, 1983

Day, C., *Building With Heart: A Practical Approach to Self and Community Building*, Devon, 1990

—, *Places of the Soul: Architecture and Environmental Design as a Healing Art.*, Glasgow, London, 1990

Dissanayake, Ellen, *Homo Aestheticus: Where Art Comes From and Why*, New York, 1992

Doczi, György, *The Power of Limits: Proportional Harmonies in Nature, Art and Architecture*, Boulder, Colorado, and London, 1981

Dumond, Don E., *The Eskimos and Aleuts*, London, 1977

Eibl-Eibesfeldt, I., H. Haas and H. Glück, *Stadt und Lebensqualität*, Stuttgart and Vienna, 1985

Eiseman, Fred B., *Bali: Sekela and Niskala, Vol. I: Essays on Religion, Ritual and Art, Vol.II: Essays on Society, Tradition and Craft*, Singapore, 1990

Engel, Heinrich, *The Japanese House*, Tokyo, 1964

Faegre, Torvald, *Tents: Architecture of The Nomads*, New York, 1978; London, 1979

Farb, P., and G. Armalagos, *Consuming Passions: The Anthropology of Eating*, New York, 1980

Faris, James C., *The Nightway: A History of a Navajo Ceremonial*, Albuquerque, 1990

Fathy, Hassan, *Architecture for the Poor*, Chicago, 1973

—, *Natural Energy and Vernacular Architecture*, Chicago and London, 1986

Fenzl, Kristian, *Design als Funktionelle Skulptur*, Vienna, 1987

Fitzhugh, W., and S. Kaplan, *Inua: Spirit World of the Bering Sea Eskimo*, Washington, D.C., 1982

Fleming, Ronald Lee, and Renata von Tscharner, *Placemakers: Creating Public Art That Tells You Where You Are*, New York, 1987

Forty, Adrian, *Objects of Desire: Design and Society*, London, 1986

Gablik, Suzi, *The Re-enchantment of Art*, London, 1991

Gallagher, W., *The Power Of Place*, New York, 1953

Gerardin, Lucien, *Bionics*, London, 1968

Goldstein, Sanford and Seishi Shinoda, (eds.), *Akiko Yosano: Tangled Hair, Selected Tanka from Midaregami*, Rutland and Tokyo, 1987

Gonick, Larry, *Neo-Babelonia: A Serious Study in Contemporary Confusion*, Utrecht, 1989

Grillo, Paul Jacques, *What is Design?* Chicago, 1961

Hale, J., *The Old Way of Seeing: How Architecture Lost Its Magic*, Boston and New York, 1994

Hall, Edward T., *Beyond Culture*, New York, 1976

—, *The Dance of Life: The Other Dimension of Time*, New York, 1983

—, *The Hidden Dimension: Man's Use of Space in Public and Private*, New York, 1966; London 1969

—, *The Silent Language*, New York, 1959

Hamlyn, H. (ed.), *New Design for Old*, London, 1986

Harris, Harold, *Stranger on the Square: Arthur and Cynthia Koestler*, London, 1984

Hawken, Paul, *The Ecology of Commerce: A Declaration of Sustainability*, New York, 1993

Hein, Piet, 'Superellipsen: en enkel løsning af et alment problem', *Dansk Kunsthaandwaerk*, No. 4, 1964 (with translation by Victor Papanek)

Hertel, Heinrich, *Structure, Form and Movement: Biology and Engineering*, New York, 1966

Heythum, Antonin, *On Art, Beauty and the Useful*, Stierstadt im Taunus, 1955

Hillier, Bill and Julienne Hanson, *The Social Logic of Space*, Cambridge, 1984

Hiss, Tony, *The Experience of Place*, New York, 1991

Howell, Sandra C., *Design for Aging*, Cambridge, 1980

Huntley, H.E., *The Divine Proportion: A Study in Mathematical Beauty*, New York, 1970

Illich, Ivan, *Tools for Conviviality*, London and New York, 1973

—, *Toward a History of Needs*, New York, 1977

Ivy, Robert Adams, *Fay Jones*, Washington, D.C., 1992

Jackson, J.B., *Discovering the Vernacular Landscape*, London and New Haven, 1984

Jenny, Hans, *Cymatics: The Structure and Dynamics of Waves and Vibrations*, Basle, 1967

Kakuzo, Okakura, *The Book of Tea*, Tokyo and Rutland, Vermont, 1983

—, *The Ideals of the East, with Special Reference to the Art of Japan*, London, 1903; Tokyo and Rutland, Vermont, 1963

Kamakura, Junichi, et al, *Ekiben: The Art of the Japanese Box Lunch*, San Francisco, 1989

Kis-Jovak, J. I., et al, *Banua Toraja: Changing Patterns in Architecture and Symbolism Among the Sa'dan Toraja, Sulawesi, Indonesia*, Amsterdam, 1988

Koestler, Arthur, *The Act of Creation*, London and New York, 1964

Kohr, L., *Development without Aid: The Translucent Society*, Llandybie, 1973; New York, 1977

—, *The Overdeveloped Nations: The Diseconomies of Scale*, New York, 1977

Koncelik, Joseph A., *Aging and the Product Environment*, New York, 1982

Lanoue, David G. (ed.), *Issa Cup of Tea Poems: Selected Haiku of Kobayashi Issa*, Berkeley, 1991

Laubin, Reginald and Gladys, *The Indian Tipi: Its History, Construction and Use*, Norman, Oklahoma, 1957

Lawlor, Anthony, *Sacred Geometry*, London, 1982

—, *The Temple in the House: Finding the Sacred in Everyday Architecture*, New York, 1994

LeGuérer, Annick, *Scent: The Mysterious and Essential Powers of Smell*, New York, 1992

Lip, Evelyn, *Chinese Geomancy*, Singapore, 1979

Lopez, Barry, *Arctic Dreams: Imagination and Desire in a Northern Landscape*, New York, 1968

Lovelock, James, *The Ages of Gaia: A Biography of Our Living Earth*, London and New York, 1988

—, *Gaia: A New Look at Life on Earth*. New York and Oxford, 1979

—, *Healing Gaia: Practical Medicine for the Planet*, London and New York, 1991

Lucie-Smith, Edward, *A History of Industrial Design*, New York, 1984

Lyle, John Tillman, *Design for Human Ecosystems: Landscape, Land Use and Natural Resources*, New York and Wokingham, 1985

Mackenzie, Dorothy, *Design for the Environment*, New York, 1992 (published as *Green Design* in UK)

Maertens, H., *Der Optische-Maassstab: die Theorie und Praxis des ästhetischen Sehens in den bildenden Künsten*, Bonn, Germany, 1877

Mails, Thomas E., *The Pueblo Children of the Earth Mother: The Heritage, Culture, Crafts, and Traditions of the Anasazi Ancestors of the Pueblo Indians* (2 vols.), New York, 1983

Mander, Jerry, *Four Arguments for the Elimination of Television*, New York, 1978

—, *In the Absence of the Sacred : The Failure of Technology and the Survival of the Indian Nations*, San Francisco, 1992

Mann, A.T., *Sacred Architecture*, Shaftesbury, 1993

Margolin, Victor, *Design Discourse*, Chicago and London, 1989

Markovich, Nicholas C., et al (ed.), *Pueblo Style and Regional Architecture*, New York, 1990

McCamant, Kathryn and Charles Durrett, *Cohousing*, Berkeley, California, 1988

McKibben, Bill, *The End of Nature*, New York, 1989; London 1990

Mollerup, Per, *Design For Life*, Copenhagen, 1992

—, *Good Enough Is Not Enough: Observations on Public Design*, Copenhagen, 1992

Mollison, Bill, *Permaculture: A Practical Guide for a Sustainable Future*, Covelo, Calif., 1990

Montù, Aldo, *Sezione Aurea e Forme Pentagonali*, Milan, 1980

Moore, Curtis and Alan Miller, *Green Gold: Japan, Germany, The United States, and the Race for Environmental Technology,* Boston, 1994

Moore, Pat, *Disguised,* Waco, Texas, 1985

Morgan, William N., *Ancient Architecture of the Southwest,* Austin, Texas, 1994

Nabokov, Peter and Robert Easton, *Native American Architecture,* New York and Oxford, 1989

Norman, Donald A., *The Psychology of Everyday Things,* New York, 1988

Oedekoven-Gerischer, Angela, et al (ed.), *Women In Design/Frauen im Design* (2 vols.), Berlin, 1989

Papanek, Victor, *Design for Human Scale,* New York, 1983

—, *Design for the Real World: Human Ecology and Social Change* (rev. edn), London, 1985; Chicago, 1992

Paturi, Felix R., *Nature the Mother of Invention: The Engineering of Plant Life,* trans. M. Clarke, London, 1976

Payer, Lynn, *Medicine and Culture,* New York, 1988; London 1989

Pearce, Peter, *Structure in Nature is a Strategy for Design,* Cambridge, Mass., 1978

Pearce, Peter and Susan Pearce, *Experiments in Form: A Foundation Course in Three-dimensional Design,* New York, 1978; London, 1980

Pearson, D., *The Natural House Book,* London, 1989

Postman, Neil, *Technopoly: The Surrender of Culture to Technology,* New York, 1992

Powell, Robert, *The House In Asia,* Singapore, 1993

Purce, Jill, *The Mystic Spiral,* London, 1980

Rapoport, Amos, *House, Form and Culture,* Englewood, N.J., 1969

Rossbach, Sarah, *Feng Shui: The Chinese Art of Placement,* New York, 1983

—, *Interior Design with Feng Shui,* New York, 1987

Rudofsky, Bernard, *Architecture Without Architects,* New York, 1964

—, *Are Our Clothes Modern?* Chicago, 1947

—, *Behind the Picture Window,* New York and Oxford, 1955

—, *The Kimono Mind,* London and New York, 1965

—, *Now I Lay Me Down to Eat: Notes and Footnotes on the Lost Art of Living,* New York, 1980

—, *The Prodigious Builders,* New York, 1977

—, *Streets For People,* New York, 1969

—, *The Unfashionable Human Body,* New York, 1971; London 1972

Rybcynski, Witold, *Home: A Short History of an Idea,* New York, 1986; London 1988

—, *The Most Beautiful House in the World,* New York, 1989

Rykwert, Joseph, *On Adam's House in Paradise,* New York, 1972

Sale, Kirkpatrick, *Dwellers in the Land: The Bioregional Vision,* San Francisco, 1985

—, *Human Scale,* London and New York, 1980

Schafer, R. Murray, *The Tuning of the World: Toward A Theory of Soundscape Design,* Philadelphia, 1980

Schmid, Peter, *Bio-Logische Architektur: Ganzheitliches bio-logisches Bauen,* Cologne, 1988

—, *Bio-Logische Baukonstruktion,* Cologne, 1986

Schumacher, E.F., *Good Work,* London and New York, 1979

—, *A Guide for the Perplexed,* London and New York, 1977

—, *Small is Beautiful: A Study of Economics as if People Mattered,* London 1973: New York, 1974

Schwenk, Theodor, *Sensitive Chaos: The Creation of Flowing Forms in Water and Air,* trans. O. Whicher and J. Wrigley, London, 1965

Scully, Vincent, *Pueblo: Mountain, Village, Dance,* London and New York, 1975

Shigenari, Takeshi, *Techno-Aid: Aid for Children with Handicaps,* Tokyo, 1988

Sommer, R., *Design Awareness,* San Francisco, 1972

—, *Personal Space: The Behavioral Basis of Design,* Englewood, N.J., 1969

—, *Social Design,* Englewood, N.J., 1983

Spain, Daphne, *Gendered Spaces,* Chapel Hill and London, 1992

Sparke, Penny, *Design in Context,* London, 1987

—, *An Introduction to Design and Culture in the Twentieth Century,* London, 1986

Spretnak, Charlene, *States of Grace: The Recovery of Meaning in the Postmodern Age,* San Francisco, 1991

Stewart, Hillary, *Cedar: Tree of Life to the Northwest Coast Indians,* Seattle and London, 1984

Storr, Anthony, *Music and the Mind,* London and New York, 1992

Tanizaki, Junichiro, *In Praise of Shadows,* trans. T. J. Harper and E.G. Seidensticker, London, 1991

Thayer, R. L., *Gray World, Green Heart: Technology, Nature, and Sustainability in the Landscape,* New York, 1994

Thompson, R. Farris, and S. Bahuchet, *Pygmées?* (with accompanying music on CD), Paris, 1991

Thompson, D'Arcy Wentworth, *On Growth and Form,* new edn, Cambridge, 1942

Tiger, Lionel, *Optimism: The Biology of Hope,* London and New York, 1979

—, *The Manufacture of Evil: Ethics, Evolution and the Industrial System,* London and New York, 1987

Todd, John, and Jack Nancy, *Tomorrow is Our Permanent Address,* New York, 1979.

—, *Bioshelters<Ocean Arks<City Farming: Ecology as the Basis of Design,* San Francisco, 1987

Too, Lillian, *Feng Shui,* Singapore, 1993

—, *Practical Applications of Feng Shui,* Singapore, 1994

Torre, Susan (ed.), *Women in Architecture: A Historic and Contemporary Perspective,* New York, 1977

Tsuzuki, Kyoichi, *Tokyo Style,* Kyoto, 1994

Uelsmann, J. N., *Process and Perception,* Gainesville, Florida, 1985

Vaihinger, H., *The Philosophy of 'As If',* trans. C. K. Ogden, London, 1924

Vanlengen, Johan, *Manual del Arquitecto Descalzo: Como Construir Casas y Otros Edificios,* [Manual for Barefoot Architects: How to Build Homes and Other Structures], Mexico D.F., 1982

Vasquez, P.R., and A.L. Margain, *Industrial Design and Human Development,* Amsterdam, 1980

Vlatseas, S., *A History of Malaysian Architecture,* Singapore, 1990

Vogel, Steven, *Life's Devices: The Physical World of Animals and Plants,* Princeton, 1988

Von Frisch, Karl, *Animal Architecture,* London and New York, 1974

Wann, David, *Bio-Logic: Environmental Protection By Design,* Boulder, Colorado, 1990

Waterson, Roxana, *The Living House: An Anthropology of Architecture in South-East Asia,* Oxford and Singapore, 1990

Watson, O. Michael, *Proxemic Behavior,* The Hague and Paris, 1970

Weihsmann, H., *Das Rote Wien: Sozial-demokratische Architektur und Kommunalpolitik, 1919-1934,* Vienna, 1985

Weisman, Leslie Kanes, *Discrimination By Design: A Feminist Critique of the Man-Made Environment,* Urbana and Chicago, 1992

Westrum, Ron, *Technologies and Society: The Shaping of People and Things,* Belmont, Calif., 1991

Weyl, Hermann, *Symmetry,* Princeton, 1952

White, Philip, *Green Pages: Ecological Guidelines For Design,* Eindhoven, 1993

Whiteley, Nigel, *Design For Society,* London, 1993

Whyte, L. L., (ed.), *Aspects of Form: A Symposium on form in Nature and Art.* London, 1951

Whyte, William H., *City: Rediscovering the Center,* New York, 1988

Williams, Robert, *The Geometrical and Biomorphic Foundations of Natural Structure,* New York, 1971

Wyman, Leland C., (ed.), *Beautyway: A Navaho Ceremonial,* New York, 1957

Yamamoto, Akira, 'Culture Spaces in Everyday Life', *University of Kansas Publications in Anthropology,* No.11, 1979

Yi-Fu Tuan, *Passing Strange and Wonderful,* Minneapolis, Minnesota, 1993

SOURCES OF ILLUSTRATIONS

Pete Addis/Environmental Picture Library: 31. ANP Foto, Amsterdam: 194. Aram Designs, London: 178 left. Architectural Association/Peter Cook: 117. Architectural Association/Charlene Koonce: 91. Architectural Association/Carlos Nino: 128. Atelier International/Cassina S.p.A.: 177 right. Timothy Beddow/The Hutchison Library, UK: 124 below, 125. Photo courtesy Anthony Belluschi Architects: 104. Photo Hedrich Blessing: 95. From K Blossfeldt and E Weber, *Art Forms in Nature,* 1932: 98 left. BMW (GB) Ltd: 239. Courtesy Bancroft Library, University of California. Photo Roy Flamm: 2. © The Field Museum, Chicago, Il. A18488: 122 right. Photo Cimma Marketing Ltd: 198 right. National Museum, Copenhagen: 231. Photo F.C./A-M. Cousteau: 47. Photo courtesy Keith Critchlow: 100. Drawings by Barry Crone: 208, 209. Photo Richard Davies: 132. Photo courtesy Christopher Day: 97. Photo Design Synergy, Melbourne and Singapore: 73. John Egan/The Hutchison Library, UK: 87. Photo Paolo Favoli: 81. Flymo: 192. Fuji Photo Film (UK) Ltd: 157. Photo Ben Gibson: 23. Photo Vadim Gippenreiter: 121 below. GOOD GRIPs ® GADGETS OXO International, New York: 58. Büsch-Reisinger Museum, Harvard University, Massachusetts: 50. Hasbro UK Ltd: 213. Health and Safety Executive, Employment Department Group: 38. Photo courtesy of Heibon-sha Co Ltd: 245. Jimmy Holmes/Environmental Picture Library: 30. Honda (UK) Ltd: 191. Photo © Greg Hursley: 92 below, 93. The Hutchison Library, UK: 116 below. Irene R Iengui/Environmental Picture Library: 33. Commissioners of Public Works, Ireland: 123 below. Photo Irish Times: 102. Japan National Tourist Organization: 149. © 1994 Photo Joel and Shin Koyama: 96 below.

Courtesy Barry Lopez (drawn by David Lindroth): 230 below. Photo © Norman McGrath: 92 above. Michael Macintyre/The Hutchison Library, UK: 116 above, 141, 145. Photo Hans Mann: 109. MAZDA Cars (UK) Ltd: 150. Memphis S.R.L., Milan: 54, 152. Henk Merjenburgh/Environmental Picture Library: 22. Photo NASA: 18. Dartmouth College Archives, New Hampshire, USA: 144. Photo David Heald. © The Solomon R Guggenheim Foundation, New York: 96 above. Albright-Knox Art Gallery Buffalo, New York. Gift of Darwin R Martin: 177 left. Photo Richard Nickel: 151. Photo OXFAM (Ian Davis): 130. Edward Parker/The Hutchison Library, UK: 148. Photo Penhallow Marketing Ltd: 241 below. Photo Sandak Inc., Stamford, CT, USA: 129. Photo Stadtverkehrsbüro, Salzburg: 106. The Design Centre, Singapore: 214, 215. Philip Steele/ICCE: 26, 27. Ezra Stoller © Esto: 90. Photo © Yoshio Watanabe, International Society for Educational Information, Tokyo: 246. Photo Hasan Uddin-Khan: 101. Drawings by Smit Vajaramant: 20. Venice Academy: 94 left. Photo Philip Watson: 198 left. Photo Martin Weaver: 80. Archiv Hochschule für Architektur und Bauwesen, Weimar: 122 left. Photo Hallfried Weyer: 120 below.

The following illustrations were supplied by the author (some drawn by students under the author's guidance): 34, 36, 37, 44, 45, 51, 52, 56, 60, 62, 63, 67, 68, 83 below, 89 above, 98 right, 120 above, 121 above, 123 above, 124 above and centre, 133, 140, 156, 161, 163, 171, 172, 178 right, 179, 181, 199, 200, 206, 207, 219, 220, 221, 224, 225, 226, 228, 229, 232, 233, 237, 241 above, 242.

The following illustrations were drawn by John Kaine: 66, 89 below, 94 right, 103, 136, 195, 243.

INDEX